POWER
& PURITY

POWER
&PURITY

Cathar Heresy in Medieval Italy

CAROL LANSING

OXFORD
UNIVERSITY PRESS

OXFORD
UNIVERSITY PRESS

Oxford   New York
Athens   Auckland   Bangkok   Bogotá   Buenos Aires
Cape Town   Chennai   Dar es Salaam   Delhi   Florence   Hong Kong   Istanbul
Karachi   Kolkata   Kuala Lumpur   Madrid   Melbourne   Mexico City   Mumbai
Nairobi   Paris   São Paulo   Shanghai   Singapore   Taipei   Tokyo   Toronto   Warsaw

and associated companies in
Berlin   Ibadan

First published in 1988 by Oxford University Press, Inc.
198 Madison Avenue, New York, New York 10016

First issued as an Oxford University Press paperback, 2001

Oxford is a registered trademark of Oxford University Press

Library of Congress Cataloging-in-Publication Data
Lansing, Carol, 1951–
Power and purity : Cathar heresy in Medieval Italy / Carol Lansing.
p.   cm.
Includes bibliographical references and index.
ISBN-13 978-0-19-514980-7
ISBN 0-19-506391-0; 0-19-514980-7 pbk.
1. Albigenses—Italy—History.   2. Albigenses—Italy—Orvieto—
History.   3. Italy—Religion.   4. Orvieto (Italy)—Religion.
I. Title.
BX4891.2.L36   1997
273'.6—DC20   96-44937

3 5 7 9 8 6 4

Printed in the United States of America
on acid-free paper

This book is dedicated to my sons,
Nicholas and Philip Gould.

Acknowledgments

THE ARCHIVAL RESEARCH FOR this book was funded by research fellow-ships from the Fulbright Foundation and the American Council of Learned Societies and a summer stipend from the National Endowment for the Humanities. Without their support the study would not have been possible. Friends and colleagues have helped me in numerous ways. The gifted and generous director of the Orvietan Archivio di Stato, Marilena Caponeri Rossi, consistently helped with sources and paleographic prob-lems, and her staff invariably responded with courtesy and speed to my endless requests. Lucio Riccetti, the leading historian of medieval Orvieto, has many times given help and suggested documents. I am especially grate-ful to Sabine Eiche. Dom Luigi Farnese of the Archivio Vescovile has been kind as well. Paolo Corsi provided excellent microfilm copies.

I owe a great debt to Marvin Becker and to conversations that began when I studied with him at Michigan. Tom Tentler has been an unfailing source of support and challenging ideas, as well. Ed English gave generous and meticulous help with particularly difficult documents as well as thoughtful comments on chapters. Dyan Elliot and George Dameron read portions of the work and made challenging and useful suggestions. Many colleagues and former colleagues have aided me with aspects of the project. Anne Barton gave invaluable help with references. The students in my undergraduate seminars on medieval heresy raised provocative questions and helped me to clarify my ideas.

Vorrei ringraziare specialmente Mario e Monalda Rosati di Osarella e Orvieto.

Contents

POWER
&PURITY

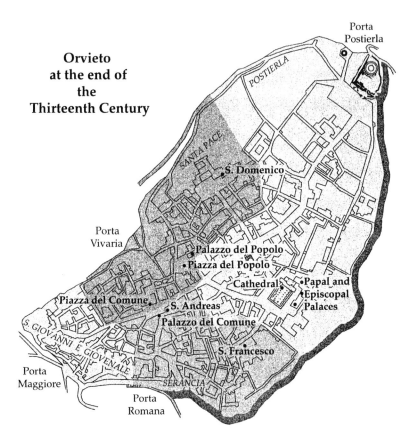

FIGURE 1-1: Map of Orvieto at the end of the thirteenth century. (Map by Michael De Gennaro.)

*I*ntroduction

IN THE ITALIAN TOWN of Orvieto at the end of the twelfth century, debate over the sacred and its relation to authority centered on whether a corpse was rotting. Cathar missionaries had enjoyed considerable success among Orvietans. Catharism was a dualist faith that spread in southern France and Italy in the twelfth and thirteenth centuries. The papacy considered it heretical because the Cathars attacked Catholic teachings and the authority of the clergy: the missionaries in Orvieto preached that no aspect of the material world or the human body can be sacred. In response, Pope Innocent III sent a young Roman named Pietro Parenzo to serve as papal rector and to combat heresy in the town. When Parenzo was abducted and murdered, the bishop blamed the Cathars, installed Parenzo's body in the cathedral, and rejoiced that the corpse, instead of decaying, gave off a sweet perfume and performed miracles. One day in 1200, as pilgrims moved towards Parenzo's tomb in the cathedral, someone hurled a piece of rotten meat at the procession from an upstairs window of a nearby house. The gesture scoffed at Parenzo, the bishop, and the pilgrims, a vivid denial of the bishop's claims for the purity and sanctity of Parenzo's corpse.

The Cathar faith enjoyed a long and remarkable success in Orvieto. Decades after this incident, in 1268–69, two Franciscan inquisitors sentenced eighty-five people for heresy, a group that included nine former civic officials, along with their families. Among them were important and powerful men—civic treasurers, a prior of the guilds, and council members, as well as merchants, moneylenders, and a group of furriers. The friars called a number of them "the progeny of a brood of vipers," which meant that they belonged to families that had been heretical for generations. One man was named as a descendant of one of Pietro Parenzo's killers.

Two of the sentences describe the beliefs of these Orvietan heretics. One is very brief: a youth is quoted saying that he believed the Cathar holy persons to be the best people in the world and salvation to be possible through them. A second recounts the faith of a furrier named Stradigotto. He believed

> that this world and all visible things were created by the devil; that human souls are spirits that fell from heaven and will only be saved through the hearts of the Cathars; that there will be no future resurrection of humankind; that the priests of the Roman Church do not have the power to absolve men who have confessed and are contrite from sin; that those living in matrimony are living in a state of damnation; that baptism in material water as it is performed in the ritual of the Roman Church does not aid in salvation.[1]

Stradigotto, by this statement, was a dualist who believed that the physical world was the work of the devil. The creation of humankind was a disaster, in which angels who were pure spirit fell from heaven and were trapped in bodies. The goal of human life is salvation through purification, possible only "through the hearts of the Cathars." The sentence stressed ideas that derive from the conviction that physicality is the source of evil and can in no form be made sacred. Thus, a resurrection of human flesh is unthinkable, and baptism in water can have no spiritual value. In this view, marriage is a state of damnation because the procreation of children only perpetuates the cruel imprisonment of spirit in flesh. The Catholic clergy have no power through the sacraments: they cannot absolve sin or aid in salvation.

Catharism was a collection of dualist beliefs and practices that was adopted by some western Europeans beginning in the mid–twelfth century. The faith, derived from the Bogomils of tenth-century Bulgaria, enjoyed its greatest success in western Europe in the independent towns. Cathar ideas were taught by holy men and women called perfects, who lived lives of voluntary poverty, abstained from sexual relations, and ate a rigorous diet. Perfects stayed in modest hospices, and traveled in pairs to preach and minister to the laity. Most Cathar believers did not emulate the austere lives of the perfects, but lived the ordinary life of the laity. They heard the perfects preach and took part in rituals that included a bow of formal reverence to the perfects and the consolation, a laying on of hands by a perfect that purified the soul, enabling its escape from the material world at death. Despite sporadic efforts by the papacy, bishops, the early inquisitions, and mendicant preachers, as well as some secular authorities, the Cathar faith enjoyed considerable popularity in many Italian towns in the 1240s and '50s. Catharism only faded in Italy after vigorous attacks by local inquisitions, often backed by powerful Guelf regimes, that began in the late 1260s.

This is a study of medieval Italian Cathars, with a focus on the Cathar community in the town of Orvieto. Study of the Cathars has often been relegated to the historiographical margins, and considered specialized research in the history of medieval heresy. The argument of this book is that the struggle over the Cathar faith was at the heart of a set of crucial and interrelated changes in thirteenth-century Italian towns: the creation of independent civic authority and institutions in association with the restructuring of Catholic orthodoxy and authority and the narrowing of gender roles. This set of changes marked the establishment of a political and institutional order with clear ideological underpinnings.

Cathar dualism was an important focus for these changes. Historians of medieval and early modern Europe have shown that ideas about authority and the social order often found expression in understandings of the human body.[2] Theorists associated orderly relations within the body with just order in society. Anatomical hierarchy mirrors the social structure, in which ignoble body parts, like digestive organs, rendered service to nobler, more spiritual ones. Rational authority is needed to control irrational members, of the body and of the body politic. Even debates in medical theory over the relations between organs could become, as Marie-Christine Pouchelle has argued, a "muffled echo" of social conflict.[3] Dualist condemnation of the material body thus opened possibilities for a critique of the hierarchy of authority—in particular, in the thirteenth century, the interrelations of ecclesiastical and secular power—a critique neatly implied by the tossing of rotten meat at the procession honoring Parenzo's corpse. In turn, condemnations of dualism as heresy reinforced not only Catholic teachings on the sacraments but the social and political order. For example, Innocent III's policies brought together contested views of the body and political ideology. It was in explicit opposition to the Cathar presence in the papal states that Innocent both urged the definition of marriage as a sacrament based on present consent and redefined heresy as treason, *lèse-majesté*. Both definitions reinforced the authority of the clergy: priestly authority over marriage and sexual relations, and papal sovereignty over the Christian community.

The focus of this study is the Cathar community in the town of Orvieto. Why focus on one town? The society and culture of Italian towns were intensely local, in the thirteenth century as today, so that general narratives often fail to do them justice. To understand the Cathars in a social and political context requires a careful look at one community.[4] A narrative broadly tracking Cathars throughout Italy would be a useful but very different kind of book. Most accounts of Italian heresy fall into one or the other pattern: they are either detailed local studies or more general analyses. At best, these two approaches are not somehow opposed but inform each other.[5] This book is poised between the two approaches, intended to provide a vivid evocation of the Cathars in one important community, to compare them with other towns, and to draw on that understanding to open larger questions about Italian Cathar belief and popular attitudes.

Why Orvieto? Despite its small size, the town played a surprisingly central role in thirteenth-century affairs. A fortress town of spectacular beauty, built on a high stub of volcanic rock, it lies on the major road between Rome and Florence. Orvieto was critical to papal efforts to build an independent state, and ambitious thirteenth-century popes from Innocent III to Boniface VIII were deeply engaged in Orvietan affairs. Especially after 1260, popes resided there with their huge courts for extended periods. Orvieto became an important cultural crossroads, visited repeatedly by Charles of Anjou; it was the residence of scholars like Hugh of St. Cher, Albertus Magnus, and Thomas Aquinas; the geometrician and papal physician Giovanni Campano; and the sculptors and architects Arnolfo di Cambio and Lorenzo Maitani.[6] The town later faded in importance with the transfer of the papal curia to Avignon.

Close papal involvement in Orvietan affairs shaped the contest over Cathar dualism. Catharism, in fact, took hold during a territorial dispute with Innocent III, and the early struggle over the spread of Catharism was intertwined with disputes over the nature and extent of local jurisdiction by the papacy. By the mid–thirteenth century, the town was playing an important and influential role in the contest over Catharism and the larger problem of the definition of political and ecclesiastical authority.

The Cathar Community

Catharism can be studied in two interrelated ways. First, one can reconstruct the social and political roles, motivations, and beliefs of the Cathars themselves. Second, one can analyze their repression: the ways their opponents defined them as heretics who threatened the whole of Christian society and then used that threat to reshape their own authority. This study attempts both, treating first the Cathars and then the efforts of Catholic authorities to define and repress them.

It is a premise of this study that there were important Italian Cathar communities, existing in dialogue with Catholic orthodoxy but not created by it. What precisely does this statement mean? It is not true that a large number of people converted to a well-organized dualist church. Only in the imaginations of anti-Cathar polemicists did the Italian Cathars effectively create an antichurch, with a defined membership and an institutional and sacramental structure parallel to Rome.[7] However, families of Cathar believers demonstrably persisted in a number of towns for decades. They are an elusive subject because the major sources for their identities are the sentences of the inquisition that repressed them.[8] These are notoriously problematic records. For Orvieto, direct confessions and the testimony of witnesses do not survive. The register of sentences, judging from the marginalia, was preserved as a treasury record. The sentences were also retrospective, based on earlier sentences that are now lost, and on testimony describing events that took place decades earlier, and they generally record not beliefs but actions.

This information from the inquisition, while incomplete, is probably largely correct. Because thirteenth-century Italians used heresy sentences as political weapons, there is a strong temptation to conclude that heresy charges had little foundation in religious differences, and were instead trumped up by the men in power to punish political opponents. For Orvieto, this conclusion would be an error: the people sentenced for heresy were in fact Cathar sympathizers and believers. These, after all, were small towns. Many of the accused were from prominent families long and publicly linked to the Cathar faith. People knew who the Cathars were; some of them at times had actually preached their faith from public tribunals. In Orvieto, a scattering of the people sentenced were clearly not the political enemies of the regime in power, notably the nobleman Rainerio Munaldi Raineri Stephani.[9] Finally, contemporary documents reveal webs of interconnection and mutual support among households and individuals accused of Catharism, including marriages. Cathars aided each other, for example, in carrying out strategies to protect family property from the threat of confiscation because of an inquisitorial sentence. These interconnections support the view that they formed Cathar communities.

Who were they, what roles did they play in the town, and why did they maintain Cathar beliefs and practices? This question has animated a long tradition of scholarship on heresy and the interrelations between politics and religious belief. Some older research on medieval heresy pictured a dichotomy between social and religious motivation, debating whether heretics were primarily driven by political and socioeconomic motives or by religious faith. Scholars have long since concluded that the division is an artificial one. Most would argue in one form or another that heretical motivations were primarily religious, but that social, economic and political concerns played a role.[10] This study attempts to trade the complex interrelations between political concerns and religious beliefs that motivated the Italian Cathars.

I began this study because I was fascinated with the attractiveness of Cathar dualism. Catharism seemed a bleak and pessimistic faith that rejected the dominant tendencies in twelfth- and thirteenth-century spirituality. In a period marked by a new naturalism and emphasis on the spiritual possibilities of the created order, Cathars preached a flat denial. No aspect of the physical world could be made sacred. Catharism thus seemed a pessimistic anomaly in a time of new valuation of the human body; a new emphasis, for example, on the teaching that the sexual consummation of a marriage can perfect the sacrament. I expected to find in Catharism a profound expression of social and cultural alienation, the pessimism of an older nobility left behind by the dramatic social growth of the thirteenth century. That expectation proved simply to be wrong.

Instead, the Italian Cathar communities were integral to Duecento politics and society. Accounts of the social diffusion of Catharism have relied
in part on outdated views of the social structure and a tendency to understand local developments in terms of international politics. Some scholars
have simply concluded that Cathars belonged to all social classes, or that
they tended to come from the middle ranks of Italian society.[11] Many,
however, have accepted the view that the faith tended to spread vertically,
linking families of the minor nobility with clients.[12] Ironically, this view
derives in part from the pathbreaking archival scholar Luigi Fumi's 1875
analysis of the Orvietan evidence. Fumi argued that the faith first attracted
Ghibelline nobles disaffected because of papal territorial ambitions, then
spread to their clients. Fumi's reading of the Orvietan evidence is problematic. It relies on the persistent idea that Guelf-Ghibelline rivalry can be
read back to the beginning of the thirteenth century. Later chronicles
often narrated this period in terms of clear factional divisions: Luca Manenti, writing in the fifteenth century, assumed that the Monaldeschi-
Filippeschi, Guelf-Ghibelline division of the second half of the century
shaped Orvietan politics as early as 1211.[13] Recent scholarship has shown
this approach to be anachronistic. Political divisions in the early thirteenth
century had more to do with complex internal competition; factions developed out of local concerns and only later allied themselves with larger
parties. The view that the Cathar faith attracted disaffected aristocrats
and then spread to their clients also relies on unproven assumptions about
vertical social ties in medieval Italian towns.

The heart of this study is a reconstruction of networks of association
among Orvietan Cathars, understood against the background of the kinds
of kinship and patronage ties that probably structured the city's life. I
have found that the Orvietan Cathars generally were linked not by vertical
dependence but by the horizontal ties of family and profession. Their
most evident political allegiance was to the popular movement that sought
to build a strong, independent commune. At the center of the Orvietan
Cathar community was a group of rising new families at the forefront of
political and economic change. The Cathars included men who were
building the new popular and corporate institutions that became the institutional foundation of the city-republics. Cathar leaders in Orvieto were
civic treasurers, guild priors, rising bankers, and prosperous artisans.

Were they typical of Italian Cathars? There are significant elements of
continuity with the Cathar communities in Florence and Bologna. The

problems of comparison are complicated by the different nature and periods of the evidence, as well as the varying political development of the towns. Nevertheless, Florentine Cathars in the 1240s clearly included comparable minor elites and rising merchant houses. For Bologna, the evidence survives from decades later and describes prosperous artisans, many of them associated with the leather trades.

Why these social groups? Stradigotto, the Orvietan Cathar leader whose beliefs were listed in his sentence, was an emigrant from Siena who built a successful fur business. He owned his own shop in the center of town, and he and his nephew Gezio loaned large sums of money at interest. As a member of the furriers' guild, Stradigotto also had a direct representative in the town's governing councils. Understanding him in terms of social alienation is problematic. Why did a prosperous, successful man like Stradigotto invite Cathar perfects to his shop to preach, and even urge his friends to run the terrible risks associated with caring for fleeing perfects in the countryside?

To answer this question requires first the recognition that not all Cathars believed the same thing: different ideas and practices had resonance for specific individuals and groups. Furthermore, Cathar beliefs are better understood not as a pessimistic anomaly but within a more general climate of religious doubt. It is useful to think not in terms of a sharp division between two camps, Cathar and orthodox believers, but of a broad spectrum of beliefs and concerns, with Cathar perfects taking one cluster of positions. Some people were untroubled by the Catholic sanctification of the body. People venerated both austere Cathar perfects and the miracle-working bodies of the saints. Some Cathars were deeply committed to the absolute goodness of God, and believed in a dualist God not implicated in any way in physical suffering, pain, or corruption. Other Cathars did emphasize the dualist condemnation of marriage and sexuality. Cathar ideas, seen in this broader context, were not anomalous and bizarre but answered questions that troubled many believers.

I initially posed this problem in terms of cosmological belief: What attracted a person like Stradigotto to dualism? This emphasis now seems to me misplaced: many Cathars simply did not share my fascination with abstract dualist cosmology. The best guide to understanding the Orvietan Cathars for me has been Emile Durkheim. Durkheim pointed out in 1913 that while theorists of religion look to find a system of ideas, believers look to experience and practice; for them the function of religion is "to make us act, to aid us to live."[14] Stradigotto's veneration of the ascetic perfects is an expression not of alienation but of admiration for a pure spiritual ideal, an ideal that could support new social forms. The most common thread in the testimony of people accused of Catharism was enthusiasm for the holy lives of the perfects. People believed that because the perfects were *boni homines*, good men, salvation was in them and not in the clergy of the Catholic Church, who were too compromised by secular entanglements. The ideal renunciation of sensual appetite by the perfects was a demonstration of human strength and possibility. Thus, as Durkheim argued, asceticism ultimately speaks to social needs: social organization requires self-restraint and sacrifice. The merchant and artisan elite in the early thirteenth century confronted directly the problem of the restraint of the self-interest that led to internal conflict and faction, and the construction of a peaceful and stable vita civile. Cathar perfects were exemplars of uncompromising morality and self-restraint.

Furthermore, Cathar preaching stressed the protection of the sacred from contamination. These men engaged in building independent civic political and economic institutions in the early thirteenth century often worked in opposition to local jurisdictions claimed by Catholic institutions: bishops, monasteries, the papal curia. Tension over conflicting claims of civic independence and ecclesiastical authority were especially acute in Orvieto, as in Viterbo and Bologna, because these towns formed part of the papal states. Beginning in the late twelfth century, there were periodic struggles with the Roman curia over land and prerogatives. Some Orvietans perceived the Catholic clergy and Catholic religious practice to be hopelessly contaminated by secular entanglements. The pope placed the town under an interdict that denied Orvietans access to the sacraments to force them to give up the strategic fortress of Aquapendente; the miracles of the local Catholic saints supported the bishop in his legal disputes over lands and rents. Some people called the cathedral a den of thieves and the local clerics rapacious wolves, venerating instead Cathar perfects who preached and represented in their persons an ideal spiritual purity, a sacred realm unsullied by material concerns. Thus in Orvieto, and probably in other towns of the papal states as well, Catharism became an alternative understanding of the relations between public authority and the sacred, an understanding that by disengaging the sacred could sustain the creation of independent corporate institutions and celebrate heroic self-sacrifice.

For some men and women, Catharism offered a powerful account of human identity and capacity. Dualism opened the possibility of a radical critique of contemporary understandings of gender and sin. Cathars believed that the body is a cruel prison and physical life in all its forms, especially marriage and the procreation of children, a diabolic plot to contaminate and trap the spirit. If marriage and procreation are deplorable, what is the status of sexual difference itself? A Bogomil treatise that circulated in western Europe saw sexual difference as an alien imposition rather than integral to identity. On these grounds, women were allowed roles denied them in the Catholic Church: they could become perfects, travel, preach, and administer the consolation. This practice denied contemporary understandings of the differences between male and female natures.[15] This challenge was fundamental; ideas about sexual difference justified the medieval social and institutional order, with its limits on the legal capacities of women, including their roles within marriage and the household, in the political and economic life of the towns and within Catholic institutions. To what extent did Italian Cathars take up these ideas and practices? The evidence is frustratingly meager, but there were Cathar women, particularly in Florence, whose practice violated contemporary gender norms.

Repression and Heresy

As for the second approach to the Cathars, analysis of their repression and persecution, the most influential study has been Robert I. Moore's *The Formation of a Persecuting Society.* Moore's view develops from a point long recognized by scholars: the idea that heresy is by definition relative, since it can exist only in relation to orthodoxy.[16] Moore puts this point neatly: heresy, like beauty, lies in the eye of the beholder. Heretical groups were, in some ways, the creation of their opponents. Moore opened the implications of the relative nature of heresy by analyzing it as an aspect of the way medieval European authorities defined themselves through the construction of deviant groups. For Moore, heresy was the creation of an administrative and clerical elite eager to build and preserve their power. These men wrote papal and imperial legislation that depicted religious difference in terms of heresy, deviance, and treason.[17] People were stereotyped as patarene heretics, Ghibelline traitors, sodomites. The threat of heresy served in part to justify the considerable expansion of Catholic bureaucracy and authority in the thirteenth century. It also acted as a counterpoint to Catholic doctrine. The sacraments, elevated clerical status, the very definition of membership in Christian society were understood in opposition to the threat of heresy. This interpretation means that the idea that heresy was a threat to society did not originate in popular attitudes. Instead, Moore argues, a bureaucratic elite sought to preserve and build their own power through the invention of an external threat, including not only heretics but homosexuals, lepers, and Jews. The rise of heresy is better understood as an aspect of the rise of persecution.

For historians of Italian towns, where politics and religion were always hopelessly intertwined, parts of this argument are familiar. In civil wars, the winners often penalized the losers by labeling them heretics, so that heresy sentences served to justify the actions of a dominant regime. From the 1260s, the victorious Guelf faction lumped together their opponents—who admittedly were often antagonistic to the papacy—and labeled them heretics. The tragic figure of Farinata degli Uberti in Dante's *Inferno* is an example. Farinata, in fact, was a leader of Florentine Ghibellines who was condemned after death, along with his kinsman Bruno, for Cathar heresy. Heresy charges justified the winners' appropriation of ecclesiastical offices and substantial property.

The threat of heresy also aided in the definition of the ideological basis of civic and church authority. In Orvieto, this process was not subtle. The pope, bishop, and town executives appropriated Eucharistic symbols, symbols that were the most powerful Catholic answer to Cathar disdain for the body. It was in Orvieto that Urban IV promulgated the universal Corpus Domini feast and Thomas Aquinas probably wrote its liturgy. Orvietan civic and church officials celebrated the Corpus Domini through a public procession, a display of their power and authority in which they carried the relics of a local Eucharistic miracle. The Corpus Domini relics served at the same time to confound heretics, to demonstrate the truth of Catholic teaching on the body's potential for sanctity, and to define authority.

Ideas about Cathar heresy played a role in the definition of gender norms. The debate over Catharism is fascinating in the light of Michel Foucault's view that the body itself is discursively constructed. Foucault analyzed the history of understandings of sexuality in terms of a long process he called normalization, in which certain actions and views of the body came to be considered normal and other possibilities excluded. Whether one accepts Foucault's analysis in terms of discourse, there seems to me no question that a process of definition of the human body and human identity was taking place in the late twelfth and thirteenth centuries, most evidenced in a normalization of gender and sexuality. Catholic polemicists took up the question of gender by depicting Cathar practice as a violation of nature. Male and female natures were defined in ways based on the medieval Catholic view of marriage as intended for the procreation of children. Cathars, polemicists argued, violate nature: condemning childbirth, they prefer incest or sodomy, which meant sex that sins against nature because its primary purpose is not the procreation of children.

This association of heresy with sexual practices that were considered unnatural contributed to a larger pattern of the definition of gender roles. The late thirteenth century imposed new restrictions on the kinds of actions thought appropriate for women, in the family, in church institutions, and in the life of the towns. To give one example, the Orvietan town council sought to ban women from entering the Palazzo del Popolo, the town hall. Civic and judicial functions were appropriate to men, and women who needed to take part in court proceedings were best questioned at home. Women's religious practices were restricted in parallel ways. The early thirteenth century had seen a proliferation of small clusters of women living in various informal ways lives of religious penance; the early Franciscan women wandered like their male counterparts, and some came close to preaching. They were startlingly similar in practice to Cathar women. By the end of the century, female penitents were subsumed within the religious orders, and Franciscan women were enclosed behind convent walls.[18] The condemnation of heretical practices contributed to new definitions of authority and gender.

The conflict between Cathar and Catholic is best understood in terms of dialogue and contest rather than repression and resistance. The construction of stereotypical understandings of heresy and their application to living individuals was a complex process, and never altogether successful. This process was not a matter of clerks imposing an ideology on a passive, gullible population. The contest, at least until midcentury, was not that uneven: the Cathars themselves included wealthy and influential families, men who played leadership roles in the community for decades. Instead, there were complex struggles over the imposition of the concept of heresy, in which mendicant inquisitors—sometimes, but not always, backed by local bishop and civic authorities—sought to impose these ideas. In many towns, including Orvieto and Florence in the 1240s, accused Cathars used force to oppose the bishop and inquisitors and did so with considerable success. Furthermore, it is clear that stereotypical understandings of heresy needed to be taught, and that antipathy to Catharism was not popular in its origins. As Moore argues, this process was not a community effort at redefinition through the excusion of deviants. The evidence is better for popular antipathy to the friars than for antipathy to the people convicted of heresy. Orvietans, like other Italian townsfolk, were not easily convinced that their Cathar neighbors were dangerous heretics.[19] As we shall see, the Orvietans sometimes cheerfully placed in high public office a person only recently convicted of heresy by the local inquisitors. Civic authorities, for reasons that might include political alliances and jurisdictional concerns, as well as personal sympathies, sometimes resisted the inquisition. In Rimini, a podestà removed the antiheretical statutes from the books and readmitted exiled heretics to the town.[20]

People sometimes just were not convinced by the friars. In Bologna in 1299, townspeople reacted to the conviction and execution of two popular local artisans for heresy with rage against the Dominican inquisition. A contemporary inquisitorial register records their comments. When the sentences were read in church, a nobleman, Messer Paolo Trintinelli, called out that this was an evil deed, that the inquisitor could have whatever he wanted written and that he, Messer Paolo, would not give a single bean for those writings. He considered the inquisitor a greater heretic than the condemned men.[21] When the two men and a woman's corpse were burned, the town rioted. People cried out that it was the inquisitor who was the heretic, the devil, the antichrist. Some explicitly called heresy the creation of the Catholic Church. A Phylippa said, "It is the friars who make men heretics"; a Domina Margarita similarly stated that heresy comes from the friars.[22] These people recognized the political uses of heresy charges and were acutely aware of the relative nature of heresy and orthodoxy: "heretic" is a label one side imposes on the other.

Definitions and Sources

What does it mean to term the people sentenced by the inquisition Cathars? In part to do so is simply convenience: calling them "probable or accused Cathar believers or sympathizers" is cumbersome. To do so also implicitly accepts the inquisitors' approach to the problem, labeling as Cathars people who heard the perfects preach, reverenced and aided them, and received their blessings. This label indicates not beliefs but actions that challenged clerical authority.

What was the connection between these actions and Cathar dualist belief? A fairly sophisticated and cohesive Cathar theology existed, but it is not at all clear these ideas were effectively communicated to most ordinary believers.[23] Many convicted Cathars did not know or accept anything like a Cathar orthodoxy. Stradigotto, who was well informed about Cathar teachings, was exceptional. Many people sentenced for heresy simply admired the Cathar holy people or took up some elements of their teaching. Evidence of accused Cathars without clearly dualist beliefs is plentiful, including the case of a Bolognese artisan convicted of Catharism who was accustomed to donate wine for the Eucharist to the local Carmelites.[24] The most bizarre mingling of Cathar and Catholic belief, as I will show, is the irresistible case of Armanno Punzilupo, who, despite strong Cathar leanings, was buried in the cathedral in Ferrara and for a time venerated as a saint. Armanno scrupulously confessed to Catholic clergy and did penance. He certainly considered himself an orthodox member of the *ecclesia Dei.*[25] Two Orvietans venerated both the Franciscans and the Cathars. They seem to have been untroubled by this contradiction, as were some clerics.

The assumption that most non-Cathars knew and accepted Catholic beliefs is also problematic.[26] It was only at the Lateran Council in 1215, and in part as a result of struggles over heresy, that Innocent led the Catholic Church in setting down guidelines for lay instruction and practice. Accurate instruction of the laity was a staggering problem, and most believers—Catholic and Cathar—did not grasp orthodox belief and practice very clearly. Religious categories were blurred. Perhaps the clearest dividing line was acceptance of the Cathar consolation, which implied belief that Cathar and not Catholic Christianity offered a chance at salvation. Even this test can be problematic, since some individuals apparently accepted both Cathar consolation and Catholic baptism and confession. Ultimately, for the inquisitors, heresy was defined by disobedience of Catholic authority rather than by doctrine.[27]

I have preferred the label "Cathar" to that of "heretic." The categories "heretic" and "orthodox" are relative: one person's heretic is another's orthodox believer. There is an important distinction between a Cathar and a Cathar viewed as a heretic. This difference was familiar in the late thirteenth century: again, in Bologna in 1299, people outraged by the execution of the pursemaker Bompietro called out that not Bompietro but the Dominican inquisitors were the heretics. When Cathars were called heretics or patarenes by their opponents, they were given not only a religious but a political and social label, which they themselves would not have accepted, as deviants and even as traitors. It seems to me that a study of Cathars should distinguish between their beliefs and the ideas imposed on them by opponents. Therefore, I have also struggled to find a label for the Christian believers who were not drawn to Catharism and remained in communion with Rome. Terming them orthodox implicitly accepts the anti-Cathar position, denying that Cathars by their own lights could be orthodox as well. Furthermore, it is not clear that non-Cathar Christians were all orthodox. I have chosen the term "Catholic" as the least value-laden, and ask readers to set aside any anachronistic suggestion of post-Tridentine Roman Catholicism.

The problem for a local study of a heretical group is to judge first what characterized the movement itself and then what ideas were imposed on it by opponents. This project entails picking through contemporary texts in an effort to uncover what can be known of the people linked to Catharism themselves: who they were, their socioeconomic and political roles, perhaps even their beliefs. Then their beliefs and actions can be differentiated, to some extent, from the ideas about heretics imposed on them by their opponents. This delicate problem is complicated by the nature of the sources for medieval heresy. For the most part, four kinds of documents survive. First, there are a few Cathar texts that circulated in western Europe, including several Bogomil accounts and one work, the *Liber de Duobus Principiis*, written by a thirteenth-century Italian.[28] These described a complex Cathar theology and have been exhaustively analyzed by a number of scholars. The problem with these texts for the purposes of this study is that it is not at all clear that the people accused of Cathar sympathies in Orvieto or most other Italian towns were familiar with them or had heard preachers recount the teachings contained in them. Again, it would be rash to conclude that everyone sentenced by the inquisition for association with Catharism had a clear grasp of Cathar or, for that matter, Catholic orthodoxy. A few texts also exist that record statements of beliefs by Cathar perfects and give us some access to Cathar preaching. Often they have something of the tenor of folktales, collections of stories told by the perfects. The most important of these is the 1229 statement of the perfects Andreas and Pietro (included in appendix A).

The second kind of document is accounts written by Catholic clergy opposed to the Cathars.[29] While these authors were hostile, some were scrupulous and well informed, particularly the compiler of the *Summa* attributed to James Capelli. The author was careful to correct misconceptions about the Cathars: it is not true that perfects have sex orgies or strangle the sick to make them martyrs. They lead chaste, pure lives and "in austerity of abstinence they surpass all other religious."[30] Other authors, notably Ranieri Sacconi, claimed to be accurate because they themselves had at one time been Cathars.[31] Nevertheless, these Catholic authors were preoccupied with pastoral and institutional concerns and understood the Cathars as a threat to authority. They stressed the Cathar attack on the power of the clergy and the sacraments; they tended to depict the Cathars as a well-organized institution holding a consistent set of religious beliefs: Cathars as a full-blown antichurch and a major threat. This view, as Moore has pointed out, justified the scale of the Church's response, including crusade and inquisition. But this view was also, in fact, deceptive: it is doubtful that the Cathars ever—even in their heyday in the south of France—posed a serious threat to the Church headed in Rome.

A third kind of document is hagiographical: accounts of the saints and their miracles. Two important texts survive for Orvieto, the *Leggenda* of Pietro Parenzo and local testimony to the miracles of Ambrose of Massa.[32] The depiction of Catholic belief and practice in these documents reveals a great deal as well about beliefs that were not Catholic. In fact, Cathar believers appear in both texts. A remarkable hagiographical/inquisitorial text survives from Ferrara, local testimony to the miracles and heresy of Armanno Punzilupo.[33] Armanno, who was probably a Cathar perfect, was buried in the cathedral in Ferrara. For a time, a cult developed around his tomb, and people came to leave offerings and pray for miracles. The dossier of documents includes both testimony to Armanno's postmortem miracles, collected by cathedral canons who wanted to encourage the cult, and testimony gathered by the horrified Dominican inquisitors, who wanted him exhumed and burned as a relapsed Cathar heretic. The materials give a remarkable look at contemporary religious concerns that bridge the divison between heresy and orthodoxy.

The fourth kind of document is inquisitorial: depositions and sentences, sometimes copied into large registers. These are scanty. No great inquests of whole populations comparable to the 1245–46 survey of the Lauragais survive for Italy, let alone a collection of detailed depositions like the massive registers of Jacques Fournier or Bernard Gui. The central text for Orvieto is the register of sentences dated 1268, a copy probably saved by the city government as a record of its share of the fines and confiscated property.[34] Portions of other inquisitorial records also survive, from Orvieto and elsewhere in Italy, including material from Florence and Bologna that contains more extensive testimony, as well as sentences.[35] Inquisitorial texts have obvious drawbacks. People's statements about their beliefs were responses to questions shaped by the preoccupations of the inquisitors, shaped in turn by the manuals they used to understand the heresy. Furthermore, the notaries who recorded the answers were translating vernacular speech into medieval Latin. Despite these institutional and linguistic filters the answers can be startling: one Bolognese pursemaker argued that just as there are seventy-two languages, so there are seventy-two religious faiths. Inquisitorial records thus do sometimes allow us to hear—at a distance, formulated in response to hostile questions and then translated into Latin—the voices of accused Cathars and those who sympathized with them.

PART I

THE POLITICS

OF THE CATHARS

The Murder of Parenzo

THE SPREAD OF CATHAR beliefs in Italy took place during the period of the collision of civic and ecclesiastical efforts at statebuilding. That conflict gave the Cathar movement a distinctive character. Historians of heresy have long insisted on the primacy of religious motivation for heretical movements, and I do not dispute that approach: it would do the Italian Cathars a bizarre injustice to deny the spiritual force of their movement. At the same time, in the thirteenth century, political and religious ideas were interwoven: beliefs about the nature of the sacraments were closely linked to beliefs about the nature of authority. The brilliant pope Innocent III recognized this fact and directly tied his understanding of papal sovereignty to the definition of heresy. Therefore the success of Catharism in Orvieto and the other Italian centers of the faith is best understood in the context of contemporary politics. This chapter explores the association between ecclesiastical statebuilding, the early Cathars, and efforts to repress them as heretics.

Ecclesiastical statebuilding was a long-term consequence of the great reforms of the late eleventh and early twelfth centuries. Popes, bishops, and abbots became acutely aware of the need to maintain resources that would allow the church's institutions to have autonomy: freedom from lay control. The papal curia saw with clarity that the way to avoid lay domination was to establish an autonomous papal territorial state. From the time of the energetic English pope Adrian IV, the papacy actively worked to develop its holdings into an effective state. Papal bureaucracy was gradually reorganized to create the most effective record-keeping, tax collection, and propaganda effort in Europe. The *Liber Censuum*, or *Book of Cencius*, was an important benchmark. Comprising a list of rents, copies of donations, and other documents, it was begun by the papal chamberlain in 1192 to serve as evidence to justify territorial and financial claims.[1] Adrian and his successors sought to extend papal dominion over a series of strategic sites in Lazio and medieval Tuscany. Their efforts were held back for a time by the conflicts with the Holy Roman Emperor Frederick Barbarossa, but renewed during the moment of imperial weakness at the end of the twelfth century.

On a smaller scale, some Italian bishoprics by the late twelfth century had been badly weakened by loss of lands and prerogatives to lay nobility and competing church institutions. In the Orvietan case, conflicts between the bishops and cathedral canons compromised episcopal power and authority. Energetic bishops struggled to shake off both lay and competing ecclesiastical claims, to regain and consolidate their old authority and jurisdictional rights, and to reclaim lost lands.[2] Some ambitious bishops emulated the lay nobility and sought to consolidate control of their holdings as territorial lordships.[3]

Ecclesiastical statebuilding took place against the background of the rise of the independent city-states. The late twelfth century was a period of remarkable institutional creativity, as townsmen sought ways to build communes that were free from outside jurisdiction. Growth and the drive for independence were fueled by rapid expansion of town populations and urban economies. Among the rising communes was the city of Rome itself, which sought local autonomy in direct opposition to the popes. In some towns, citizens guaranteed their own independence through the extension of the commune's control over its region, forming militias and launching campaigns to subdue rural nobles and neighboring towns, forcing their submission to civic authority. Rising communes thus were often at odds with episcopal ambitions and often directly opposed the expansion of papal rule.

Orvieto was at the center of these events. It held a critical strategic position in the papal state, and local resistance to papal jurisdiction was intense. It was in this political turmoil that the early Cathar missionaries arrived in the town and began to attract converts. A uniquely detailed contemporary text reveals the links between the repression of Catharism and conflicts over expanded papal and episcopal authority: a saint's passion, the *Leggenda* of Pietro Parenzo. Parenzo, the Roman rector sent by Innocent III to govern Orvieto and combat heresy, was assassinated in 1200, purportedly by Orvietan Cathars. His passion was written quickly, probably by a cathedral canon. The author was concerned to exonerate the bishop, rebuild episcopal fortunes, and, to that end, get Parenzo canonized. He tells the tale in terms of the invasion of Orvieto by heretical missionaries, orthodox defense, martyrdom, and triumphant post-mortem vindication. The text has often been read by historians of heresy as a straightforward narrative of the early struggle over Catharism in the town. The *Leggenda* is better understood as delicately positioned within local conflicts over episcopal ambitions and the larger contests over papal jurisdiction and political authority.[4] This chapter first looks briefly at late-twelfth-century Orvieto, the town's fractious relations with the papal curia, and the bishop's campaign to rebuild his jurisdiction and his cathedral roof. Then I focus on the *Leggenda,* and the relationship between the spread of Catharism, the extension of papal jurisdiction, and the murder of Parenzo.

Pope and Bishop in Orvieto

Orvieto had considerable strategic value for the papacy. It sits on a volcanic rock six hundred feet above the floor of the Paglia River valley. The sheer face of the rock was a considerable defense against assault. The town dominated a bridge over the Paglia River, on the major road north to Arezzo and Florence. This formidable military position, and perhaps also the town's loveliness, attracted the papacy, and from the mid–twelfth century on, papal efforts to strengthen their hold over the Tuscan Patrimony of Saint Peter centered in part on Orvieto. In 1155, Adrian IV chose the site for a meeting with Frederick Barbarossa. The planned meeting in Orvieto was forestalled when the emperor arrived early, but Adrian in 1157 agreed to a convention in which the Orvietans took an oath as feudal tenants, effectively recognizing papal sovereignty. In exchange, the Orvietans received three hundred libre, silver pounds, for help in maintaining the security of a stretch of the Via Cassia, the ancient road running north from Rome toward Siena.[5] Orvieto thus became a self-governing commune within the Patrimony. Adrian also initiated what was to become a long tradition of extended visits to Orvieto by the papal curia, and Orvieto, like Viterbo, developed a special status as a papal city.

At the end of the century, Orvieto's relations with the papacy became strained over its efforts to expand and reinforce papal jurisdiction in the region. In 1197 the death of Emperor Henry VI and the ensuing dispute over his successor opened an opportunity, and papal forces began to strengthen military defenses in the Patrimony, building new fortifications at Radicofani and Montefiascone and asserting control over existing fortresses of strategic value. Aided for once by troops from the city of Rome, the papacy inflicted a military defeat on the town of Narni and was able to claim a castle at Otricoli.[6] Orvieto was next in line. Not only was the town itself an important fort on a crucial road, but Orvieto also claimed Aquapendente and the adjoining Val di Lago of Bolsena, both northwest of Orvieto. The Val di Lago was a valuable grain-producing region, and Aquapendente was the town that commanded the bridge where the great medieval trade and pilgrimage road, the Via Francigena, crossed the Paglia. This location gave the town crucial strategic value. In the twelfth and thirteenth centuries, although a variety of north-south routes were used, the bulk of the traffic passed not near Orvieto and then north to Florence, but to the west of Orvieto, following the Via Francigena to Siena.[7] The papacy, the Orvietan commune, and the German emperors were all eager to have Aquapendente under their direct control, and the town changed hands endlessly. Frederick Barbarossa occupied it in 1161, built a fort, and maintained an imperial administration until 1177. The Aquapendentans themselves preferred independence and periodically rose in revolt, including an 1196 rebellion against Orvietan rule. In April 1198, Innocent III sought to claim the town.[8] He placed Orvieto under an interdict for usurping papal jurisdiction over it, and he recalled the bishop to Rome for nine months. According to Master John, the author of the *Leggenda* of Pietro Parenzo, it was this forced episcopal absence that allowed heresy to take hold in the city.[9]

In fact, the bishopric was in a sad state. As in many towns, the Orvietan bishops in the second half of the twelfth century were besieged on all sides.[10] They were threatened by their vassals and petty nobles, by the cathedral canons, by a schismatic bishop, by the new commune, and by papal ambitions as well. A plaintive commentary on these difficulties was written by Bishop Ranerio after his accession in 1228. Ranerio inventoried episcopal property and wrote notes on a compilation of episcopal documents, explaining the dismal state of the see. He looked for his explanation back to a mid–twelfth century conflict between the bishop and the canons of San Costanzo over control of episcopal rights and property. In 1149 Bishop Ildribando removed the canons from services in the cathedral, relying instead on parish clergy. Then in 1154 he gave in to pressure from the canons and restored to them the use of the cathedral and half the revenues from penances and burials. Ranerio's explanation of this series of events is scandalous. He writes that Ildribando was originally procurator of the see during a vacancy. The procurator administered the episcopal estates and collected the revenues on behalf of the bishop. Ranerio believed that Ildribando caved in because he was intimidated by the canons, who held him in disrepute because of a "lapse of the flesh."[11] It was fear of the canons and their knowledge of his lapse that inspired him to give away control of episcopal property. A priest from the bishop's table was so grieved by the bishop's actions, Ranerio tells us, that he burned the episcopal records. This story, for Ranerio, explained the absence of extensive episcopal documents. The gesture is a curious one: Why destroy rather than preserve records of lost property?

After Ildribando's time, the job of procurator fell to the canons, enabling them to exploit the see during a series of long vacancies.[12] Adrian IV supported them, and during the visit in which he received the oath of the city he confirmed the possessions and privileges of the chapter, surely a political trade-off. A seven-year episcopal vacancy, 1161–68, was the time of the greatest disaster, according to Ranerio. The see was in the keeping of Rocco, the prior from San Costanzo, "and those who should have been the guardians and shepherds of the vacant see were rather destroyers and wolves, usurping the father's goods." Another underlying problem was probably usurpation by lay vassals and tenants, aided by kinsmen among the canons. A member of the Monaldeschi family, Matteo di Pietro Cittadini, was mentioned as a canon in May 1180.[13] The Monaldeschi came to hold important episcopal property at Caio, perhaps as the bishop's vassals.[14]

Episcopal problems were compounded when Frederick Barbarossa, in the course of his contest with Alexander III, appointed his own, schismatic bishop to the see. It was perhaps this threat that led Bishop Rustico at his 1168 investiture to strengthen the canons further, confirming the restitution made to them by Ildribando. As Ranerio commented, the beleaguered bishop also rewarded his supporters with grants of episcopal property in the contado.[15] Rustico, unlike his predecessors, nevertheless had the stature to exercise authority over a major civic office. In February 1170 he acted together with the town's executives or consuls to grant privileges to a official whose exact function is murky but clearly powerful, since he was titled the master of bridges and the popolo.[16]

Subsequent bishops made some efforts at repair. Rustico was succeeded by Ricardo (1178–1202), an able and combative man who worked to recover and even extend episcopal prerogatives, becoming embroiled in a number of legal disputes.[17] One great success came in November 1181, when Rocco, the prior of San Costanzo, returned to the bishopric the baptismal parish of Santa Maria de Stiolo and the men of Caio.[18] Still, even in 1228, when Ranerio took inventory, he was shocked at the state of episcopal property. The movable wealth of the bishop consisted of an old set of vestments, two chests, a few books, a modest amount of grain and spelt, a lame mule, and nine wine casks, seven of them empty and two full. Of his other furnishings and goods, Ranerio writes, "he had been miserably despoiled."[19] In 1239 Ranerio was forced to pawn episcopal treasures, including two crosses and a book of antiphons, to raise funds to pay episcopal expenses.

The cathedral itself was left badly dilapidated for decades, a highly visible symbol of episcopal weakness. The focus of Orvietan worship of necessity was not the cathedral, Santa Maria Maggiore, but the church of San Andreas, in the heart of the town on the ancient forum that was to become the piazza comunale. Ildribando's concessions to the canons in 1154 had included a promise that he would repair the cathedral roof and walls. The 1170 meeting with the consuls and the master of bridges and the popolo did take place in the choir.[20] However, the church was in bad shape in 1200, when Master John tells us that it was used only at Christmas, Easter and the feast of the Assumption of the Virgin and was left empty at other times with scarcely three lamps to light it. Part of the roof had given way, allowing the rain in, and grass grew inside the building, so that it looked like a meadow.[21] There is an ironic clue that Orvietans cared about the state of their cathedral: one of the Cathar missionaries, a woman called Milita, established a reputation for piety through her efforts to have the roof repaired.[22]

Was the arrival of Cathar missionaries yet another disastrous blow to the bishopric, or a heaven-sent opportunity, an external threat that gave episcopal supporters a potent justification for strengthened episcopal authority? Evidently it was both. The early Cathar missionaries in Orvieto were successful in attracting followers, a success that was surely linked to the miserable state of the bishopric. This point is often made about the success of the Cathar movement in the south of France: it was the weakness of local church institutions that fostered heresy. One close parallel is Toulouse, which became a major Cathar center: the bishop in 1206 was so deeply in debt that he was afraid to have his mules walked out to be watered, for fear of their confiscation by his creditors.[23] At the same time, the bishops and their supporters were quick to use the threat of heresy to rally support and rebuild. Ironically, perhaps townsmen were alienated not so much by episcopal poverty as by the bishops' aggressive efforts to recover their estates and extend their revenues and jurisdiction.

Cathar and Papal Rector

The *Leggenda* of Pietro Parenzo describes the spread of Catharism in Orvieto and the 1199 death of the Roman rector Parenzo. The author, Master John, was probably a canon of the cathedral who went on to serve as bishop in 1211–12.[24] He mentions his other writings, which included a book attacking heresy, now lost. The *Leggenda* is clearly a contemporary account written by someone with intimate knowledge of local personalities and events, who viewed the appearance of the Cathars and the Catholic response as an active episcopal partisan. The text is constructed not as a conventional saint's life but as a passion narrative.[25] Master John simply left out standard hagiographical topics, including the saint's origins, Roman childhood, and either early sanctity or religious conversion. Instead, he set the tale entirely in Orvieto, against the background of the dangerous infiltration of heresy. Parenzo's career began when he rode in like a new sheriff in Dodge City to clean up the town. Master John concentrated on the events immediately leading up to Parenzo's martyrdom, the death itself, and his post-mortem miracles and vindication. For Master John, the political and military conflicts in the late-twelfth-century city were a clear struggle between heresy and orthodoxy, and he does not hint that Parenzo may have been unpopular with those who resented papal overlordship and feared the loss of civic independence. Perhaps for Master John, these opponents were ipso facto heretics as well. The political circumstances of the events strongly suggest that hostility to Parenzo had much to do with local antagonism to a controversial and ambitious bishop and especially with opposition to the expansion of papal jurisdiction. It may be that the episcopal response was a combined assault on heresy and on those who sought to usurp episcopal property, as was true in late-twelfth-century Vicenza.[26] The connection was explicit in the thought of Honorius III.[27]

Master John tells us that heresy was originally spread in Orvieto by a Florentine, Diotesalvo, together with Hermannino of Parma and Gerardo of Marzano, during the tenure of Bishop Rustico (1168–76). Rustico was understandably distracted: Frederick Barbarossa was occupying the nearby town of Aquapendente and had named his own imperial bishop to the Orvietan see, Pietro degli Omodei. The heretic Diotesalvo taught, Master John explains, that the Sacrament of the Body and Blood of Christ is nothing; that the baptism taught by the Roman Church effects nothing for salvation; that prayers and charities do not benefit the dead; that Pope Silvester and all his successors are bound to be tormented with eternal punishment; that all visible things are the creation of the devil and subject to his power; that the good will be be equal to the Blessed Apostle Peter in merits and rewards; the evil will suffer punishment like that of the traitor Judas.[28] Most historians have concluded that Diotesalvo was a Cathar missionary from Florence, an early Cathar center. The catalogue of his teachings is not consistent: the reference to the diabolic creation of all visible things suggests Cathar dualism, but the emphasis on eternal reward and punishment does not. Cathars generally did not believe in damnation any more than they believed in any purgatory other than life on earth. Perhaps Master John's knowledge was limited, despite his lost book on heresy, or quite possibly Diotesalvo did mingle Catholic and Cathar teachings.

Bishop Rustico's successor, Ricardo, threw the original missionaries out, but they were followed by two women, Milita of "Montemeato," perhaps Monte Amiata, and another Florentine named Julitta. According to Master John, these wolves in sheep's clothing fooled the bishop and the Orvietans by taking on the appearance of fervent orthodox piety. They attended divine services so frequently that the bishop even thought to admit them into a clerical confraternity. Milita, like another Martha, promoted the repair of the cathedral roof, while Julitta, like Mary, embraced the contemplative life. They appealed to women, and "the greater part of the matrons of the city and some of their friends began to venerate them as the most holy of women." "Under the pretext of religion" they drew many men and women into heresy.[29] Master John drew on contradictory contemporary understandings of female nature in suggesting that it was feminine deception that made the spread of heresy possible and matrons who were most fooled. Still, it is clear that some Cathars were established in the town in the last decade of the century.

When Bishop Ricardo realized that he had been tricked by the women's pretense of piety, he consulted with a council of canons, judges, and other prudent men, evidently turning to other civic and ecclesiastical authorities to build political support. Then the bishop began to pursue the heretics. He condemned some to death by hanging, others to be burned at the stake, and others to the loss of their citizenship and perpetual exile. Unrepentant heretics were buried outside the cemetery. No outside source allows us to check this account and judge the actual scale of the episcopal effort, but it is not at all clear that the bishop had the popular support and police power needed for a serious initiative against his opponents, Cathars or not. Furthermore, if people were executed for heresy it was by a local statute that is no longer extant, since capital punishment for heresy was only decreed in the constitutions of Frederick II, dating from 1224.[30] Master John's account serves to exonerate Bishop Ricardo by underscoring his energetic efforts to carry out his episcopal responsibility and combat heresy. It was not the bishop who was at fault.

In fact, Innocent III's interdict, imposed because of the dispute over Aquapendente, Master John tells us, allowed heresy to spread. During the interdict, Innocent detained Bishop Ricardo in Rome for nine months. This was disastrous. In his absence, the faith spread freely and Cathars preached in the open. A certain "doctor of Manicheanism" called Peter Lombard moved to Orvieto from Viterbo and called a council with other learned Cathars. Manicheanism was of course a common medieval label for heresy. The learned doctor Peter Lombard always provokes an indignant orthodox footnote: he was emphatically not the Catholic theologian called the Master of the *Sentences,* the author of a standard theological textbook.[31] A multitude of nobles and people came to hear the Cathar preaching, Master John reports, and so many became heretics that they preached in public against the Catholics. The heretics began to say that in case of war the Catholics could be exiled from Orvieto and the fortress town made a bastion of the Cathar faith.

Master John thus neatly pinned the blame for the spread of heresy not on the bishop but on the bishop's involuntary absence. The author heavily underscored the scale of the threat to orthodoxy: without the bishop, the town was very nearly taken over by heretics. There is an undercurrent of criticism of the papal curia: the obvious unstated implication is that it was Innocent who was at fault. At the same time, the author's bundling together of opposition to the papacy and attraction to heresy may well reflect the actual mood of the Orvietans. Anger at a papal interdict that restricted their access to the sacraments in order to force the town to give up Aquapendente probably did make Orvietans more receptive to the preaching of the perfects, more impressed by their voluntary poverty and austerity. Perfects probably did preach openly in the town, as did Cathar believers decades later. A Cathar council at Orvieto is also possible, though it is documented in no other source. The proposed expulsion of all Catholics is surely a fantastic overestimation of Cathar numbers.[32] In sum, there is no compelling reason to deny Master John's assertion that Cathar missionaries did preach in Orvieto in this period, although he had reason to emphasize the scale of the threat they posed to the Catholic Church.

Finally, Master John tells us, the Orvietans in desperation sent a messenger to Rome requesting help of Pope Innocent and the Romans, and the Roman popolo in response sent a young man, Pietro Parenzo, to serve as rector.[33] Parenzo's appointment was a delicate political choice. Parenzo's family and political ties, left unmentioned by Master John, are revealing: he derived from a family that probably rose in the papal administrative service.[34] At least from 1148, they claimed senatorial office. The Roman Senate and popolo, after their 1143 assertion of republican independence, were often at odds with the papacy, a conflict complicated by emperors who played off the rivalry, using both diplomatic and military means. Popes for the most part were simply unable to control the town, and a newly elected pope typically could secure Roman fealty only by payment of a large customary bribe called the *donativum* to prominent Romans. Parenzo's family was among the Roman republican leaders. A "Iohannes Parentii" appears among the senators ratifying an 1188 settlement with Clement III over control of civic honors; when in 1219, in the course of a conflict with Honorius III, the Senate corresponded with the emperor Frederick II, it was a Parenzo who wrote to offer the emperor a Roman coronation. In 1225 a short-lived Roman regime hostile to the papacy was led by Parenzo Parenzo.[35] Innocent III, by the time of his 22 February 1199 consecration, had achieved some control over the Roman Senate, and probably was able to use the donativum to extract oaths of obedience.[36] It was shortly after his consecration that Parenzo was appointed to the rectorship in Orvieto. The appointment was thus a neat political choice, perhaps a concession to a major senatorial family. Innocent's later refusal to canonize Parenzo may have had to do not only with personal knowledge of the youth's character and piety but with the family's politics and clout: perhaps Innocent was loathe to allow them a saint.

Innocent's efforts against heresy and his efforts to extend papal monarchy were closely linked.[37] His decretal attacking heresy in Viterbo, "Vergentis in senium," issued on 25 March 1199, was already in preparation in February, when Parenzo was sent to Orvieto. The decretal for the first time defined heresy as a form of lèse-majesté, high treason in Roman law, an offense against the divine majesty of Christ. This definition relied on an understanding of the sovereign status and unique judicial authority of the pope as Christ's representative: the pope alone is able to judge that heresy, as an attack on the faith that is the foundation of Christian society, constitutes an attack on papal sovereignty. In effect, a "heretic was a rebel against his sovereign, the pope."[38] "Vergentis" provided that lay authorities were to punish heretics through the confiscation of all their property and goods, effectively disinheriting their descendants. Any who aided them were to be excommunicated.[39] Innocent thus interwove a new definition of heresy as treason with a new definition of papal sovereignty: the two were bound up together.

The appointment of Parenzo was part of the larger effort to expand papal jurisdiction in the towns of the Patrimony. After Innocent's election, rectors were quickly sent to a number of towns. The Orvietan messenger who complained of the threat of Cathar heresy and wolves among the flock and asked for aid thus offered Innocent an irresistible political opportunity. By the same token, Parenzo's arrival, for some Orvietans, marked the town's subordination to a papal appointee, even while the dispute over Aquapendente was left unsettled. Master John mentions several times in the *Leggenda* the close association of Parenzo with a Roman judge named Henrico, and he even casts Henrico in the implausible role of disciple. Like Christ's disciples, Henrico dined with Parenzo the night of his betrayal and death. Judge Henrico's presence in Orvieto surely meant the expansion of papal legal jurisdiction, though little evidence remains other than the mention of heresy cases in the *Leggenda*. In practice, rectorial justice, as Phillip Jones points out, usually "consisted largely of proceedings for disobedience."[40]

Some Orvietans did resist. Master John tells us that when Parenzo took office in February 1199, the Orvietans greeted him with great relief and rejoicing, a scene evoking Christ's entry into Jerusalem. But Master John also mentions opposition and civil war. The ensuing conflict is portrayed as a struggle between heresy and orthodoxy, but it surely had as much to do with Orvietan resistance to papal overlordship as it did with Cathar dualism.[41] One of Parenzo's first acts as rector was to prohibit the traditional carnival games, on the grounds that their violence offered a means of concealing homicides.[42] The heretics, Master John writes, reacted with violence: on the first day of Lent, the whole city began to fight with swords, lances, and stones, in the main piazza and the towers and palaces surrounding it. Parenzo courageously rode through the middle of the conflict and remained miraculously unharmed. Then he punished some of the participants by destroying the towers and palaces involved. In effect, internal fighting broke out; some Orvietans violently opposed Parenzo and were served with the traditional punishment of political opponents, the destruction of their urban properties.

Parenzo acted in concert with the bishop, as Master John tells the story. Their authority was closely intertwined: the rector even shared the episcopal palace. The two began their efforts against heresy with an amnesty. Up to a certain date, heretics were allowed to return freely to the Church. After that time, the heretics suffered public whippings, exile, and the destruction of their houses.[43] They imposed monetary fines that, Master John tells us, made their avaricious owners weep real tears.[44] Perhaps this reference was to Cathar merchants or moneylenders, stereotypically avaricious. Again, there are few clues either to the scale of this effort or to its targets, and it is not at all clear how much political and military support Parenzo could muster. There is good evidence that Orvietans were unhappy about the weight of his fiscal exactions, which included securities posted to guarantee good behavior.[45] When Parenzo was abducted, the first demand of his kidnappers was that he return their money.

As Parenzo's death approaches, the *Leggenda* follows more closely the conventions of a martyr's passion. Parenzo returned home to spend Easter with his household, and he presented himself to Innocent during the traditional papal procession from Saint Peter's to the Lateran. He told the pope that the heretics were threatening him with death because he had punished them. Innocent sent him back to Orvieto with all his sins absolved in advance in case the heretics should happen to kill him. As his wife and mother grieved, the young man returned to Orvieto. Meanwhile, the Orvietans he had punished and who opposed his presence met and decided to force him to repay their pledges and renounce his overlordship. The plotters also, Master John writes, planned to demand that he consent to and even favor their perfidy. Parenzo's servant Radulph was promised a bribe to betray him and thus plays the role of Judas in the passion.

Master John gives a lively and detailed account of what followed, including dialogue, which is presumably imaginary. At Parenzo's last supper, a dinner with the Roman judge Henrico, the traitor Radulph accepted food directly from his lord's hand. Later, when Parenzo had removed his shoes and prepared for bed, Radulph and the other plotters kidnapped him, wrapped his head in hides, and carried him off. The disorganized kidnappers argued over their destination and ultimately took him to a hut outside town. They demanded that he repay their pledges, relinquish dominion of the city, and, if he wished to survive, make a formal agreement strengthened by an oath that he would never harm their sect but rather give it aid and favor.[46] These demands seem contradictory: Why, if Parenzo was to renounce his office and presumably return to Rome, demand an oath of support for Catharism as well? The inconsistency derives from the author's casting of the account in terms of a conspiracy to protect heresy, rather than opposition to the papal rectorship and fiscal exactions. This opposition does not mean that the conspirators could not have been Cathars or Cathar sympathizers as well.

Parenzo agreed to return the pledges, but he was unwilling to give up rule of the city or swear to support their sect. He was killed, according to Master John, almost by accident after one of the kidnappers lost his temper and struck him on the mouth, knocking him to the ground, where some dust in his mouth served as the sacrament of communion. The rest stabbed him. The corpse, after some indecision on the part of the murderers, was left under a tree. The men who first found the body assumed at first that it was the corpse of "some murdered merchant," a sad commentary on the safety of a major road in 1199. When they recognized the rector and his death was revealed, the bishop, clergy, and all the people came running; the whole town, Master John tells us, grieved. "Even the court wept," he writes, "because while there was law in the city, he who had adjudicated and enforced it was gone, and the laws and decrees were forced to become silent by the death of their patron."[47] Parenzo's death brought an end to his judicial proceedings and to the enforcement of law. The identification of Parenzo with justice—and the idea that his saintly power derives from the fact that he was murdered because of justice—is a theme in the *Leggenda*.[48]

Bishop Riccardo quickly used the death of Parenzo to bolster his authority. The rise of a cult around the murdered rector is a clear case of the political use of sainthood. The corpse was first carried to San Andreas, the church on the old forum that, because of the dilapidation of the cathedral, was the center of lay worship. Conflict broke out over whether to bury the body there. Some, including the Roman judge Henrico and presumably the bishop, thought the cathedral more fitting. San Andreas and the forum were a center of communal power distanced symbolically and geographically from the episcopal complex.[49] The bishop's side prevailed, since the martyr's corpse was moved to the cathedral. To do so was appropriate, Master John wrote, as the man who was killed by blasphemers of Jesus Christ and his Virgin Mother could thus by his burial bring greater honor and reverence to the church dedicated to her. It was also fitting that the patron of Orvieto be buried in that church where he had often discussed with Ricardo, bishop of Orvieto, how best to clear the Church of "the filth of heresy."[50]

In fact, the roof was still so bad that it rained directly in on the new saint's tomb. The location of the tomb was part of the episcopal effort to reconstruct the cathedral as the center of episcopal authority and lay worship, a reconstruction that was both physical and symbolic. In 1200, the bishop used the cathedral to exercise his authority when he established an episcopal rental contract in the church, before the altar of Saint Thomas.[51]

Parenzo's early miracles underscore the bishop's interest in centering the cult on the new tomb in the cathedral and associating it with episcopal authority. The martyred Parenzo quickly developed a reputation for healing, particularly the restoration of sight to the blind. Master John tells us that the cult enjoyed dramatic success, drawing great crowds to the cathedral. People prostrated themselves at the tomb and remained there for days, praying for the saint's aid, and many had their prayers granted. The cathedral that had been so dimly lit now enjoyed miraculous lights, now scarlet, now golden. The miracle stories mention local skepticism of the new cult, and Master John emphasizes the ways in which opposition was confounded by the power of the saint. When, for example, the prior of Santa Trinita, who was involved in a legal fight with the bishop, expressed incredulity, he suffered a supernatural punishment.

One story conveys the flavor of Parenzo's miracles. A rural priest named Lambert had been separated from the communion of the clergy and deprived of his benefice because he was thought to be involved in heresy. Since his brother Pepo suffered from a recent paralysis of his fingers, Lambert begged to be restored to his clerical office so that he could support his brother and the man's wife and children, who had no other resources. The bishop did not relent. Pepo, like many other ill people, visited the tomb of the martyr. Lying at the tomb and deploring his sins, Pepo humbly asked the martyr to restore his hands. They were instantly and miraculously cured. Master John testifies directly: he personally saw them, first in their damaged and then in their restored condition.[52] The doubting priest Lambert was not returned to his benefice, but the humble and devout Pepo received a miraculous cure. The tale underscores both the confounding of the bishop's opponents and the saint's merciful patronage. Other miracles involved not the bishop's enemies but his supporters. Messer Munaldo Petri Cittadini, as discussed later, contributed two miracles. He belonged to the Monaldeschi, the family that may have started out as episcopal vassals and went on to become the leaders of the Guelf faction and, from 1334, the lords of the city.

The Early Cathars

Who did murder Parenzo? According to a fifteenth-century Orvietan chronicler, an important rural noble family, the Prefetti di Vico, was ultimately responsible for the killing. Some contemporary evidence supports this statement. Some of the murderers fled to a Prefetti property; the Prefetti were later deprived of their castle, perhaps as punishment. Luigi Fumi, the late-nineteenth-century historian of Orvieto, on these grounds understood the early heretics to have been Ghibelline nobles and their clients, whose disaffection from the Catholic Church was a reaction to papal policies in the region.[53] Scholars now argue that the Ghibelline proimperial faction per se did not exist in 1199. Still, the Prefetti may have been involved in the death, and they probably were threatened by papal territorial ambitions. They were not great friends of the town either: this was also the period when the commune pressured rural nobles to submit to civic authority and surrender their castles, as did the Prefetti. The communes, including Orvieto, were far better able to subdue rural nobles than was the papacy.

Who were the early Cathars? There is a heartbreaking reference in Bishop Ranerio's inventory of episcopal property to three notebooks concerning the heretics, now long lost. The *Leggenda* does mention social categories, as we have seen: pious matrons, urban nobles who owned towers on a central piazza, and perhaps merchants or moneylenders, as well as Lambert, the priest who lost his benefice. More detailed evidence comes from the 1268 sentences of the Franciscan inquisitors, who demonstrably consulted earlier records that have since been lost. Several members of urban lineages were explicitly described in these sentences as deriving their heresy from their progenitors or belonging to a house of heretical persuasion.[54] Their involvement extended back several generations, although only one is explicitly traced to the twelfth century. The moneylender Cittadino Viviani Avultronis, according to his sentence, came from progenitors implicated in Parenzo's murder. However, of course, his unnamed progenitors could have been involved in the death without being Cathars.[55]

These inquisitorial sentences emphasize the roles of rising houses with strong urban interests rather than older nobles like the Prefetti. The most notorious longstanding Cathar family was the Toste, whose cluster of houses, palaces and a tower in the *rione* (neighborhood) of Santa Pace suggests a fairly recent urban presence. Toste were prominent in Orvieto in the early decades of the century. Two of them assented to a treaty with Siena in 1202.[56] Another Toste agreed in 1212 to a settlement between Bishop Giovanni and an important episcopal vassal, the Bulgarelli counts at Parrano.[57] In 1221 Ranuccio Toste and Ranerio Toste were among the Orvietans who consented to a pact with Siena.[58] In 1229 the Toste played a central role in an agreement between the walled village or castrum of Montepulciano and the Orvietan commune, which led to a Florentine alliance: the pact was made in a Toste house.[59] They served in the civic militia: Ildebrandino Ricci was among the Orvietan prisoners released by the Sienese in 1235.[60] Despite their lack of titles, due presumably to their long association with heresy, the Toste are best described as minor nobles of recent, probably urban origins.

The Lupicini were another older family: probably some were consuls in the late twelfth century.[61] A Johannes Lupicini agreed to a pact with Siena in 1202.[62] By the 1220s, they were prominent in public life: Provenzano is mentioned as a witness in 1222 and served, as discussed later, as communal treasurer or *camerarius* in 1239.[63] He went on to hold popular offices in the 1250s. Amideo similarly appears as a witness during Provenzano's term as treasurer, in 1239.[64] He was active in the 1250s, witnessing, for example, the 1251 submission of Aquapendente, and serving as a rector as late as 1266.[65] The Lupicini were prosperous in the mid–thirteenth century, judging from their high tax assessments. There are no clues to urban financial interests. To my knowledge, despite the antiquity of the family, they are not mentioned with titles, though Provenzano's grandson was a Ghibelline knight killed in battle in 1289.[66]

The Toncelle were probably a more recent lineage. Judging from the surname, Toncella was the lineage founder; his father Arone appears in a list of Orvietans of 1202.[67] Toncella served as civic treasurer in 1215.[68] The family owned a house and tower in San Andreas.[69] They had titles, which were surely derived from the commune. Toncelle by the time of the 1292 catasto nevertheless held substantial rural property. I have seen no evidence of mercantile or banking interests. Both Toncella and his son Artone died as consoled Cathars.[70] His son Messer Domenico persisted in both traditions, public service and Catharism.[71] He, too, was civic treasurer as early as 1234, taking part in the settlement of a dispute between the commune and the bishop in which the commune paid a large sum in exchange for the bishop's lifting of a ban of excommunication from the town and its residents.[72] As discussed later, he enjoyed a distinguished career and for a time virtually ran the commune as prior of the arts. Another Toncelle son, Messer Matteo, was very prominent in public life but never accused of Catharism; one of his sons, Pietro di Matteo, became an influential jurist.[73] Other individuals were described in their 1268 sentences as deriving from heretical houses, but they are less well documented.

Orvieto at the turn of the century, then, was divided along combined political and religious lines. Parenzo was disliked by Orvietans both because of his efforts to punish heresy and because he represented submission to papal overlordship. The assassination was directly motivated by anger over his fiscal exactions.

Who opposed Parenzo? The aggressive policies of the papacy must have alienated older landed nobles, like the Prefetti di Vico, whose prerogatives were genuinely threatened by papal ambitions. But other people were directly affected by the papal rector, particularly townsfolk, men from prosperous new families who benefited from the independent commune, holding important offices in civic administration. By the 1240s men from these families played major roles in the popular associations and popular rule.

What, then, explains the early success of the Cathar preachers? Surely opposition to papal ambitions played a part, as did the squabbles of the local clergy: the bankrupt bishopric, half-ruined cathedral, and rapacious canons. Master John writes that the miracles of Pietro Parenzo restored popular devotion to the cathedral, even among "those liars who had called the church a den of thieves."[74] Not all the clergy deserved this, as the reference in the *Leggenda* to a clerical confraternity suggests. Pastoral care cannot have been good; parish clergy must often have been ill-educated. In 1234 Bishop Ranerio required two priests to swear that they would renounce their concubines, Clara and Benvegnate. They would no longer have carnal relations with them, nor eat and drink with them, nor live in the same house. One of the men was the priest at a major rural parish in Allerona.[75] These priests are best seen not as corrupt but as old-fashioned, and little differentiated from the laity.

The regular clergy were not exempt from the charge of corruption. In 1220, when Honorius III passed at least three summer months in Orvieto, he expelled the "black monks" from the venerable abbey of Santi Severo and Martirio, just outside the city. Ranerio noted in his episcopal chronicle that they had been abusing the Rule and had not been corrected by the bishop.[76] They were ultimately replaced with Praemonstratensians. But probably some Orvietans were troubled not by old-fashioned priests or lazy monks but by the energetic and expansionist bishop and pope.

Cathar perfects, in contrast, were exemplars of Christian piety and poverty, uncontaminated by worldly ambition. Their purity had great attraction not only for laymen but for alienated clerics like Lambert, who lost his benefice because he was drawn to the Cathars. This point has often been made in the scholarship on the Cathars, and the Orvietan evidence supports it. When accused Cathars were questioned about their beliefs, the most common response was to stress the holy lives of the perfects. In them, and not in the Catholic clergy, lies the path to salvation.

As I argue later, the perfects as exemplars of abstinence and self-control offered an ideal closely suited to civic life—to the need for citizens to put aside self-interest and pursue communal good. The *Leggenda* of Parenzo also underscores how movingly Cathar perfects articulated their faith. As Master John tells us, a multitude of Orvietans converted to heresy after they heard the learned Cathars preach.

The importance of heroic abstinence and preaching to the success of the Cathars was well understood by Innocent III, who, after all, permitted Francis to establish his new mendicant order. Innocent visited Orvieto in 1216, shortly before his death.[77] While in the town, he took an interest in the local churches, and he consecrated an altar for the Augustinian canons. It was on this visit that he refused to canonize Parenzo. The pope was only too aware of the strong Cathar presence in Orvieto as well as Viterbo, and perhaps his decision to launch a new crusade from the city during his visit was an effort to counter the perfects and rebuild Catholic piety. This must have seemed preferable to making Parenzo a saint; again, Innocent may have doubted his character. Anna Benvenuti Papi has pointed out the importance of crusade as a Catholic response to heresy.[78] Innocent used a dramatic sermon to inspire Orvietans to go on crusade, a sermon that has been seen as part of a new type of popular preaching, inspired by the threat of heresy and anticipating the preaching campaigns of the mendicant orders. A contemporary account describes a huge crowd of Orvietans gathered in a meadow just outside the town, listening so devoutly to the pope's sermon that they were oblivious to the downpour that soaked them.[79] The author also states that more than two thousand men and women from the area took the cross; the claim is not substantiated in any other source.[80]

The early spread of Catharism in Orvieto thus was shaped by a distinctive political climate. Religious divisions combined with tensions over the rise of papal monarchy and the real implications of the town's membership in the Patrimony, as well as local conflicts over the power and authority of the bishop and his allies. Parenzo as papal rector, working in alliance with the bishop both to extirpate heresy and to impose some measure of papal authority through judicial proceedings and the exaction of large securities, was the perfect focus of these conflicts. There is no way, at a distance of eight centuries, to solve the mystery and identify his murderers and their individual motives with any certainty. The author of Parenzo's passion portrayed them as Manichee heretics, but it is very clear that opposition to his judicial proceedings and fiscal exactions was a critical motive. Surely the two were bound up together. The early Cathars who can be identified derived from rising urban families and were prosperous townsmen who worked to build independent civic institutions and then benefited from them. It is not surprising that they resented papal interference and the presence and exactions of the rector. Motives that modern scholars have sought to isolate as either political or religious were in practice interwoven. After all, in contrast to the aggressive and highly politicized pope and bishop, the austere Cathar perfects were men and women who had made themselves entirely disinterested. Like Francis, they must have seemed genuinely saintly.

Orvietan Society and the Early Popolo

ONLY ONE CONTEMPORARY reference to Orvietan Cathars survives from the first four decades of the thirteenth century.[1] The faith did not die out during this period. The inquisitors of the mid–thirteenth century were convinced that it persisted and, as I have shown, considered a handful of individuals and families to be longstanding Cathars and the involvement of some houses to date back to the time of the murder. When the Franciscan inquisitors of 1268–69 pursued the Orvietan Cathars, the sentences they imposed were retrospective: they mentioned events long past and ancestors involved in her-esy, and in some cases they convicted the dead. As a result, there is enough evidence to construct a list of a large part of the Orvietan Cathar community as it existed in the 1240s and '50s.

This chapter provides the context needed to make that list meaningful: a portrait of the social makeup and institutional structure of the larger community. I turn first to Orvietan society, drawing on tax surveys and wills to analyze something of the population, the distribution of wealth, and the patterns of family structure. Because scholars have argued that Cathar beliefs were spread through networks of clientage, I set out the meager evidence for thirteenth-century urban clientage. Then, I turn to the crucial political transformation of the period, the rise of popular political institutions. The last section describes the failure of the early efforts against heresy. Chapter 4 locates the Orvietans linked to Catharism within this social and political context and compares them with what is known of the Cathars in Florence in the 1240s.

Orvieto was in many ways typical of towns in central Italy in the thirteenth century, more typical than the heavily studied cities of Florence or Venice. Every town was, of course, different; Orvieto's identity was shaped by its fortress site on a major road and by its complex ties to the papal curia. Nevertheless, Orvietan social structure and political institutions followed the general pattern of towns of medieval Tuscany, which is to say that they underwent a gradual social and political revolution from the late twelfth century on. That revolution was the result of growth, prosperity and effective political autonomy.

Social Structure and Family

The proportions of Orvieto's growth can be sketched by tracing the gradual appearance of new neighborhoods and churches on the plateau, and especially in the suburbs below it, in the course of the thirteenth century. The major cause of growth, as elsewhere, was local emigration. The effects are clear from a magnificent document, a *catasto*, or tax survey, compiled in 1292, near the peak of demographic expansion. The survey names the head of each propertied household in town and countryside and then lists their holdings in rural land and their value.[2] It includes only heads of households and only rural land. The list allows us to estimate the population size and the rough distribution of landed wealth. Of course, social groups that did not own land are left out: the clergy, domestics, landless laborers, vagrants. Elisabeth Carpentier, whose analysis of the text forms the basis of this discussion, estimated the landless at 10 percent, a very conservative figure.[3] She argues for an urban population in 1292 somewhere between fourteen and seventeen thousand.[4] The figure for the contado and district she places somewhere between nineteen and thirty-two thousand.[5]

This breakdown is deceptive. Perhaps the most significant information to emerge from the 1292 catasto is that, at least for people with property, the division between urban and rural populations is artificial.

Town and countryside were so closely integrated that virtually everyone in the survey but poor peasants were considered town residents and were assessed there. All the titled nobles were surveyed in town, except for two men who had only scattered holdings in the Orvietan district and lived primarily in another town. A purely rural nobility did not exist. The vast majority of the people identified as country residents were small peasant proprietors, with a pitiful average holding of a hectare and a half.[6] Conversely, virtually all townspeople who could afford it did own some land in the country.

On the whole, the Orvietan townsfolk who do appear in the 1292 survey enjoyed some prosperity. The catasto offers a glimpse of the social structure and distribution of wealth; the surveyors recorded for each household the number of pieces of rural land, the land's location and borders, and its size (i.e., one and a half hectares), type (i.e., woods, pasture, vineyard), and assessed value. There are many problems with this evidence; notably, in a study of heresy, the question of whether tax assessors discriminated against former heretics by inflating their assessments.[7] Nevertheless, the catasto enables us to look not only at the size of a family's holdings but at the land's location, rough quality, and value.

Orvieto had a small hierarchy of great landowners and then a striking number of modest proprietors: city dwellers with a few plots of land near the town, and peasants with tiny holdings.[8] A handful of old feudal nobles appear, all titled counts: the counts of Montemarte, a branch of the Aldobrandeschi, and a local house, the Bulgarelli.[9] Then, eighty households were headed by men termed *domini*, titled lords, a diverse group that included not only dubbed knights but jurists and guildsmen who held the title because of their service as guildsmen executives of the town, the Signori Sette, or Seven. The average assessed value of their holdings was close to four thousand libre.[10] Another 173 hearths were headed by people called *filii domini*, sons of lords, with average holdings at 2,350 libre. This titled group comprised roughly 9 percent of the population and owned just over half the land, 55 percent of the acreage owned by townsmen. Not all of their land was of high quality, however: the big estates of the old feudal counts in particular included large tracts of woods and scrub, land of low estimated value.[11]

Among these propertied classes, social divisions were indistinct, as urban and rural sources of wealth and status were intermingled. A few of the lords derived from branches of the older comital families, but most were more recent. Members of older noble houses took on urban occupations: the Monaldeschi lineage, for example, derived from twelfth-century landed proprietors, probably episcopal vassals; they owned a *fondaco*, or urban workshop, and by 1292 they included merchants and jurists. Members of recent urban houses like the Toncelle—who served as civic treasurers from the first decade of the thirteenth century—held substantial lands. The jurist Pietro di Matteo Toncelle was a major landowner, with rural property valued at 2,197 libre.[12] Only two men are actually called merchants in the document, but in fact families like the Monaldeschi and the Miscinelli, identified in the catasto simply as lords, demonstrably owned shops and engaged in merchant ventures.

One hundred and one hearths were headed by people called *magistri*, masters, including twelve notaries, five doctors, and many master artisans. Most held smaller parcels of land of high value, typically small plots near the town. These were gardens and vineyards, their produce probably used for the family table.[13] The wealthiest master artisan was a blacksmith, with land valued at 891 libre. In all, 246 identifiable artisans appear. A few groups were particularly prosperous, including the textile and leather trades and the potters who made the jugs for Orvietan wine.[14] In effect, Orvieto included a tiny older landed nobility, a large petty elite, and a prosperous artisanate, all with close ties to the countryside. The landless poor are not visible in the survey.

Orvietan patterns of family structure and inheritance were flexible, even among elites. This situation contrasts markedly with that of the elites in the large cities—a contrast with important implications for understanding Orvietan social networks, including those relating to heresy. Scholars argue that twelfth- and thirteenth-century Italy saw a dramatic shift in elite family structure. Families began to define themselves as descent groups—groups of men united by shared ancestry, with that ancestry traced through the male line. Family identity came to be marked by the possession of a surname, often derived from an original ancestor, perhaps a fictional one. This development suggests that elite families thought of themselves as permanent and clearly defined groups, patrilineages. The new pattern generally originated in the countryside but was reinforced in towns.[15] The pattern enabled groups of men to share crucial resources, including urban properties, honors, and patronage rights.

The patrilineage was linked to a new exclusion of women and the female line. Lineage members dowered their daughters and often excluded them from any further inheritance; similarly wives lost most permanent claims on their husband's properties other than dotal rights. The limitation of the claims of women facilitated lineage efforts to maintain shared resources intact over a number of generations. Men passed their patrimony to sons—or more distant patrilineal kin, in the absence of sons—in equal, undivided fractional shares. In Florence, the pattern enabled large groups to share strategic urban properties: fortified towers, palaces, lucrative and prestigious ecclesiastical patronage rights.[16] Women were largely excluded from the ownership of the shares of these resources. The great Roman baronial houses of the thirteenth century similarly used the exclusion of women to build landed patrimonies over the course of generations.[17]

According to this custom, a man dowered his daughters and excluded them from future inheritance. Roman noble testators sometimes explicitly excluded the female line: "We entirely exclude female descendants from our succession," reads one will.[18] Legally, a woman's dowry was held on her behalf by her husband or, in the absence of a husband, her father or brothers; when a husband died, the estate was obligated to repay the wife's dowry.[19] Often, men wrote wills offering their widows support while they remained in the household and sought to recover the dowry, but allowed them no permanent claim on the estate other than their dotal rights.[20]

Orvietans tended to be more flexible, and they perhaps were more typical of medieval Italians than the great noble houses of Florence or Rome.[21] The patrillineage, after all, served most usefully as a way for elites to maintain control over strategic properties like urban forts. Families without great assets had less incentive to operate as patrilineages and could afford to be flexible. The most systematic Orvietan evidence is in the *Liber donationum.*[22]   In this register, begun by the city government around 1260, a notary made copies of wills, codicils, and donations that described property transfers that were taxable because they were valued over 25 libre in the currency of Cortona.[23] The first volume contains eighty-eight thirteenth-century wills. Unfortunately, because they were copied purely for fiscal reasons they are excerpted versions and are sometimes incomplete. Of the eighty-eight wills, sixty are legible and name the heirs. Seventeen are the wills of women, forty-three of men.

Some men did follow the patrilineal custom characteristic of Roman elites. Eighteen of the forty-three male testators in the *Liber donationum* had legitimate sons and made them their heirs. According to patrilineal custom, in the absence of sons the estate was left to more distant kin, traced through the male line. In 1258, the Orvietan Maffeo Berizi gave his daughter a dowry but no further inheritance. The heir instead was his brother, who was charged with handing over the unpaid balance of the dowry to the daughter and her husband within six years.[24] However, patrilineal exclusion of women from ownership of any portion of the estate beyond a dowry was not the invariable rule. In 1258, Angelo Egidii, an oil dealer, made his son his heir and dowered his daughter, but if either child died without heirs the other was to have the whole estate.[25] In five cases, men without sons named their daughters as heirs. In 1255, Benvenuto di Angelieri Corduli made his minor daughter his heir; in case of her death the estate was to go to the three children of his father's brother, Bonaventure Corduli.[26] A Florentine or Roman nobleman would have dowered his daughter and left the property to the male cousins in the male line. In 1254, Giovanni di Rollando Caballi after careful provision for his wife and even gifts to his wife's sister, made his daughter his heir.[27]

Some Orvietan men simply named all their children or grandchildren as heirs. In 1257, Dominico Capaczani left his estate divided among a group identified as the children of Venture and Jacobo, probably his grandchildren. At least one of them was a female named Rosa, who also received an affectionate bequest of furs and livestock.[28] Thus, while Orvietan men did not disinherit their sons and grandsons, they often named their female descendants as heirs as well. In 1258 Donadeo di Ranutio Ugolini of Civitella named as his heirs his three children. Two were sons, Guidone and Ranaldo, and the third was a daughter, Ringratiata.[29] Dricto di Guidone Inglisci in 1247 named his seven children his heirs, in equal amounts. Three of them were daughters. If the females chose to marry, their dowries were to be named by their mother and brothers. The text, which is an abbreviated copy, does not specify that dowered children were to be excluded from other inheritance; perhaps exclusion was assumed as the usual practice in Roman law.[30] A few men apparently without living wives or children passed their property to the female line entirely.[31]

Orvietan men thus at times passed property into the female line. On occasion they even emancipated their daughters. Legal emancipation freed an individual from *patria potestas,* paternal authority as defined in Roman law, and enabled an individual to be an independent economic and legal actor.[32] A fascinating female emancipation was enacted in 1253 by Domenico Toncelle, a prominent civic official who was surely a Cathar. Domenico belonged to an identifiable lineage, but as I discussed in chapter 2 a recent and urban one: the Toncelle who was the probable source of the family's name was his father.[33] In 1253 Domenico emancipated his daughter Odolana and then gave her his urban property, an undivided half share of a tower and building site, owned with his brother Matteo.[34] The tower was a genuine urban stronghold: it ended up in the hands of Matteo's descendants and was used as a civic prison in the last decades of the century.[35]

Domenico's action was a startling violation of patrilineal custom. In the absence of sons, he would be expected to pass this military property to his brother or his brother's sons. Were the men in the family at odds? They divided over religion, since Matteo and his descendants apparently were Catholic. However, they cannot have broken entirely, since Domenico in 1257 did donate a pasture, vineyard, and arable land to Matteo on behalf of his two sons, Domenico's nephews.[36] Perhaps the donations to Odolana were efforts to foil inquisitors and protect property from the threat of confiscation after a heresy conviction, and perhaps this maneuver was only momentary. However, there is no evidence of an inquisition active in Orvieto in 1253, and it is not clear that transferring ownership to a daughter rather than male kin would be a more effective shield. For a member of the Florentine elite, the donation of a tower share to a daughter would have been an unthinkable violation of patrilineal custom. Family towers were the ultimate symbol of patrilineal identity and power; the tower society pacts of the late twelfth century repetitively forbade passage of any share of a tower to women.[37] Odolana, after all, might marry and pass her half of the tower into the hands of family enemies. Her emancipation and her receipt of the tower share suggests the relative unimportance of patrilineal ties in at least one elite Orvietan family.

How did these patterns of inheritance—in which undowered daughters might receive equal shares—work out in practice? An extensive text in the *Liber donationum*, dating from 1291–92, suggests the complex family arrangements this pattern could create, and is a reminder that a will was only one stage in the transmission of a family's property, and that personalities could be crucial to these difficult decisions. Pietro di Giovanni Corclelli had been married at last twice and had to provide for eight living children: five daughters and three sons. Three daughters had been dowered and married, and a fourth was to receive a dowry as well. One son was an Augustinian friar, living in Rome and Florence. Pietro was left with the need to provide for one daughter and two sons. He emancipated them all, including the daughter, and gave them considerable urban and rural property. The daughter, who is called Suor Caratenuta and evidently pursued some form of religious life, lived separately from her brothers. Her lack of a dowry suggests that she was not expected to marry. Caratenuta received a third of the rural property—as an undivided share—and the use of a residence in town, which she was to share with her mother, Pietro's wife. The house was also to serve as repayment of the mother's dowry. In addition, Caratenuta received a certain amount of furnishings and supplies. The sons got the rest of the estate, including an adjoining house and all the assets in Pietro's shop.

Pietro insisted in the donation on continuing provision for the whole family, clearly trying to do his best by a large and quarrelsome brood. Another daughter, Bartholomea, was expected to marry and would have a dowry of two hundred libre. Her married sisters explicitly had the *tornata*, the right to return at need to the paternal household and receive support. The Augustinian brother, Phylippo, had an annual allowance of three libre for clothing. And if the two brothers did not treat their father's widow, Adalascia, well, so that she could not or would not stay with them, she was to receive extensive support from the estate; her clothing needs were spelled out in great detail.[38]   In effect, the dowered daughters were excluded from further inheritance, while the undowered daughter did receive an apparently proportional share. This arrangement did not necessarily mean a permanent loss of property to the female line, since Sister Caratenuta probably would produce no heirs and and might ultimately pass the rural property back to her brothers or their children. However, family relations were strained, and women were less restricted by custom than men in their testaments: she might well leave the property to her sisters' children or to a church.

Orvieto did not have the numerous large and violent noble patrilineages characteristic of Florence or Siena. Patrilineal practices were apparently more recent and of less use to a family. Surnames were used erratically in most documents. The most common form of surname in Orvietan Latin records was identification of a person as *de filiis* _____, literally "of the sons of so-and-so." This usage directly evoked the name's origin in a patronymic, suggesting that its use as a surname was within a few generations. One podestà, for example, was named in Latin Stefanus de filiis Stefani, literally "Steven of the sons of Steven."[39] The great Roman baronial lineages were identified in this way: the Orsini were the *filii Ursi,* sons of the Bear.

Lineages themselves were relatively small. The 1274 records of the composition of vendettas after the notorious killing of several members of the Pandolfini lineage by a group of Filippeschi include lists of kinsmen agreeing to the reconciliations. A lineage faced with a vendetta had a strong motive to insist that all of the kinsmen of their opponents formally consented to the reconciliation. Nevertheless, the lists are short. Nine men called the filii Pandolfi took part. In another vendetta, seven filii Grece made peace with nine filii Bramanni.[40] The filii Grece seem typical. Apparently the descendants of Ugolino Grece, they were a new lineage of a mere three generations. By comparison with Florentine elites, lineages do not seem rigorously exclusive, and surnames are often left unmentioned. It is not always apparent who belonged to the lineage and who did not, as in, for example, the list of twenty men initially banned in seven thousand libre for the Pandolfini homicides.[41] How many were Filippeschi and how many were allies or clients is not evident.

Again, the key to this flexibility is the lack of a motive for more rigorous patrilineal practices. There is little evidence of urban properties held in fractional shares among lineage members comparable to those in Florence or Rome. The closest instance I have seen is the 1270 sale of a complex of central property, in Serancia, to a sindic acting for the commune. The property included a tower, shop, houses and building sites. It apparently belonged to the descendants of Jannis Ranuzii. Guido, a grandson, was selling an undivided half share. The other half belonged to his father's brother and to that man's son. A long list of nobles also consented and renounced any rights in the property.[42] Even joint fraternal properties—like the tower Domenico Toncelle shared with his brother until the donation to his daughter—are rare. They did exist at lower social levels, where they meant a shared household. One exquisite text of 1269 sets out a classic *fraterna*—joint fraternal household—in which two brothers and their wives lived "as one family, at one bread, at one wine."[43]

Clientage

If patrilineal ties were relatively weak, what of the vertical lines of clientage? It may be that urban-rural clientage was strong, but there is little to suggest close ties of clientage among those who primarily lived in town. Evidence for clientage is notoriously difficult to find for historical periods or social classes that left behind no letters begging for favors.[44] Ties at this level are elusive, even in sources from the ancient Roman world, which most scholars think was riddled with patronage.[45] For thirteenth-century Orvieto there are only scattered clues. There is little evidence for patterns of rentals or even loans, both potentially aspects of clientage. A 1295 list of men fined for illegal mourning at the funeral of the son of a Muntanari nobleman includes a person identified as "Fredo who stays by the house of messer Muntanari."[46] In the overcrowded, ramshackle conditions of a late medieval town, it is possible that Fredo literally stayed in the street by the Muntanari house, a humble client who might run an errand or do a chore and therefore had a place at the funeral.

The *Leggenda* of Pietro Parenzo refers to people who are called *clientuli*, little clients. They appear in the account of the miraculous healing of Messer Munaldo Petri Cittadini. He had become so weak in the legs and feet that he was unable to stand unless lifted by his clientuli. They carried him to the shrine of the saint, where he was cured, probably much to the relief of the clientuli.[47] Judging from their role, they were household domestics. In addition, a woman called Complita is termed the *rustica* of Munaldo and his brother. For fourteen months she was afflicted with a twisted neck, giving her an appearance so horrible that no one from the Monaldeschi household was willing to enter her home to receive *hospitium*, hospitality. Her obligation to provide Monaldeschi family members with hospitality—probably food—suggests that she was not a free tenant but a serf. Complita was driven by the prayers, threats, and blows of the household to seek a cure at Parenzo's tomb; after remaining there for six days she was miraculously healed.[48] From her perspective this coerced cure was a mixed blessing, since the Monaldeschi now were willing to come to her for obligatory hospitality. These stories reveal the Monaldeschi making use of their dependents, people who might be considered clients, as they helped the bishop to build up the cult of the martyr.

The strongest evidence of clientage is the 1240 testimony of Orvietan witnesses to the miracles of a contemporary Franciscan healer Ambrose of Massa, a text I explore in detail in chapter 6. The language and attitudes of patronage suffuse the testimony. Supplicants came to the saint and asked for a *mercedem*, a free gift. In return, they promised a return gift and lifetime service. For example, when a child fell from a window, his father held the lifeless body in his arms and made a vow: Saint Ambrose, I vow to you my son, so that you will deign to aid me by your glorious merits. If you do this, I will remain in your service for all time and will bring an image of wax to your tomb.[49] Two exchanges take place: one between Ambrose and God, in which the saint uses his merits to attain the miracle, and the other between the saint and the parents, in which the saint's influence is traded for a gift of wax and lifetime service. Maestro Pietro, a smith, and his wife Clara made a vow to Ambrose, seeking that God by the saint's merits heal their dying month-old infant. They promised in exchange to give Ambrose lifetime service and, startlingly, not a wax image but love.[50] Pietro, in fact, testified to another miracle as well, part of his service to his patron.[51] These stylized exchanges do suggest the strength of patron-client relations in the Orvietan community. Religious and political patronage reinforced each other.[52] Peter Brown, among others, has indicated the ways in which early medieval saints—paralleling the bishops—stepped into the roles of the ancient patrons.[53] The *Leggenda* of Pietro Parenzo suggests this pattern in the episodes in which the saint intervened in jurisdictional disputes involving the bishop.

Surely—as Sydel Silverman has suggested for the mezzadria, forms of share-cropping in modern Umbria—economic ties closely overlapped with forms of clientage. Modern studies have shown that optimal conditions for patronage exist when free smallholders live near the powerful and they are economically interdependent.[54] These conditions were notably present in thirteenth-century Orvieto, where 75 percent of the peasant proprietors owned bits of land worth less than one hundred libre.[55] They must have relied for wages and other forms of support on their neighbors, not only great landed proprietors but well-to-do townsmen and petty nobles.[56] This exchange was reciprocal. When landlord-tenant relations were hostile and coercive, landlords suffered. The canons complained in court in August 1291 that a laborer on their lands did not do his work at the appropriate season.[57] Urban landowners needed not only labor but goodwill and protection from their country neighbors. Unguarded resources in the country were at risk; the court records bristle with accusations of crimes against rural property: cutting wood, damaging a vineyard, picking the crops, or allowing livestock to graze in a planted field.[58]

Clientage defined relations among rich and poor neighbors in the countryside, but it was probably less significant in town. It is useful to consider the entire system, not only individual patron-client ties but the role of patronage in the overall social system. What resources were allocated through patronage? Patronage is typically a bad deal for the client, since patrons might promise more than they delivered, and often could coerce. What might clients get—or at least seek? For medieval rural smallholders, the answer is clear: as with the Roman poor, they sought "security against violence . . . or food, clothing and shelter."[59] Their patrons received labor and modest assistance as well as some protection from petty crime. For townsfolk, it is not clear what needs could be served by urban patrons that were not better met by horizontal forms of association, including guilds, confraternities, and military associations. The relative weakness of elite patrilineal ties reinforces this conclusion. Research on patronage suggests that vertical relations can inhibit "the class or status forms of horizontal solidarity." [60] Patronage, because it favors some individuals over others, subverts horizontal ties. But nothing is more apparent in mid-thirteenth-century Orvieto than the success of horizontal networks of association, at least among the prosperous. [61] In Florence, people might turn to the big noble patrilineage in the neighborhood for a loan, for physical protection in times of civil war, or for influence with a judge or tax collector. Little Orvieto was not dominated by powerful noble patrilineages. The relative weakness of these vertical ties helps to explain the strong horizontal networks of association among Cathar households.

The Rise of the Popolo

Despite its formal membership in the papal states, Orvieto developed independent political institutions, like the other towns of the period. In the thirteenth century, prosperous artisans and petty elites gradually developed and refined new political forms based in networks of corporate association, a pattern termed the rise of the popolo. In Orvieto, as elsewhere, popular officials took power by the late 1240s and '50s. This political development is crucial for an understanding of the Orvietan Cathars. In this period, they were, in effect, tolerated. While the papal curia and the bishop may have defined Cathars as deviants and traitors, local Orvietans did not systematically view them that way and efforts at repression were ill-supported. Further, people who were well-known Cathars often held high popular office.

By the mid-1240s, popular institutions were clearly in place. The rise of the Orvietan popolo is documented largely by mention in contemporary documents of institutions and offices considered popular; often these institutions were copied from other towns. There is little evidence of the violent social conflict between knights and popolo that marked other cities. [62] It may be that lines of political division were less clear in this small, prosperous town. The first reference to rectors of the popolo is from 29 October 1244, when the three rectors included the probable Cathar Raniero de Arari.[63] In an action characteristic of popular interests, they restored to a tailor from Apulia a horse, sword, lance, and other gear.[64] The goods were taken from him by a Pietro Velle and associates, Orvietan citizens who were probably on guard duty. Their restoration was a gesture that placated a well-to-do artisan trader, protected commerce, and affirmed the law. The Carta del popolo, a popular constitution, existed by 1244 as well.[65]

By January 1247 the whole popular organization was in place, with the exception of the capitano del popolo. In a gesture just as characteristic as the restoration of property to a passing trader, the organization went into debt, pledging *beni comunali*, collectively owned resources, like woods in the countryside, to local nobles in order to borrow the funds to pay the podestà. A loan from four men, Messer Monaldo Ranieri Stefani, Messer Rainuccio Transmundi, Petro Gulielmi Pepuli, and Rainuctio Ardiczonis, was used to pay the podestà his salary. The popular officers included the rectors and the twenty-four leaders of the guilds and popular societies, *signori delle arti e delle società*. The popular constitution, or Carta del Popolo, is mentioned as well.[66] The loan was secured with two years' restricted use of the beni comunali in Ficulle, Carraiola and Fabro. This concession was substantial and potentially risky: it might become difficult to regain the property. The creditors were even allowed to post six guards there in case of a threat from the armies of the pope and emperor or their allies. This arrangement again suggests that political divisions were less sharp than in Florence or Perugia.

The first outsider capitano del popolo is mentioned in 1250: it was to the capitano as well as the councils and rectors of the popolo that the Ghibelline Manfred Lancia petitioned.[67] The office was relatively unimportant in the period: it was only with the revival of the popular movement associated with the rise of the political leader Neri della Greca in the 1280s that the capitano del popolo came to wield real power. In the earlier period, the prior of the guilds and popular societies played this powerful role.

What interests were represented by the new popular institutions? Our models of the popolo are drawn from larger towns like Bologna, Florence, and Perugia. In Florence, the popolo represented the rise to power of new commercial interests: greater and lesser guildsmen taking power in opposition to an older military nobility. Popular institutions were in part designed to protect popolani from the need for a noble patron. Occasionally, there was sharp hostility between the two networks of alliance. Does this description apply to Orvieto? Popular institutions had a double organization, by neighborhood and by profession, in the form of guilds. In most towns, guilds predominated; in Orvieto, the rioni, or neighborhoods, were at least equally important. In effect, socioeconomic divisions were less distinct; the strong social antagonisms of the Florentine or Bolognese popolo less evident. The Orvietans did not adopt, for example, the careful Florentine provisions to protect popolani from noble military intimidation. In Florence the capitano del popolo offered popolani an alternative to a noble patron, someone to whom they could turn when threatened; judging from the relative weakness of the office in Orvieto, the Orvietans did not feel a similar need.

What did animate the Orvietan popolo? The evidence is scanty, but three concerns are clear. First, in the 1250s Orvieto engaged in an ambitious reconquest of their district, their subject territory. Daniel Waley wondered whether popular groups traded participation in these military campaigns for constitutional concessions. But in fact, the campaigns were popular policy. It was the leaders of the popolo themselves who opposed papal and imperial territorial claims and drove the reconquest. There was a long series of submissions to Orvietan authority, as for example in March 1248, when Monaldeschi nobles and their associates agreed to terms with commune over an important fort, the Rocca Sberna.[68] Second, a central concern of the popolo at Orvieto—as in Perugia, as Maire Vigueur has pointed out—was to preserve and build the beni comunali, properties that were at risk of usurpation by nobles. An inventory of the beni comunali was drawn up as early as 1244.[69] Third, as Lucio Riccetti has shown, the Orvietan popolo had a strong interest in public works. The city gates, for example, were repaired in 1247.[70] This concern extended to the expansion of civic bureaucracy: it was popular leaders who initiated the *Liber donationum*, the compilation of wills, emancipations, and other notarial records that resulted from the legal requirement that copies of important property transfers be recorded in order to be taxed. In sum, the popolo sought to build a strong, prosperous, and independent commune.

Early Efforts against the Cathars

The Orvietan popolo effectively tolerated Catharism: the Cathar sympathies of some popular leaders were hardly a secret, and there is little evidence of any successful repression of the Orvietan Cathars. In August and October 1239, when a judge acting for the podestà issued warnings to five men who were minor nobles of the contado, they were enjoined not to receive in their houses or lands heretics or counterfeiters, not to disturb churches and hospitals, not to disturb for ten years the citizens of Orvieto, and not to allow any persons subject to them to commit attacks or robbery. Instead, they were to protect Orvietans and their property at need.[71] This action was clearly part of the effort to restrain the rural nobility and place them under the control of communal law; perhaps it is significant that these minor nobles were perceived as harboring heretics. It is also worth noting that the communal treasurer taking part in these proceedings himself came to be a well-known Cathar, Provenzano Lupicini.

A Dominican inquisition was attempted by 1239. It is ill-documented and cannot have been very effective. The inquisitor was Fra Ruggiero Calcagni, who achieved greater success and notoriety in Florence. The Dominican presence at this time was a weak and perhaps unpopular one. They had only arrived in Orvieto between 1230 and 1232, just a few years after the Franciscans. They probably stayed initially in a preexisting house or hospice and then constructed a church with the aid of the city government.[72] Fra Ruggiero's sentences are long lost, but at least ten of the people sentenced in 1268 were initially questioned by him. The Cathar response to the first inquisition was confident and violent. A group of men broke into the Dominican convent and attacked the inquisitor and the other brothers. Perhaps they hoped to scare them off. A sentence records the testimony of two participants, Bartolomeo and Rainerio de Tosti. Summoned by the inquisition, they at first denied any involvement. Bartolomeo later confessed that "he believed the lives of the Cathars to be good and had seen them and spoken with them in many places" but had initially denied it out of fear of the inquisitor.[73] It was his brother Rainerio who laid violent hands on the inquisitor Fra Ruggiero and gave him a bloody beating. The attackers also included Rainerio and Bartolomeo's kinsman Cristoforo de Tosti, Provenzano Lupicini, and perhaps Bivieno and Giuliano di Biagio.[74] Their actions were utterly at odds with the pacifist Cathar faith but followed a pattern characteristic of factional conflicts between minor urban nobles in the duecento: the Tosti and Lupicini treated the Dominicans like any political or military opponent and launched a retaliatory attack. They saw their conflict with the Dominicans primarily in political terms, since of course they would not have believed that the friars had any special religious authority.

The Dominicans, with support from the podestà, were able to exact a dramatic penance from the attackers and their families. The Lupicini conviction describes what was imposed on him, his accomplices, and all of his *familia*, or household. They were led before the populace barefoot, stripped to their shirts, and with ropes around their necks, and they abjured heresy.[75] This public humiliation did not end the Lupicini public careers: Provenzano was right back in office on 27 December 1239. Two years later he served as consul and even tramped out into the fields with the other consuls to adjudicate a dispute over ownership of produce from property claimed by the bishop.[76] Despite the inquisition's evident weakness, it persisted at least for a time: in 1240 Fra Ruggiero heard the heresy confession of Ildebrandino Ricci de Tostis.[77]

The next evidence of conflict is a single text from January 1249, a decade later. It refers to a prior heresy condemnation by Fra Ruggiero of seven men. Five were Tosti, three of them the brothers of Cristoforo; the other two were Giuliano and Bivieno di Biagio. Little is known of Giuliano and Bivieno; they came from nearby Todi. It may be that the seven were the people convicted of the attack on the Dominicans a decade before. They must, at any rate, have taken oaths and abjured heresy. Since their condemnation, according to the text, Giuliano di Biagio and Ildebrandino Tosti had broken their oaths, violated ecclesiastical immunity, and returned to the heresy they had previously abjured. As a result, they had been condemned in huge amounts, one thousand libre each. They attempted to escape the penalty with the aid of their brothers, Cristoforo Tosti and Bivieno di Biagio. Their strategy was bizarre: they visited the notary who had written their sentences. "Threatening him with death, [they] forced him to falsify certain documents which had been made against them."[78] The action is fascinating because of its implications about the contemporary understanding of the power of a legal document. The convictions were certainly already notorious; it is not at all clear how falsified documents could have been convincing evidence. How could they serve any purpose?

When the podestà then attempted to enforce the inquisitor's sentence against Giuliano and Ildebrandino, their families resisted by gathering with their weapons in their houses, arming their towers, and "exciting men to sedition and war."[79] Again, they followed the pattern characteristic of factional conflicts. Bivieno di Biagio, who, according to the condemnation, had been a Cathar believer for thirty years and excommunicate for nine, more than once spoke from a public tribunal in the piazza comunale, attacking the podestà's blindness in his persecution of the Cathars.[80] The surviving document is the inquisitor's sentence of January 1249, which condemned Bivieno to a huge fine of two thousand libre in Pisan currency and the permanent destruction of his houses and towers.

The conclusion that leaps from this document is the futility of these inquisitors' efforts: even with the aid of the podestà they were unable to enforce their sentences effectively. There is no evidence that the heavy sentence against Bivieno was carried out; in fact, there is little evidence of an Inquisition in Orvieto after this date, until 1263. A few references in the 1268 sentences do imply efforts against the Cathars, but it is not clear when they took place. The sentence of a woolworker mentions that he took the corpse of the perfect Josep of Viterbo down from the scaffold and buried it. Perhaps Josep was hanged at Orvieto in the 1250s. But my guess is that the commune did not pursue heresy, and that the hanging—if it happened in Orvieto—took place after the revived Franciscan inquisition of 1263. The Dominican inquisition had little support either from the populace or from those in power in the town. As chapter 4 demonstrates, a number of prominent popular leaders and their households, like Provenzano Lupicini, were publically known to be Cathars.

$\mathcal{T}$he Cathars

I HAVE SHOWN THAT in the first half of the thirteenth century Cathar believers in Orvieto were not a desperate, persecuted minority. They lived, for the most part, in an atmosphere of tolerance or perhaps wilful ignorance, and people known to be Cathars enjoyed successful, public careers. Outside powers, including the pope and the emperor, promulgated laws that identified Cathars as dangerous deviants, heretics, and traitors, but few Orvietans evidently gave much credence to this view of their Cathar neighbors. The early inquisitions had little impact: the recently arrived Dominican inquisitors cannot have attracted much local sympathy, since the Toste, Lupicini, and others who attacked their convent and thrashed the inquisitor suffered little in consequence. Public penance for heresy was ineffectual in changing popular opinion. Certainly, people were willing to do business with known Cathars, and some of them prospered. Cathars were embedded in the local community and power structure.

Who were the Orvietan Cathars? They are best understood in a number of interrelated networks. Cathar households often were interconnected by marital, professional, and financial ties, both because the faith spread among groups of people, and because Cathar believers over time tended to associate with each other. This situation is hardly surprising: it was demonstrably true in towns like Toulouse as well.[1] The Orvietan Cathars can be grouped into three clusters: popular officials; petty nobles, money-lenders, and merchants; and furriers and other artisans. These circles, particularly the first two, very much overlapped.

However, the three circles do not include all the local Cathars. First, perfects have been omitted; their antecedents are difficult to recover, since perfects were generally named in the extant records by given name and place of origin, but not by surname, patronymic, or former profession. Only occasionally does the evidence surrounding a perfect allow any secure identification. A single perfect demonstrably came from Orvieto, the Jacopo of Orvieto mentioned in the heresy sentence of Miscinello Ricci Miscinelli.[2] The others came from places like Viterbo, Florence, or Lombardy and visited Orvieto as holy persons. The perfects listed in the inquisitorial sentences also varied in their degree of involvement with the local community. Some were passing strangers; some ministered to the community for a time. It is not clear that even they belonged in the way that a local resident was a member of the community. Second, a number of the people sentenced for Cathar heresy do not fit into these circles; in several cases, particularly people of low status who lacked surnames and did not own land or hold public office, little evidence survives. The handful of people who fall into this important but ill-documented category are described in chapter 7. Third, surely some people were never mentioned because they eluded the inquisition entirely. My guess is that those Cathars who escaped attention were not members of the wealthy and influential families targeted by the friars, but folk of lower status and individuals who did not come from longstanding Cathar households. This reconstruction, then, is necessarily incomplete and biased toward propertied elites, but probably does include the core of the Orvietan Cathar community.

Minor Elites

One fact that was both effect and cause of toleration is the presence of many Cathars in popular offices from the 1240s, many of them from a small cluster of merchant and moneylender families. Three men closely

linked to the Cathars held popular office in the late 1240s: Ranerio Raneri de Arari, Ranieri Adilascie, and Martino Martini Guidutie. Ranerio
Raneri de Arari was one of the new rectors of the popolo in 1244.
Camera, who was the widow of Rainucci de Arari and was condemned
for heresy in 1268, was probably his mother.[3] She described her son's role
in heresy as an active one in her confession to the Inquisition. She received
perfects in her son's house and gave them food and drink at her son's
request.[4] The family engaged in some merchant ventures: Ranerio and his
brother Bonifatio restored mules and their accoutrements to Florentine
merchants as a part of an exchange in 1240.[5] They had kinsmen associated with local petty nobles: Bonifatio Dominici Ranucti de Arari and
Bartolomeo Boncompagni Ranucti de Arari served as guarantors for a
Monaldeschi nobleman, Pietro Munaldi, in the 1248 submission of the
fortress of Sberna.

Ranieri Adilascie was a rector of the popolo in February of 1247, with
Martino Martini Guidutii acting as a witness.[6] In April of the same year
Martino, acting as consul of merchants, received repayment for a substantial loan made to the podestà and four men, one of them Ranieri Adilascie. The loan was needed to increase a sum paid to the Florentines.[7] Both
men performed military service for the commune; Ranieri Adilascie was
captured by the Sienese and then released in 1235. His sons divided
between the two faiths. Pietro, called Pietro Coroza, who held popular
office as one of the anziani, or advisors of the capitano, in 1262, was
sentenced for heresy.[8] Another son, Jacobo, became a canon at San Andreas and was present when Domenico Toncelle's widow, Syginetta, was
sentenced for heresy, a moment that was perhaps quite painful for him.[9]
Pietro Coroza was condemned post mortem; there is no direct evidence
that the father, Raineri, was Cathar as well.[10] While Ranieri was an important early popular leader linked to the Cathars, he did not emulate the
high-minded disinterest of the perfects: he probably embezzled the substantial income he received from the town's collective property, since his
heirs were required to repay it.[11]

The Guidutie were a family of merchants and convinced Cathars, and
Martino was important enough to hold office as the merchants' consul in
1247. He served in the civic militia and heard Cathar preaching on a
military expedition at Todi. The family lived in Santa Pace, the Toste
neighborhood. Their house was predominantly Cathar, judging from the
heresy convictions of Martino's sisters. The family's ties are suggested by

their marriages. Matthea, who married the Cathar moneylender Miscinello Ricci Miscinelli, is identified in her heresy sentence as a devout Cathar who often sent offerings to the perfects and received the consolation during an illness.[12] Another sister, Albasia, married to Pietro Frascambocca, was also condemned. Amata, the wife of the late Enrico Martini, perhaps Martino's brother, was still living when she was sentenced in 1268 and lost her dowry and goods to the inquisition.[13] Enrico's sons (and probably hers as well), Mathutio and the late Barthutio, were also condemned.[14] Martino's post-mortem condemnation was as a relapsed heretic; he was first sentenced by Fra Ruggerio, presumably in the inquisition of 1249.[15]

In the 1250s and early 1260s, during the first popular ascendancy, a startling number of well-known Cathars served in high office.[16] Domenico Toncelle was the most prominent, the man who emancipated his daughter and gave her a half share of an urban tower in 1253. One of the witnesses to the donation was a member of the Toste lineage, considered leaders of the Cathars.[17] Domenico capped a long public career with the job of prior of the guilds and *società*, popular societies, in 1255 and 56. The office was very powerful, judging from the formal resubmission of the strategically crucial town of Aquapendente. The town had taken advantage of the imperial presence in the 1240s to escape the Orvietan yoke. When it was forced to resubmit to Orvieto in 1251, it did so to the Orvietan podestà, and Toncelle was present as witness. The conditions imposed by Orvieto were stringent enough to provoke another Aquapendentan rebellion, again suppressed. In 1256, Aquapendente chose a Friar Lorenzo to represent the town "before lord Domenico Toncelle prior of guilds and his council [of anziani] and commune of the city of Orvieto, to accomplish and fulfill the decrees of lord Domenico and the commune of the city of Orvieto."[18] Strikingly, it was Toncelle, as guild prior, who was imposing conditions on the town. In 1259 the lords of Bisenzio submitted the Martana island to Orvietan authority, and again Lord Domenico Toncelle, prior of the guilds and società, was preeminent, his presence listed even before the podestà.[19] Toncelle was killed while in office; versions in the chronicles differ, but he was probably cut down by the Filippeschi Bartolomeo di Pietro Gani in the Piazza San Andreas in 1259.[20]

A number of other men later convicted of Catharism served with him. Provenzano Lupicini, who had taken part in the 1239 attack on the Dominicans and was by this time an old man, was an anziano in 1256. Another Cathar, Benvenuto Pepi, served as anziano with him. When Benvenuto's widow, Benamata, was sentenced in 1268, she confessed that her husband had received heretics in his home sixteen or eighteen years before and that she had believed in their teachings for about six years. This timing places the period of her Cathar belief—roughly 1250–58—during his term as anziano.[21] Little else is known of them. Amideo Lupicini, like Provenzano, continued to be active in public life: he witnessed the 1251 submission of Aquapendente and he served as guild prior in 1255 and rector of the popolo as late as 1266. Petrus Ranieri Adilascie was one of the anziani of the capitano in 1262, serving with one of the Toste, Rayneri di Stradigotto.[22] (This man was the first identifiable Toste to hold public office in the century.)

Martino Guidutie's sister Matthea married into the Miscinelli. This connection leads us to the second, overlapping circle of Cathars, minor nobles, merchants, and moneylenders. This circle centered on the Toste and their associates, families that played no formal role in the popolo. The Miscinelli lineage, in part Cathar, is evident in Orvieto at least from 1202, when Ranieri Miscinelli was one of the Orvietans who took an oath establishing an alliance with Siena. His son was given the romantic name of Nanzilotto, or Lancelot; he sold property in 1222. Benedetto Miscinelli witnessed a 1212 marriage dispute in the bishop's court; as discussed in chapter 6, it is just possible that the would-be husband in the case was also a Miscinelli, Oderisio or Ricco.[23]

Matthea's husband Miscinello Ricci Miscinelli is mentioned in a record of 1251, when property sold to the Ghibelline leader Manfred Lancia bordered on his rural lands. He was explicitly identified in his heresy conviction as a usurer. His branch, the Ricci Miscinelli, in fact were prominent moneylenders and did extensive business with the Sienese. Cambio Ricci and his brothers received repayment of substantial funds in Siena in 1257.[24] Ultimately, the Miscinelli were confined as Ghibellines in 1315; to my knowledge none ever served in civic office in Orvieto.

The Ricci Miscinelli were Toste neighbors. At least in 1287, members of the family owned property in Santa Pace adjoining the Piazza del Popolo.[25] The piazza had been built in part on land confiscated and purchased from the Toste.[26] Four Miscinelli were convicted of heresy, including Matthea and three men who were apparently brothers: her husband, Miscinello Ricci, Cambio Ricci, and Petrutio Ricci. Miscinello, probably first questioned by Fra Jordano, was sentenced as a heretic "from long ago."[27] All three men's sentences released their debtors and required the restitution of usury. Cambio Ricci Miscinelli confessed to contact with perfects at the shop of the furrier Stradigotto, whose nephew lent money as well.[28] Petrutio Ricci Miscinelli was also condemned but was given a variant punishment.[29] The young trumpet player Petrutio Guidi Becci also lent money at interest.[30]

The most notorious Cathar lineage was the Toste. As I discussed in chapter 2, they were a family of minor nobles who lived in a cluster of houses, palaces, and a tower in the rione of Santa Pace and who, despite their association with Catharism, were influential in public life in the early decades of the century.[31] Toste economic interests are difficult to uncover. Their rural holdings cannot be reconstructed, since the modest 1292 catasto returns of Toste heirs date from long after their lands were decimated by the confiscations of the Inquisition. In 1239 a man and his wife donated their urban houses to members of the Toste but retained their use, suggesting relations of clientage.[32] The Toste were not a lineage with purely rural interests, and their status was not much more exalted than their merchant neighbors. Two family members, Bartholomeo and Ranerio di Rainuccio, were required in their inquisitorial sentences to repay usury, implying that they lent money at interest.[33] One had become a notary by 1270.[34] Fourteen living Toste, drawn from three generations, were sentenced by the inquisition in 1268. They included the supposed Cathar ringleader, Cristoforo, his son Ranucetto, and his daughter Tafura.[35] The two sons and five grandsons of Ricco were sentenced, as were Bartolomeo Rainuti and his brother, son, and grandson.[36]

Several households closely associated with the Toste were Cathar as well. Bartho Francisci, his wife, Belverde, and a nephew or grandson Neri were their neighbors in Santa Pace.[37] Bartho witnessed a 1239 donation of a house in San Andreas to the Toste.[38] A 1259 will reveals a web of association. Berardina, the widow of Johane Marini, left her daughter Tecta, wife of Bartolomeo Rainuti Toste, funds invested with a merchant, along with the revenues from her half share of a flock of sheep and goats. The testament was enacted in the house of Bartho di Pietro Saraceni. Berardina was thus a Toste mother-in-law. She was condemned post mortem for heresy. Apparently a longstanding Cathar, she had her son Rainuccetto given the consolation just before his death.[39] Her house in San Giovenale was to be destroyed, although marginal notes to her sentence indicate that no property was found. Probably the marriage of her daughter Tecta with Bartolomeo Toste was a conscious alliance between Cathar houses. Bartolomeo and his brother were condemned as well, though Tecta was not.[40]

Berardina's funds were deposited with another Cathar, the merchant Giovanni Claruvisi. He was fined four hundred libre for heresy; his wife, Vianese, testified to the inquisition that he had received heretics in his house; she was condemned as well.[41] He may have been a cloth dealer, as was his son: an estate inventory of 1282 includes a substantial debt to his son Pietro for black cloth.[42] Finally, Berardina's will was enacted in the house of Bartho di Pietro Saraceni, though Bartho did not appear as a witness; both he and his wife Adalascia were also sentenced for heresy.[43] The property may have been the old palace of Pietro Saraceni, used to transact official civic business at least since 1204. Other accused Cathars just touch on this network of associations, in bits of evidence. Some were neighbors, like Ranerio Zamfrongini, whose rural lands in Rubiaglio bordered on those of the Lupicini and Toncelle.[44] Others were merchants and shared at least guild membership with the Guidutie: Ingilberto Tignosi is identified as a merchant in his post-mortem sentence of 1268.[45] He may have been related to the Tiniosi whose house was the site of the wedding invalidated by the bishop in 1212, and perhaps to the Cathar leader in Viterbo called J. Tiniosi who so troubled Innocent III.

Furriers and Artisans

A network of Cathar artisans developed by midcentury as well. The artisans who can be identified were prosperous guildsmen: not landless laborers but rather well-to-do households that owned shops and garden plots. They centered on the shop of the Sienese emigrant furrier Stradigotto.[46] His importance in the local Cathar community is suggested by his sentence in the *Liber inquisitionis:* it is the only one that includes more than a terse list of incriminating actions, meetings with perfects, or receipt of the consolation. Stradigotto's confession of faith is reported as well.[47] Whether he first contacted the heresy in Siena or in Orvieto is unknown, though it is known that he lived at least twenty years in Orvieto. He was first questioned by the Dominican inquisitor, Fra Ruggiero Calcagni, placing him in Orvieto sometime between 1239 and 1249.[48]

Stradigotto's role in spreading heresy again challenges the idea that Catharism spread along vertical social lines, and that nobles converted

first, then passed the faith along to their clients. By midcentury, the Orvietan evidence suggests just the opposite. It was Stradigotto, the master
artisan, who was encouraging the spread of the faith. He was associated
with nobles through his trade and perhaps through moneylending: in
1264, his grandson or nephew Gezio transferred to him a large debt owed
by three nobles, one of them the Cathar Messer Rainerio Munaldi Rainerii Stephani.[49] And one of the Miscinelli mentioned visiting his shop to
hear the perfects preach. But these links were perhaps a consequence and
not a cause of his Catharism.

Stradigotto was central to a small network of Orvietan artisans linked
to heresy. Another former Sienese, a man called Amato, stated that it was
at the suggestion of Stradigotto that he received two perfects in the house
where he lived, listened to their preaching and made them reverence, as he
was taught by Stradigotto.[50] Blanco, an Orvietan furrier, testified that it
was at the urging of Stradigotto that he listened to the preaching of a
Florentine perfect in Castellonchio and led Nicola of Casalveri and his
associate, and many other heretics, to many places. He once carried a
salted fish to perfects in hiding, on Stradigotto's behalf.[51] The people
convicted included a shoemaker, a tailor, and a smith. It was a woolworker,
Symeone the grandson or nephew of Egidio Seccadinari, who removed
the corpse of the perfect Josep from the scaffold and buried it with devotion.[52]

Stradigotto's fellow furriers were very much involved. Another furrier,
Viscardo, was convicted by the inquisition, and his house destroyed. He
was dead in 1265 when the inquisitors gave the site where the house had
stood to his widow, Bellapratu, in recompense for her dowry. She took
up residence in the household of a fourth furrier, her son Frederico, who
probably lived in Serancia.[53] Bellapratu was surely a valuable addition to
the household, as a skilled furrier in her own right. She gave Frederico
the building site in exchange for food, clothing, and other necessaries.[54]
Her donation is curious, since he stood to inherit the property anyway; it
would have been more usual for him to administer it while she retained
ownership. Perhaps they feared that she would be condemned for heresy,
and the donation was an effort to avoid a reconfiscation of the land by
the inquisition. The fact that two of the witnesses to the donation were
fellow Cathars, the furrier Blanco and Filippo Busse, supports this explanation.[55] And certainly fears of more heresy condemnations were justified.
Three years later Bellapratu was condemned along with Frederico's wife,

Grana and Blanco and Filippo as well. The two women had flown and were sentenced in absentia to wear the yellow cross and to suffer the confiscation of their goods. Frederico was not condemned and, in fact, successfully appealed a fine of forty soldi for an unspecified offense just a year later, in 1269.[56] Whether the building site was reconfiscated I do not know. There is an odd 1280 reference to a donation in the house of the furrier Guiscardo, suggesting that the house still stood, long lost to the family but still remembered as the property of Bellapratu's husband, though he had been dead at least fifteen years.[57]

It was a close associate and fellow Cathar who probably turned them in to the inquisitors: Filippo Busse. Filippo's profession is unknown; he was prosperous enough to own a house, in San Giovenale. When Filippo and his wife, Clara, sold the property, Frederico the furrier acted as their guarantor, suggesting very close ties. After their heresy sentences, the inquisitors had the house destroyed because the consolation had taken place there, and the buyer was left trying to recoup her investment. Filippo's tale is thus a sad one: according to his sentence he was captured and imprisoned for heresy and after "various prudent interrogations" was convinced to confess and implicate his friends.[58]

Perhaps the connection between furriers and heresy in Orvieto was purely accidental, the result of Stradigotto's gift for persuasion. However, a similar connection between leatherwork and heresy existed in Bologna. Catharism persisted late in Bologna and was pursued by a Dominican inquisition in the late 1290s. The testimony given to the inquisitors, however, refers to 1265–70, when the faith was spreading.[59] Lorenzo Paolini found 101 people identifed as Cathar perfects or believers in Bologna from 1270 to 1299. Twenty-six were women. Fifty-nine people were identified by profession. Of that group, a startling twenty-one were involved in some aspect of the leather industry: they included pursemakers, curriers, and shoemakers as well as furriers.[60]

A circle of pursemakers was central to the Cathars in Bologna, one of them Bompietro, whose beliefs are explored in chapter 5. Bompietro had learned his trade, as well as his Cathar faith, from his father, Giovanni, a pursemaker emigrant from Ferrara. Giuliano sheltered a female perfect, Maria, who lived in a small building attached to his house. Onebene, a Mantuan living in Bologna, mentioned two perfects he met in Mantua, both furriers. Another perfect, a Bolognese, according to Onebene, stayed in the houses of Messer Bererio and Guillielmo of "Ansandris," where he worked at making purses.[61] The Bolognese evidence, then, reveals numerous Cathars involved in tanning and the production of leather goods. Fragments of published evidence suggest that there was also a handful of Cathar leatherworkers in Toulouse. The most dramatic is the mid-thirteenth-century testimony, quoted by A. P. Evans, of a man apprenticed in a leather shop. He called his employer a heretical leatherworker, and implicated the man's father, his business associate and seven apprentices, as well as a few customers.[62] The leather shop, like Stradigotto's fur shop, was a small hub of the Cathar faith.

These scattered references hardly constitute a mass movement. They do suggest that in a few well-documented towns, Cathar dualism had a special attraction for people engaged in work with leather and particularly with fur. This pattern recalls the venerable argument that heresy expressed socioeconomic discontent and the debate over whether the persistent association between heretics and weavers implies that heresy drew disaffected laborers.[63] The consensus since the 1970s is that that view is not sustained by the evidence. As Herbert Grundmann commented in 1962, heresy came first: weaving was a convenient profession for itinerant holy men.[64] Furriers and pursemakers were not disaffected laborers. None of the people mentioned as Cathars were ordinary tanners. A few tanners do appear in the Orvietan sources: termed *conzadori*, they tanned hides—oxhide, goatskin—to be used for harness, containers, and heavy shoes.[65] Stradigotto and the other Orvietans instead were *pelliparii*, tanners and preparers of furs. They tanned and prepared raw skins; the actual tailoring was done by specialists.[66] As David Herlihy has suggested, this preparing of furs was almost a new profession. The fur trade in Italy changed dramatically in this period with a shift in elite clothing style. In the early Middle Ages, fur was generally worn hair outward. In the twelfth and thirteenth centuries, perhaps under the influence of Constantinople and the Muslim world, elites turned furs inwards, using them as linings.[67] Clerics, as well as laypeople, wore overgarments with the fur turned inward, under an outer covering typically made of commercially woven wool. Thirteenth-century furriers, then, prepared the light, supple furs appropriate to this use: not only game—squirrel, rabbit—but commercially raised imported lambskin.[68]

Tanning furs was a complex process.[69] The furs were first soaked in a series of solutions of brine. This was probably done in the countryside, at least in the Orvietan case.[70] It was foul and stinking work. It also required running water, which was at a premium on the Orvietan plateau but easily available in the valley below. Several of the Orvietan furriers listed in the 1292 tax records owned rural land adjoining a river. They probably hired wage laborers to perform the noisome initial stages of tanning. Franco D'Angelo, studying thirteenth-century Palermo, has argued that the filthy aspects of tanning were done by slaves or by marginal laborers, transitory people of very low status.[71] In Orvieto a slave would have been a rare luxury, but it seems reasonable to suppose that the unskilled work of moving wet skins from one vat to the next was done by ill-paid wage laborers. The later stages of preparation involved the delicate work of scraping, curing, softening, and piecing together the small hides. This work required highly skilled artisans and took place in town, judging from contemporary references to urban shops. Statutes from many Italian towns support this view restricting, for example, for sanitary reasons, the beating of skins in the street to soften them.[72]

The furriers and leatherworkers who show up in the Orvietan and Bolognese sources were prosperous artisans. The furriers probably employed laborers, who may well have been alienated but are invisible to us. Orvietan leatherworkers had become a large and prosperous group of artisans by the time of the 1292 catasto. There is one reference in the catasto to a pillizaria, a furrier's shop: Clariello, who himself owned property, is identified as living "in pillizaria." The catasto calls eleven men pellizarii. None of them were identifiably descendants of the households linked to heresy. They were doing well. Durante the furrier owned nineteen pieces of land, valued in total at an impressive 695 libre.[73] The rest were more modest, ranging from a man with a single holding, a vineyard valued at fifteen libre, to a furrier's son, Brother Meo, son of Girardino the furrier, whose substantial lands, some of the on the river Faena, were valued in total at 371 libre. Clariello, the man who lived in the pillizaria, owned a single piece of land on the bank of the Paglia, valued at 110 libre. The value of these artisans' holdings in rural land thus ranged from a very impressive 695 libre to 15 libre.[74] The furriers had prosperous households, benefiting from recent commercial growth. They occasionally can be found investing in merchant ventures, or, like Stradigotto's household, lending sums of money. They had an important guild, existing at least from 1269 and probably before. And they had a direct voice in politics: their guild consul served in popular governing institutions.[75]

Were the leatherworkers, like Grundmann's weavers, Cathars who adopted the trade as a convenient means of support? Most of them—in both Orvieto and Bologna—were not perfects, but ordinary believers who helped to support the perfects. There are a few exceptions: the Mantuan Onebene's testimony from Bologna gives us a glimpse of a perfect visiting a house and stitching purses while speaking of his faith. Onebene also mentions two perfects in Mantua who were furriers.[76] But for the most part, the profession preceded the religion.

Nevertheless, the circumstances of their work surely influenced their faith. In Orvieto they did not live in the same neighborhood, though Paolini has shown the importance of neighborhood links in Bologna.[77] Their strong rural ties played an important role. They had sources of hides in the countryside and, as I've suggested, probably carried on the early phases of their work there. Stradigotto probably used some of those rural ties as he aided the perfects in hiding from the authorities. Leatherworkers' geographical mobility, due to their highly portable skills, is also striking. A number of the individuals mentioned as Cathar leatherworkers, like the Sienese Stradigotto, were emigrants from one town to another. They had interurban networks of trade contacts, trading not only in furs but in other luxury commodities as well. Bompietro, the Bolognese purse-maker burned for heresy, traded at least once in spice. As many scholars have pointed out, heretical ideas spread along the roads.[78.] Thus the web of contacts among people engaged in the trade facilitated conversation and exchange.

The Florentine Cathars

How typical of Italian Catharism were the Cathars of Orvieto? There were, of course, no typical towns or typical Cathars: every Italian community has its own history. The problem of comparison is further complicated by the differing kinds of inquisitorial sources that survive, since depositions of witnesses can give information very different from that of heresy sentences. Sources also derive from different periods. Nevertheless, a comparison with Florence is revealing. The Florentine Cathars, like the Orvietans at least in the 1240s, included petty elites and merchants, often of recent urban origins.

Florence was an important Cathar center and became the seat of a series of Cathar bishops. It was the source of the missionaries who spread the faith to Orvieto, at least according to the author of the *Leggenda* of Parenzo. There was an active and well-documented Dominican Inquisition in 1244–45, headed by Fra Ruggiero Calcagni, the friar who had been beaten up a few years earlier by Provenzano Lupicini. Florentine efforts against heresy were far more violent than the Orvietan: the extant records mention eleven people burned for heresy in Florence or nearby towns. These records include eleven depositions, brief summaries of another twenty depositions, and a few sentences.[79]

Depositions to an inquisitor must be read with care. People were caught in terrible uncertainty, under pressure to protect fellow Cathars but threatened by the possibility that their fellows might confess and implicate them. And they were, of course, fearful of the violence of the inquisition: their property might be confiscated, their houses destroyed, their ancestors, if considered Cathar, disinterred from the cemetery. Several people implausibly told their questioners that they did not know where their parents were buried.[80] People often changed their stories: a Lamandina in 1245 initially denied any involvement, but after her husband confessed and took up the cross, she returned and told the inquisitor that she had lied before "because of fear of her husband and of the destruction of his house."[81] Given all these factors, how much credence can be given to these depositions? My working assumption has been that people generally told the truth but edited things out. Fabrications were more risky than omissions. The best evidence supporting this assumption is that the testimony often agrees, suggesting that people thought it safer to omit things rather than make things up.

Who were the Florentine Cathars? A few scattered professions are mentioned, including a laborer in the country, a female servant, a master purse-maker, and several doctors. Elites, people identified by surnames, are very much evident. They derived from a cluster of rising banking and mercantile lineages: the Baroni, Macci, Pulci, and Nerli. Like the Toste or Toncelle in Orvieto, these were recent, predominantly urban families. Most are documented from the late twelfth century and are established not in the oldest parts of Florence but in nearby parishes. Family members occasionally held civic office. The Macci lineage included bankers by 1203; they held houses on the central piazza of Orsanmichele that were used by civic officials in 1232.[82] Two unnamed women from the lineage were involved: the wife of Cavalcante de Maccis was consoled, and their daughter and her husband reverenced the perfects.[83] As Cavalcante's name suggests, the Macci were associated with the Cavalcanti lineage, prominent early merchants and bankers.[84] The Cavalcanti in 1236 held a tower near the new market.[85] A Cavalcanti father and son were attracted to Catharism: Uguccione, who had served as consul of the merchant's guild of Por Santa Maria in 1218, admitted that he had been to hear the perfects preach.[86] His son Herrigo was described as visiting a sick man who sought the consolation and as meeting four perfects.[87] A woman from the Sizi lineage was a consoled Cathar: Biatrice the daughter of Rogerio Sizi. Dante considered the Sizi a twelfth-century family like the Macci and the Cavalcanti, but little documentation remains.[88]

The household of Rinaldo de Pulci was an important Cathar hospice. Again, they were an elite family by the late twelfth century, judging from a tower termed the "tower of the Pulci" near San Firenze, behind what is now the Piazza Signoria, in 1181.[89] Rinaldo de Pulci was an important man in 1235, one of ten guarantors of a Florentine pledge of five thousand libre to honor an arbitrated settement with Siena.[90] He is considered the founder of a major bank, the Pulci-Rimbertini. A Maria testified that after her consolation she stayed in the household of Rinaldo and his wife, Lamandina, for four months and saw many perfects there.[91] A man called Albano testifed that he and Gemma de Caccialupis received the consolation in the Pulci house from the Cathar bishop Torsello. There are depositions from both Lamandina and Rinaldo. Rinaldo told the friars that he had known of the Cathars for twelve years because Tedora, his brother's wife, brought them into their household. Their life pleased him, he considered them to be good men, he heard their preaching, and when he was at home he sent them fish, bread, wine, and things to eat.[92] Rinaldo also admitted, in response to a question, that he had held money for them: a man before his consolation deposited a sum in his house and then reclaimed it. The inquisitors added to the text following this testimony an account of further evidence against Rinaldo, to prove that he himself had received the consolation from Bishop Torsello, in his own home. Lamandina stated that she had had knowledge of the heretics for twelve years. After Margherita, the wife of Pulce, came to their house, she saw many perfects there, and twice saw the consolation performed. Perfects often came to Domina Tedora, who in fact was the wife of Rinaldo's brother; Lamandina ate twice with Tedora and others, and she often adored the perfects, including Bishop Torsello.

The Pulci were connected with another lineage, the Nerli. The consoled perfect Margherita, married to a Pulci, was the daughter of Nerlo and sister of Ghisola, Diana, Avegnente, Sophia, and probably Gherardo. The Nerli lineage established a presence in the city in the late twelfth century, and Nerlo di Ottavante and his father took the oath to a central tower society in 1179 along with the founder of the Abati lineage, Abbas de Lambarda, and others.[93] Nerlo, the father of the group known to Lamandina, had served as judicial consul for the court of Santa Cecilia in 1221.[94]

Other Cathars, identifiable only in meager references, were also petty elites: Guidone Bauncini witnessed the failed appeal of a judicial fine in 1234.[95] Albertino Malecreste may have been the descendant of a Malecrista who together with a Tribaldi, acted as a guarantor of the Alberti counts in 1200.[96] Albizzo Tribaldi, also implicated in Catharism, was a creditor of Count Guido Guerra in 1240.[97] Claro Mainetti acted as a witness to an Uberti quitclaim in 1238 and, along with an Uberti, served in a civic office charged with collecting the hearth tax from nobles in 1242.[98]

The primary targets of the inquisitor and of Bishop Ardingo in 1245 became two brothers, Pace and Barone del Baroni. The Baroni owned several houses in Florence, including one in Porta Santa Maria and another that was "high and walled," on a street between the Arno and Borgo Santissimi Apostoli. Like the Pulci house, these were used as Cathar hospices.[99] Bishop Torsello performed the consolation in them. Many perfects stayed there: "the woman Rosa" testified that she saw "in the house of Pace del Baroni six heretics praying and a meal prepared before them."[100] Three women lived for four months in both houses, while they taught and learned the Cathar faith.[101] Two perfects who were forcibly rescued from the commune's prison took refuge in the walled house. Fra Ruggiero in consequence targeted the Baroni and the house and compiled evidence from twenty-two witnesses against them.[102]

Were these families, like the Orvietan Cathars, connected with the rise of popular institutions? The problem is complex, both because the Florentine Primo Popolo, the first popular regime, is ill-documented and because of the intensity of the town's factional divisions. Houses tend to be identi-

fied in the sources as Guelf or Ghibelline rather than popular, particularly
when they ultimately became magnates or nobles, and it can be awkward
to determine when this designation is anachronistic. However, of course,
Ghibelline and popular sympathies could be interwoven. Popular institutions in fact took shape in 1244 under a Ghibelline regime and persisted
into the 1250s.[103] The Nerli, Pulci, Macci and Baroni houses came to be
identified with the Ghibellines. Five Macci, were council members during
the Ghibelline regime of the 1260s, and eight were exiled as Ghibellines.
Three Pulci served in Ghibelline councils, and three Nerli as well.[104] So
did the accused Cathar Chiaro Mainetti, who was linked to the leading
Ghibelline nobles, the Uberti.[105] But the merchant Uguccione Cavalcanti
was considered staunchly Guelf.[106] And Messer Albizo Tribaldi, who was
very much implicated in Catharism, was one of the creditors of the Guelf
leader Guido Guerra in 1240.[107] In truth, households and lineages often
swayed with the political breeze, particularly when they had substantial
financial interests at stake. Despite a long history of Ghibelline sympathies, the partners in the Pulci bank took an oath to the pope in 1263
and became closely tied to the papacy and the Angevins.[108] The Nerli
lineage was considered Ghibelline, but in 1278 some Nerli became Guelf
council members and even took the oath on behalf of the Guelf party at
the factional reconciliation achieved by Cardinal Latino.[109]

The conflict over heresy in Florence quickly became a jurisdictional
dispute, with the bishop, friars, and ecclesiastical officials on one side and
the Ghibelline podestà on the other. When the Baroni brothers were sentenced in March 1245, the podestà Pace Pesamigola supported them.
Barone was named as a member of the city's council in 1245.[110] When
Barone sought to appeal the sentence, the Florentine notaries initially refused to redact the document, on the grounds that there could be no legal
recourse against a heresy sentence, and they relented only after the podestà
required it.[111] The Baroni brothers were placed under imperial protection,
and another imperial order required that the leaders of the antiheretical
societies not hinder the podestà in the exercise of his office.[112] On 11
August, the inquisitor sentenced the Baroni to the loss of their property
and demolition of their house. On 12 August the podestà sent two mes-
sengers in procession with the standard-bearer of the commune to the
Dominican convent to order Fra Ruggiero to annul the sentence, because
it had been pronounced against express imperial order. Perhaps he was
not aware that the pope had deposed the emperor on 17 July. The inquisi-

tor responded by citing the podestà as a public defender and aider of heresy. On 24 August, Saint Bartholomew's Day, Bishop Ardingo and Fra Ruggiero preached to their followers, including the Society of the Faith, and excommunicated the podestà. In reaction, the podestà had the commune's bell rung and banner displayed to summon military support. The result was a battle in the cemetery adjoining the cathedral and even within the church, a fight that was long remembered in the city. A half-century later, the blind old Corso di Pietro Velluti still displayed his scars and claimed that he had fought in the battle. The bishop and friar, driven back, regrouped in the piazza of the Dominican convent with a group of armed supporters, and again condemned Pace and Barone.[113] The immediate result is undocumented, but it is clear that the conflict became subsumed within the larger struggle betwen the Guelf and Ghibelline factions.

Catharism in Florence, then, attracted a petty elite population somewhat like the Orvietan into the 1240s, notably rising urban houses of merchants and bankers. Catharism in Florence followed a different trajectory because of contemporary Florentine power struggles: Catharism became identified with Ghibellinism and embroiled in factional war. The evidence for active Florentine Cathars largely disappears with the exile of the Ghibellines. I know of no documentation of Cathars in the Primo Popolo or of circles of Florentine artisans drawn to Catharism at midcentury, like those of Orvieto and Bologna.

It is not surprising that Cathar ideas were popular among people who enjoyed the benefits of socioeconomic and political change. Scholars have sometimes assumed that because the Cathar faith seems to us a pessimistic, world-denying religion it must have attracted the disaffected, perhaps an older nobility displaced by rapid change. In fact, however, a disaffected, failed nobility barely existed in Orvieto, and only a few shreds of fifteenth-century evidence connect one old noble family, the Prefetti di Vico, with the Orvietan Cathars. Petty nobles— like the Monaldeschi, who were to become the lords of the town—more typically adapted to and benefited from change. And the Cathar faith was popular not with the historical losers but among the new families, often those active in the popolo.

Why these social groups? By no means do I urge a return to the old arguments that heresy was primarily socioeconomic—or political—in motivation. That approach assumes, as Talal Asad has pointed out, a blank socioeconomic movement looking for an appropriately matching cosmology. I am very much in sympathy with those who see these choices as fundamentally religious. However, again, the critical point is that the division between religious and political motives is a modern and artificial one. Cosmological and political beliefs were interwoven. For men like Domenico Toncelle or Provenzano Lupicini, Cathar dualism was not primarily a protest against Catholic teachings: Cathar rather than Catholic Christianity was normal to them. Both were instrumental in carrying out the most apparent policy of the popolo: the effort to strengthen the independent commune and to dominate the town's territory. This policy brought them into direct conflict with the territorial ambitions of the papal curia and attracted a series of papal interdictions. Surely, hostility to the political ambitions of the curia encouraged skepticism about the teachings of the Catholic Church as well. The Cathar faith radically separated the life of the spirit from quotidian, material existence. This separation is often seen by scholars in negative terms, following the inquisitorial argument that Catharism allowed people, until they received the consolation, to do whatever they chose. But perhaps for popular leaders like Toncelle or Lupicini, Catharism offered a faith that, rather than allowing libertinism, condemned the secular entanglements of pope and bishop as contamination. By implication, it allowed a free, independent commune. Furthermore, the Catholic faith in the thirteenth century provided the ideological underpinnings for political and social hierarchy. These men who built popular institutions espoused not hierarchy but a new, more egalitarian corporatism.[114]

Cathar teaching set the spiritual utterly apart from the political realm. But surely, as Durkheim claimed, the extraordinary austerity of the perfects made them social models nonetheless. Here were people capable of renouncing the gratification of their appetites and all but the most intangible self-interest. Orvietan citizens and guildsmen similarly needed to put aside immediate self-interest to form a strong and peaceful community. Heroic, otherworldly abstinence was an appropriate ideal. These were sophisticated people, skeptical of the heavy involvement of the curia and the Catholic clergy in contemporary politics and acutely aware of the political uses of sanctity. Late medieval Italians could be cruelly cynical about the clergy. When the Inquisition burned the Cathar purser Bompietro in Bologna in 1299, many locals believed that it was only because the inquisitors wanted his money or, worse yet, wanted his sister. At the same time, people had enormous respect for those they considered genuinely saintly, whether it was the Franciscan Ambrose of Massa or the Cathar Armanno

Punzilupo. It is not surprising that they venerated Cathar perfects, austere and devoted preachers who urged a spiritual faith entirely disengaged from worldly affairs.

Why furriers in particular? Perhaps the attraction of Catharism was linked to their odd, ill-defined status. They were a prosperous, rising social group. What distinguishes leatherworkers and, in particular, furriers from other skilled artisans is a certain ambivalence about the value of their work. As Bronislaw Geremek has commented, professions like those of tanners and butchers, involving work with animal carcasses, were the "accursed professions," the most despised.[115] Furriers were implicated in that foul and despised work, yet they were producing exquisite luxury goods. Again, the shift in fashion that expanded the ranks of skilled furriers suggests this ambivalence: elites wore furs but concealed them under fabric. By the late thirteenth century, only rustics wore rough, heavy furs turned outward.[116] Perhaps, as Robert Delort suggests, this new concealment of fur was an effort by elites to distance themselves from animals and from brute physicality. Hides with the fur exposed were too close to the rustic, too close perhaps to the bestial.[117] It may be that this revulsion reflected on the furriers themselves. They were a wealthy and powerful guild, and they produced delicate fashions for the courtly elite, yet, they were engaged in the foul work of tanning animal hides. Perhaps the discrepancy between their social and material success and and the dirtiness of their work drew them to Catharism: as men and women of ambiguous status and contaminated with the dirtiness of leatherwork, they were drawn to the unsullied purity of the Cathar understanding of goodness. Cathar preachers insisted on absolute purity, just in the period in which the Catholic Church blurred the boundaries between matter and spirit.

PART II

THE *B*ELIEFS
OF ITALIAN CATHARS

$\mathcal{B}$elief and Doubt

WHEN THE BOLOGNESE pursemaker Bompietro was questioned by the Dominican inquisitors in Bologna, he expressed an odd bafflement. The friars wanted to learn to which Cathar sect he belonged, and questioned him at length, but he simply did not know:

> Bompietro, asked what faith and belief and which heretical faith he held, answered that he could not differentiate well among the beliefs and sects of the heretics, but he believed that the heretics were the best men in the world and that true salvation was in them and in their faith, and damnation in the faith of the Roman Church.[1]

Bompietro placed his faith in the pure lives of the Cathar perfects and, in fact, was burned to death for it. Still, his Dominican questioners knew more about heretical sects and their teachings than he did.

This chapter explores the religious beliefs of Italian Cathars, in the context of contemporary skepticism and religious debate. What beliefs and concerns animated the conflict between the Catholic clergy and the Cathars? In exploring Cathar belief I have sought to avoid reliance on the systematizations of Cathar doctrine written by inquisitors like Raineri Sacconi and James Capelli, with their emphasis on organized Cathar churches and the theological divisions among them. Those differences have been minutely examined by several fine scholars, including Father Antoine Dondaine, and it would be difficult to improve on their analysis. Furthermore, as Bompietro's answer suggests, those differences may have been of more concern to Catholic scholars than they were to many Cathar believers. My interest is not in systematic Cathar theology but in the beliefs that drew people to the Cathar faith.

Popular faith is awkward to recover, because most surviving evidence was shaped by the preoccupations of the clerics charged with rooting out heresy. They had a strong incentive to view the Cathars as organized churches with systematic doctrine, real competitors with the Catholic Church. And they tended to emphasize beliefs that denied their own authority. However, Catharism was probably not taught as systematic doctrine, at least outside a modest number of learned perfects.[2] As Manselli has pointed out, Cathar teachings were elaborated with myths, in part to reconcile discrepancies between biblical texts and Cathar belief. Cathar teachers transmitted not points of dogma but texts that were constantly being interpreted.[3] For this reason, I have preferred the depositions of witnesses: statements made by accused Cathars. These are hardly unmediated sources: setting aside their translation from the vernacular to Latin by the recording notary, the depositions were shaped by inquisitorial questions, and the answers were only selectively preserved. Nevertheless, the texts are our best access to what people themselves said they believed.

Even so, the Orvietan evidence is sadly thin. The inquisitorial register includes no depositions; it is a list of sentences. Only Stradigotto's details his beliefs, and the list emphasizes the sacraments and the clergy's power to perform them, perhaps because his Franciscan inquisitors understood heresy as an attack on clerical authority. For this reason, I have drawn extensively on material from inquisitions in other towns. Ideally, this analysis would move chronologically, recognizing the possibility of changing beliefs and tracing both the impact of internal changes in Cathar teaching—most importantly, the arrival of an absolute dualist treatise from the east—and the effects of persecution and inquisition. Unfortunately, most sources for Italian popular Cathar belief are too late and too scanty to permit this kind of precision.[4]

I argue that Cathar beliefs existed within a general climate of religious skepticism in thirteenth-century Italian towns. It is useful to think in terms not of a sharp division between two camps, Cathar and Catholic believers, but of a spectrum of beliefs and concerns. Representatives of the Catholic Church perceived a war between heresy and faith, a perception that must have been shared by embattled Cathar bishops and perfects. But perhaps contemporaries with less vested interest saw a vaguer and more general debate, with Cathar perfects taking one cluster of positions. Cathar ideas, seen in this broader context, were not anomalous and bizarre but answered questions that troubled many believers.

Cathars also probably varied in their beliefs and religious preoccupations even more than did orthodox Catholic believers. Many Cathars rejected Catholic understandings of the body. Cathar teaching repudiated the forms of sanctification of the physical body at the heart of thirteenth-century Catholicism, including the sacraments of marriage and the Eucharist, as well as belief in bodily resurrection and the powerful relics of the saints. However, some Cathars or Cathar sympathizers were untroubled by these aspects of Catholicism. Some venerated both Cathar perfects and the miracle-working bodies of the saints. Some were deeply committed to belief in the absolute goodness of God and his lack of responsibility for any pain or suffering. Dualist teaching made sense to them because it described a God not implicated in any way in suffering, pain, or corruption. This outlook paralleled their disapproval of many Catholic clerics and their enthusiasm for the perfects, holy persons who removed themselves entirely from worldly affairs. The Catholic clergy, like the Catholic God, was too compromised by secular entanglements. These people were most concerned to maintain an understanding of the sacred as pure and uncontaminated.

The differences between Cathar and Catholic practice could be surprisingly blurred. Some professed Cathars went to Catholic clerics for confession and absolution, had godparents, and, in one case, demonstrably respected the Eucharist. There were people who reverenced Cathar perfects and received the consolation but also sought miracles from Catholic saints. The cult of Armanno Punzilupo, the Cathar for a time venerated as a miracle-working Catholic saint in Ferrara, was not as bizarre and anomalous as it seems. Many people were concerned not with the tidy belief systems that preoccupy theorists, both medieval and modern, but with experience and practice.

This chapter begins with direct evidence for the beliefs of individual Cathars, first a 1229 account of Cathar beliefs from an Italian perfect, second an uncoerced statement from a literate and well-informed Cathar believer in Toulouse, Peter Garcias. Garcias, despite his distance from Orvieto, allows us a clear look at a well-informed mid-thirteenth-century Cathar. Having established a rough Cathar orthodoxy, I turn to the more problematic beliefs of three Italians convicted of Catharism. The second section sets those beliefs in the broader context of contemporary religious debate and doubt.

Cathar Believers

The most detailed early testimony to Italian Cathar belief is a statement made to Gregory IX by two former Cathars, Andreas and Pietro. The abbot of the Florentine monastery San Miniato al Monte somehow got hold of the two men and in 1229 displayed them to the pope, who was then in Perugia. The two Cathars publicly abjured heresy and professed the Catholic faith, in a speech before Gregory and "the greatest multitude of men and women, in the presence of many cardinals, archbishops, bishops, and chaplains of the Roman church."[5] In an astonishing moment that underscores the close interconnection between belief and practice, they ate meat in the presence of the abbot, witnesses, and a recording notary, in order "to expel ambiguity" and demonstrate their repudiation of heresy. They spelled out their former beliefs at length, and the account was recorded in Latin, first by the abbot of San Miniato and then by a notary. One of the perfects, Andreas, affirmed the entire account and presumably was responsible for it. His companion Pietro did not deny it, but he admitted that he had not known many of the points in it.

The text is a clear statement of dualist belief, a Cathar reading of the Bible. It thus offers a detailed look at what one Italian perfect knew and taught in the early decades of the century. I have attempted in the following translation to preserve the tone of the original, including its occasional ambiguities. (For the Latin text, see appendix A.)[6]

> In the beginning there were two principles, good and evil. The God of light made all light and spiritual things, while the God of darkness, the devil, made all evil and all shadows and some of the angels. The devil and his angels tricked Lucifer and some of his angels, who were people of the

God of light. The devil, Lucifer, and his angels fell from heaven. One of the good angels with some of his fellows traveled to the shadows to recover Lucifer and his fallen angels. The devil, termed the great dragon, and Lucifer together created the world in six days, with the God of light permitting them to do so. They seized the good angel and his associates and took from him his crown and splendor, and used them to make the lights that are in the firmament. Lucifer repented of the trick that had deceived the God of light, and in concord with the dragon made man from the earth. The dragon wished man to be immortal, but Lucifer wished him mortal, and he was made mortal. They placed the angel who had come to rescue Lucifer and his angels, the angel whose crown they had stolen, in the body of a man, namely Adam. They made for Adam a woman associate and this race of men afterward existed in the body and forgot all of the good and retained the gods that had made their bodies. Lucifer ordered them not to eat of the tree of the knowledge of good, namely not to commingle themselves together, and the dragon made them collude together, that is commingle themselves.

Creation, then, is accomplished by the evil principle, who is a great dragon, together with the fallen angel Lucifer. Salvation history is set in motion by Lucifer's repentance. He seeks to limit the damage, first by making man mortal and the body thus only a temporary trap, and then by forbidding procreation. The God of light, while not omnipotent, is very powerful in this version, but permits actions that (apparently) will lead to the salvation of his kidnapped angel. The text continues with a dualist reading of significant events of the Old and New Testaments, assigning the Old Testament God's role sometimes to the dragon, sometimes to Lucifer, and sometimes to the good God.

When the dragon saw that man was mortal, he repented, and with the permission of the God of light, he sent a flood over all the earth; Lucifer, with permission from the God of light, preserved Noah and his associates. The dragon had the tower of Babel made and created many kinds of languages, so that if someone came from the celestial kingdom to preach, men would not understand him. Then Lucifer spoke to Abraham, Isaac, and Jacob, showing them the God of light, and so handed down the law of Moses, and they were saved. The God of light spoke through the prophets, announcing the coming of the son of God, and said that John was sent by the God of light. He said that the son of God came in the Blessed Virgin Mary, who was made of superior elements, and took flesh from her and not from these elements, and descended from heaven with one hundred forty-seven thousand angels. After death he descended to hell and brought back with him the holy fathers and the prophets and those who had obeyed the prophets. On the day of Pentecost he sent the Holy Spirit and taught the apostles all languages, contrary to the one who had confused the languages, and said that this Holy Spirit and none other has salvation.

He believes that none are saved without the imposition of hands and says that no confession of sin is required of those who come to their faith for the first time. He said that nothing can be done or given toward salvation through an evil priest or minister. He said the Roman Church does not have the Catholic faith, nor is there any salvation in it, nor can any be saved through it, and all the constitutions of the Roman Church are abominated. He condemned marriage [and the] consumption of meats, cheese, and eggs, and [he] entirely prohibited oaths. Concerning the body of Christ and baptism, no faith should be placed in the Roman Church.

The account preserves much of the medieval Catholic reading of the Bible, though some Old Testament events are understood in terms of a struggle between the devil and the repentant Lucifer. The patriarchs and prophets are still rescued in the harrowing of hell. There is a dualist emphasis on the special spiritual nature of Jesus' body. The account ends with a quick list of Cathar rules and practices that are left unexplained: a listener would not understand the rationale for the prohibition of oaths and the consumption of meat, cheese, and eggs.

The statement downplays Cathar condemnation of procreation and marriage, a point to which I return later. It is Lucifer who commands Adam and Eve not to commingle, and the devil who makes them do so. There is no mention of lust. Perhaps the most striking aspect of this account is the lack of any human responsibility for evil and the tone of curious optimism. Evil is not the result of human choice but is entirely diabolic. Humans in truth are angels, but they are temporarily forgetful of their true natures because they are burdened and limited by the body. Mortality is their great good fortune, the gift of the repentant Lucifer: their diabolic entrapment in the body was foiled by Lucifer's insistence that humans be mortal, thus able to escape and return to heaven. Mortality so frustrated the evil intentions of the dragon that it sought to wipe humankind out entirely in the Flood.

What in this odd dualist reading of the Bible attracted people? One text, which allows us to glimpse a passionate Cathar speaking freely about his religious beliefs, provides some indication. This text comes not from

Italy but from Toulouse, but it is to my knowledge the best uncoerced source describing an individual believer who has a clear grasp of Cathar dualism. The text exists because of a nasty trick. A Toulousan called Peter Garcias was persuaded by his kinsman, Friar William Garcias, to visit him in the schoolroom of the Franciscan convent and speak of his Cathar faith. Four more friars somehow concealed themselves under the roof above the schoolroom, where they could both see and hear Peter. They reported his words to the inquisition, and their depositions survive. Their accounts agree, though the emphasis is on points of interest to the inquisition, which were not necessarily the points urged by Peter. Nevertheless, we hear Peter speaking openly, perhaps even in the hopes of persuading his listener.

Peter had a sophisticated understanding based on written as well as oral sources: he told his kinsman that all those clerics who ululate in the church, singing unintelligibly, deceive simple people, but that he had a romance Passion, a vernacular text describing the death of Christ, in his home that stated things as they were.[7] His understanding of humankind and salvation derived from a Cathar reading of Genesis. "The apple forbidden to the first parents," he told Friar William, "was nothing other than the pleasure of carnal coition, and that was the apple Adam offered to the woman."[8] This condemnation of sensuality and physical pleasure is much stronger than that found in the statement of Andreas. This apple, which represents not forbidden knowledge but carnal pleasure, has been shifted from the hand of Eve to that of Adam: it is the man who desires pleasure and tempts the woman.

Peter scorned his wife and despised matrimony. Marriage effected by the Roman Church between a man and a woman, like his own marriage with Ayma, he told Friar William, is prostitution. There is no marriage other than that between the soul and God. At Pentecost it was two years that he had not lain with Ayma. Asked repeatedly whether Ayma shared his faith, he insisted that she did not: she was a stupid beast, just like Friar William.[9] Matrimony is prostitution; no one can be saved together with his wife, not even Peter with his own wife.[10] What did he mean by calling marriage prostitution? That marriage exists only to slake lust? No explanation survives.

Peter spoke with passionate anger against the Catholic understanding of the spiritual potential of the body. When Friar William asked whether the flesh would rise again, Peter, showing the friar his hand, said that the flesh would only rise again as a wooden post does, and he banged a post with his hand.[11] The body has no more capacity for sanctity than an inanimate object. Peter's beliefs were very clear: purgatory did not exist, and the charities of the living could not aid the dead. One was saved only by perfect penance in life, and a spirit destined for salvation that failed to make perfect penance in one body would return in another.[12] Did he consider that some spirits were not destined for salvation and ultimately would not return for another chance? This possibility is doubtful, given his vivid rage at the injustice of the Catholic understanding of damnation: "if he held that God who, of a thousand men he himself had made, saved one and damned all the rest, he would attack and slash him with teeth and nails as a traitor." Peter was outraged at the very idea of a God who would create people only to consign most of them to damnation. He "found him false and treacherous and would spit in his face, adding, 'let him die of gout.'"[13]

Peter revealed, then, intense dissatisfaction with the Catholic clergy and their teachings. He had the tone not of a devoted adherent of a sect, but of an intellectual, a man proud of his independent thinking who had himself discovered the truth in a book. Peter was a thoroughgoing dualist, and he flatly denied the resurrection of the flesh, slapping a post to equate the body with a dead piece of wood. He stressed to Friar William a point that was critically important to many contemporary Cathars: God's pure goodness. Peter was angered by the very concept of damnation, which implied a contaminated, treacherous God.

A similar emphasis on divine goodness appears in a rare detailed statement of belief by an Italian Cathar believer who was not a perfect: the series of depositions Bonigrino of Verona made to the inquisition in Bologna in 1296.[14] Bonigrino was a sophisticated man, a guildsman who had served in popular office in Bologna. He was questioned periodically after 1273, and from 17 July 1296 he was probably imprisoned and repeatedly interrogated about his beliefs.[15] Finally, after considerable official deliberation, he was condemned for heresy and burned at the stake.

How close is Bonigrino's testimony to his actual belief? The testimony reveals him speaking in response to specific questions, so that the topics discussed and sometimes repeated derived from his questioners. He probably had had considerable contact with Cathar preachers, since he came to Bologna from the region near Lake Garda, an area considered the center of two Cathar churches. Nevertheless, his answers express not a rote Cathar orthodoxy but individual reflection.[16]

Bonigrino was not so much committed to metaphysical dualism as to a conception of God as purely good and utterly incapable of causing human suffering. Asked whether there were two principles, Bonigrino answered no, there was one God. Asked whether God made all visible bodies, and especially serpents, dragons, scorpions and the like, he said no, clamorously affirming that the devil and not God made all things that were harmful and burdensome to humans.[17] Asked who made the human body, he answered that man has his body from his father and mother; asked whence came their bodies, he answered that all derived from Adam and Eve; asked where their bodies came from, he answered that he did not know. The Cathar view— from whatever sect—was that all bodies came from the devil. Bonigrino simply pointed to a natural process of generation. It is not all visible things but only the harmful ones that are diabolical. This view is not consistent with contemporary mitigated dualism.[18] Furthermore, Bonigrino had no obvious motive to avoid saying that the devil created all bodies, had he believed it: he was not trying to avoid implicating himself, since he confessed to all sorts of other heretical convictions.

Bonigrino believed the Cathar teaching that the souls of those to be saved were angelic spirits fallen from heaven, and he counted himself among their number. But not all souls are angelic. Bonigrino answered a question about the creator of Judas Iscariot by stating that he was made by his father and mother; they in turn derived from Adam and Eve, and whence they came he did not know. "Asked who created the soul of Judas, in which there was such great malice and evildoing that he thought to betray Jesus and commit such a great evil, he responded that the soul of Judas was not created by good God" *(bono Deo)*. Asked where Judas's soul did come from, he answered, the devil. Asked who made the devil, he answered that he did not know.

Bonigrino had little interest in a dualist identification of evil with the material principle. If Judas's soul was evil, then it was made by the devil.[19] Instead, he was very concerned to maintain an understanding of God as absolutely good. His questioners, presumably working from inquisitorial manuals on Cathar teaching, made reference to the "true God and God of light," but Bonigrino spoke not in terms of light and dark but only of the good God.[20]

On the same grounds, Bonigrino believed that God was not implicated in any form of punishment. He responded to a question about the Flood and the drowning of the Egyptians in the Red Sea with the assertion that nothing like this comes from the good God. Andreas, in contrast, had said that God did not cause but permitted the Flood. Asked whether it is a sin to exact justice from malefactors, he said that criminals like homicides and thieves can be punished according to the world but not according to God, and that their punishment does not please God. Asked whether the podestà and rectors, when they punish and kill malefactors, act against the commands of Christ, Bonigrino answered yes. Neither Christ nor the apostles ordered that men should be killed, because it is written, "Thou shalt not kill." An absolutely good God does not countenance capital punishment.[21] These ideas are consonant with Cathar teaching. Asked about marriage, he answered that it was not ordained by Christ, nor was it in accordance with his teachings. The inquisitor, who was not supposed to debate theology with heretics, nevertheless reproved him on the grounds that Christ took part in the wedding at Cana. Bonigrino answered that Christ was present there with his mother and apostles not to approve of marriage but to console and give joy to those who made the nuptials.

Bonigrino's views on the clergy and sacraments are difficult to disentangle. Asked about the clergy and whether the pope "was head of the Roman Church of Christ," Bonigrino answered cautiously that the pope and others of the Roman Church who carried out the wishes of Christ and were good men were the head of the Church, but otherwise not. Similarly, he was asked about the sacraments: whether priests sacrifice the body of Christ when they say Mass, and whether they have the power to bind and absolve. He responded that all good men in a state of penitence can sacrifice and bind and loose. In fact, all men who are good Christians can do so. His statement implies that it is their spiritual state rather than any institution or ritual that empowers them to perform the sacrament.[22] It is not obvious that by "good Christians" he meant the perfects, and not any good person, because the statement suggests acceptance of the Catholic sacraments: sacrificing, binding, and loosing. It would be curious to accept the Catholic sacraments but claim that only Cathar perfects can perform them. In effect, Bonigrino directly denied that the Catholic clergy, because of their ordination, had a special sacramental authority regardless of individual moral condition, but he did not deny the efficacy of the sacraments.

This interpretation might be taken as reading too much into a hasty remark made under terrible pressure, but Bonigrino went on to make a startling unsolicited assertion that supports it: "just as there are seventy-two languages, so there are seventy-two faiths."[23] The idea that there were seventy-two or seventy-three languages in the world was a medieval commonplace.[24] But Bonigrino placed religious faiths on the same status as languages, and he did not characterize seventy-one of the faiths as wrong. Instead, he implicitly asserted a religious pluralism: not one true church, but seventy-two faiths.

Bonigrino's views, then, had some consistency. The ability to perform a sacrament comes not from an institution but from being a good Christian in a state of penitence. Confession and absolution—and apparently even the Mass—have validity, depending on the spiritual state of the person performing the ceremony. But no church has a monopoly on truth. His pluralism is a faint echo of that bugbear of thirteenth-century theologians, the Averroistic double truth, the idea that faith and reason can lead to opposite conclusions, both of which are true. It calls to mind more directly Boccaccio's tale of the three rings in the *Decameron*, the tale in which Saladin sets a trap for a learned Jew named Melchizedek by asking him which law he considers true, the Jewish, Muslim, or Christian. Melchizedek escapes the trap with a story gracefully suggesting that there may be some truth to all three religious faiths.[25]

Bonigrino certainly was an individual thinker. He accepted much from Cathar preaching, particularly their understanding of human souls as trapped angels. But Bonigrino urged not a dualist condemnation of matter so much as an insistence on the absolute goodness of God. For him, bodies came from a physical process of generation: he did not call them a diabolic, material trap. Bonigrino did not even rise to the inquisitorial bait and deny the Eucharist, but simply insisted that only good Christians could perform sacraments. It is possible that he went to confession and even to Mass, despite his Cathar beliefs. His most remarkable statement was the idea that there are seventy-two faiths and, by implication, all have some validity. Christian sacraments are efficacious if a practitioner is good and in a state of penitence. This belief would certainly justify adoption of some aspects of Catharism and some aspects of Catholicism, since both could have some truth to them.

Bonigrino held these beliefs with passion, if the inquisitorial record is to be trusted. The medieval Church defined heresy as an act of will, the choice to persevere in beliefs despite the knowledge that they are counter to the teachings of the Church. When the inquisitor, acting on this definition, explicitly told Bonigrino that the Church and the inquisitor did not share his beliefs and faith, and asked whether he wished to persevere, and whether he was willing to die for his faith, Bonigrino said yes, he was willing to die.

His fellow Bolognese Cathar, Bompietro, shared some of these ideas. A second-generation Cathar, it was Bompietro who memorably told the Inquisitor that he did not know how to differentiate between the sects of the heretics, but believed perfects to be the best men in the world. Salvation was in them and in their faith, and not in the Roman Church. He did mention three further beliefs. Marriage was not licit according to God. It was a sin to execute criminals. He also said that he "believed nothing of the body of Christ." This statement is awkward to interpret but perhaps meant that he did not believe Christ had a material body. The sacrament in contemporary teaching was, of course, Christ's physical body. However, there is evidence that Bompietro venerated the Eucharist: he gave wine for the Mass to the local Carmelites, and just before his death at the stake he begged the Dominican inquisitors for the sacrament. They denied it, an action that outraged the community. Some of Bompietro's neighbors argued, reasonably enough, that his request for the sacrament was proof that he was not a heretic. My guess is that the request does not indicate a last-minute change of heart: the gifts of wine to the Carmelites are evidence of long veneration.[26] Possibly he venerated the sacrament but did not give credence to transubstantiation. It is also possible that when Bompietro said he believed nothing of the body of Christ, he meant that he was unsure. Certainly, he blurred the differences between the two faiths. His interest was in practice rather than theological truth: salvation is to be found in the perfects, because they are the best men in the world.

In the evidence surrounding the case of Armanno Punzilupo from Ferrara, metaphysical differences were again disregarded, and the line between Cathar and Catholic was vague indeed. Armanno was the man condemned by the Dominican inquisition as a consoled Cathar but venerated by the cathedral canons and local people as a saint.[27] A cult developed, and his tomb in the cathedral became a shrine loaded with votives and statues. Few things were more antithetical to the dualist condemnation of materiality than holy statues, save perhaps the imputation of miracles to a corpse. Veneration of saints' bodies, after all, was based on Catholic belief in the resurrection of the flesh. Nevertheless, the dead Cathar Armanno was venerated and accomplished many miracle cures. People brought wax and votive offerings, prayed for healing miracles, and believed that Armanno answered their prayers. It was only after a concerted campaign by the Dominican inquisition that Boniface VIII ultimately ruled Armanno a heretic and the corpse was exhumed and burned, the shrine dismantled, and the statues smashed. The local Cathars must have found all this not only ironic but comic, as one witness to the inquisition suggested; perhaps cynical old Pope Boniface had a laugh over the case as well.

A late fifteenth-century copy of the dossier of documents provided to the papal court survives.[28] The dossier presents a sort of *Sic et Non*, since it includes both the Dominicans' excerpts from testimony to the inquisition, selected to prove Armanno's heresy, and the cathedral clergy's collection of depositions of witnesses proving his sanctity and healing miracles. It underscores how close the parallels were between inquiries used to prove sainthood and those used to prove heresy. Armanno in life had a reputation as a kind and saintly man. He was known for his mercy toward the imprisoned, collecting charity for them and visiting them in their cells; one of his post-mortem miracles was a jailbreak. Anecdotes in the dossier show him on close terms with all sorts of holy persons, including priests, perfects, and even Waldensians. He must have spoken beautifully: his vivid turns of phrase were remembered by witnesses. It is a measure of his reputation that at his death, Armanno's body was carried to the cathedral, and a crowd gathered to gaze at it before it was interred in a tomb.

The inquisitorial texts prove Armanno's heresy largely on grounds of association and public reputation. A long list of witnesses are quoted who stated that he was a Cathar *credens*, or believer, or testified to his close association with known Cathars. Some were themselves considered Cathar: Madonna Bengepare, termed a Cathar credens, stated on oath in 1274 that Punzilupo of Ferrara was a credens of the Bagnolan Cathars. She had heard Cathars making many jokes and derisory comments about the Roman clerics, saying "How can the men of the Roman Church continue to say that we are evil men, since they made one of us a saint."[29] Other witnesses had seen Punzilupo making formal reverence to perfects: when he entered a house containing a perfect, he would graciously doff his hat, bow to the holy person and say, "Benedicite, bene, bene, bone christiane."[30] Some had heard that he had been consoled. Some arguments for his heresy are comically thin. The judge Messer Jacobino swore in 1270 that Punzilupo was a credens, a Cathar believer. Asked how he knew, Jacobino answered that he did not go to church unless rarely, he took no counsel from any wise churchman, and he had many bad things to say of the clergy.[31] Surely Punzilupo was in good company! In fact, the statement was implausible, since the canons were able to produce sworn depositions from no fewer than seven clerics who had heard Punzilupo's confessions and given him absolution.[32]

Witnesses to Armanno's heresy pointed to an intense concern with clerical practice. He was highly critical of some clergy and spoke with eloquence against them. "They were evil men and did not do the works of God, nor was salvation in them nor in the faith of the Roman Church. They were deceivers of souls and rapacious wolves who were persecuting the good men and the church of God."[33] When Martin of Campitello was led off to be burned, Armanno said to the crowd, "You see what sort of deeds these are, to burn this poor old good man. The earth should not have to sustain those who do such deeds."[34] A Cathar called Bonmercato reported that Armanno repeatedly exhorted him to stay firm in the faith of the heretics, because only in them was salvation.[35] Again, the emphasis was on practice: salvation is in those who lead pure lives.

Armanno did question transubstantiation and the Eucharist, implying to listeners that an incident in which a priest put so much wine in the chalice that he became drunk suggested a coarse motive for the Catholic doctrine.[36] At Easter he was accustomed to offer a large quantity of wine and bread to friends, with the remark that this proved the liars and rapacious wolves were wrong to say that the body of Christ could not be consumed.[37] And Armanno repeated his own memorable comment to the inquisitors: "The priests are so stupid they believe they can close God up in a pyx."[38] There is no mention in the dossier of dualist beliefs. It is impossible at this distance to know more of his beliefs, but the surviving evidence certainly suggests an enthusiasm for saintly lives without too much concern for the theology that justified them.

Some Cathar believers, at least in Ferrara, practiced Catholic as well as Cathar forms. There is no obvious reason to doubt the veracity of the priests who swore they had heard Armanno's confessions and absolved his sins. These visits to Catholic priests for absolution again suggest that Armanno venerated not religious institutions but pure individuals: for him, not all of the clergy were rapacious wolves. The contemporary emphasis on confession to a priest served to bolster clerical authority, and the denial of any need for confession and absolution undermined it. Armanno thus was not concerned to attack the formal authority of Catholic clergy, but only critical of those he considered corrupt.

A shoemaker named Castellano, a Cathar believer, mentioned his own godparents, who were fellow Cathars. Castellano joined with the people who went to view Punzilupo's corpse before its burial, and commented that he was worse than a beast, perhaps disapproving of his association with Catholics. Oldeberto of Cavriano responded "Beware of what you say, *compater,* because he was consoled along with your *comatre,"* referring to Oldeberto's wife.[39] These were people considered Cathar believers who practiced the consolation while they honored godparents and, by implication, Catholic baptism. One might argue that this behavior was only cover: avoidance of baptism would have publicly marked a family as heretical. However, godparenthood was a deeply ingrained social and religious institution, and it would have been hard to set it aside. Castellano and Oldeberto mentioned godparenthood in a way that suggests they took the relationship seriously. Again, perhaps they were untroubled by Catholic baptism with its nondualist implications.

These scanty examples of individual Italian Cathars suggest that there were not two orderly camps opposed on metaphysical grounds. Cathar orthodoxy existed or, more accurately, Cathar orthodoxies. But surely the perfects understood and taught varying versions as they interpreted their texts. Not all of them can have been able to read, and they learned the faith in intensive study with other perfects. A Florentine woman named Albensa told her inquisitors that before she received the consolation she lived in the houses of Pace del Barone in Florence for four months, in order to learn Cathar teachings from two female perfects, Fioretta and Meliorata.[40]

Most people considered to be Cathars did not know and believe an orthodox Cathar faith any more than most Catholics clearly grasped and believed orthodox Catholicism in the thirteenth century. Belief was more individual. Some, like Peter Garcias, held clear, carefully worked out dualist ideas. Others were drawn to aspects of Cathar teaching without necessarily adopting or caring about dualism. Reading Bompietro's deposition, I wondered whether he was sorting out how his beliefs fit together for the first time, in a desperate response to the inquisitor's questions. The most common thread was an emphasis not on systematic belief but on practice: the saintly purity of the perfects was the way to salvation.

The young trumpet player sentenced for heresy in Orvieto in 1268, Petrutio Guidi Becci, had the same general understanding. He was sent by his father to aid the perfects and hear their preaching and warnings. For a time, he believed that the perfects "were good and saintly men and apostles of God, and that salvation was only in them, and that those who were in the faith of the Roman Church would not be saved, but only those who followed the life of the heretics."[41] Again, he gave credence to the perfects because of their purity; it was in the life of the perfects that salvation could be found.

Armanno Punzilupo was not so much an anomaly as an extreme example of the blending of Catholic and Cathar belief and practice. I found no evidence that he taught or maintained any clearly dualist beliefs. Possibly he did, but no witnesses repeated them. The Dominicans, in their understandable eagerness to get him disinterred from the cathedral, would surely have reported any reference to explicitly Cathar beliefs. And Punzilupo's unorthodox ideas were very common points of doubt: he questioned the Eucharist and the actions and sanctity of some Catholic clergy. Popular Cathar teachings were not an anomaly in an age of Catholic faith, but rather a cluster of heterodox answers to contemporary questions about good and evil and the body, part of a more general climate of religious doubt and speculation.

Skepticism and Doubt

The thirteenth century was an age not only of faith but of skepticism.[42] As Alexander Murray has shown, preachers in Italy often complained of widespread impiety and doubt: not only did people give way to lust, pride, and avarice and neglect to go to Mass and confession, they also doubted central teachings of the Church.[43] The Dominican Giordano of Pisa spoke on this theme in sermons in the cathedral and the Dominican convent in Florence, in 1304-5: "Now tell me, how many of these unbelievers exist? Who today believes in invisible goods, the goods of Paradise, who takes care for them? People care for them not at all. They know not what they are. . . . People care today for nothing except piling up temporal wealth. Today all the world is filled with this sin." "Today, they feel safe from the threats and pains of hell and simply do not believe in them."[44] Giordano considered this disbelief a revival of philosophic skepticism. Ancient sages once doubted God's existence. They saw that good people suffered great harm, and wondered: "It cannot be that God exists. How could he sustain so much evil and so many terrible things? And again today," Giordano preached, "madmen ask this question every day."[45] Destructive doubt is a common occurrence.

Evidence of religious skepticism, once you look for it, turns out to be everywhere in the thirteenth century. There were thoroughgoing skeptics, like the wicked old Fra Giacomo Flamenghi described in testimony to the inquisition in Bologna in 1299. Fra Giacomo, who had been a monk at the Vallambrosan monastery of Montarmato for over fifty years, refused to confess, do penance, communicate, or say Mass, although he was in fact a priest. He refused to honor any religious fast, preferring, he claimed, to feast on a splendid supper with laypeople. He told his fellows that a single Lenten fast was enough for a person's lifetime.[46] He did not even attend the divine offices, neither masses nor the other hours.[47] Asked why the abbot did not correct him, several of the monks replied that the abbot feared Fra Giacomo, who was thought to have committed arson and even homicide.[48] Before the current man became abbot, Fra Giacomo had once taken him, tied him up, and dumped him in an open grave. The bishop could not correct him because the monastery was exempt from episcopal authority.

Fra Giacomo was an irreligious old man who amused himself by shocking the young monks. He told them that if he had the power he would freely kill Pope Boniface and the cardinals. Why? Boniface had arranged the death of Pope Celestine, who had been the best man in the world: Celestine was the true pope, and Boniface had no legal right to the office, although he was pope de facto.[49] The remark reveals an unexpected appreciation for sanctity: Celestine was, of course, the saintly hermit who was utterly unable to cope with the demands of the papal office, abdicated, and died shortly afterward. Fra Giacomo was only repeating a popular rumor of Boniface's involvement in his death. Giacomo also criticized the Dominican inquisition for burning two local men convicted of Catharism: the inquisitor and the brothers had committed "an evil deed and a great sin," since the two Cathars "were good men and better than the inquisitor and the Dominican brothers."[50] Again, Fra Giacomo was in good company, since other testimony in the Inquisitorial register shows that literally dozens of Bolognese agreed with him.

Other remarks express a casual skepticism. When someone disturbed by his unwillingness to fast or attend services asked Fra Giacomo, "Don't you fear sin, don't you have a soul?" he replied that a fish has a soul.[51] This statement seems to mean that a person has a soul comparable to that of a fish, but not an immortal soul.[52] He also said that there is no hell or heaven other than this world.[53] This view was not thoughtful and considered, since he also made the contradictory remark that one who does well in this world does well in the next. [54] Fra Giacomo even admitted to manufacturing miracles: he had made "false and fictitious miracles" with *aqua vite* and the veil of the Blessed Virgin, and seduced people and made a lot of money, in the town of Barletta.[55] Fra Giacomo, in sum, was an aging reprobate monk unworthy of Boccaccio only in his apparent lack of sexual peccadilloes. He could appreciate saintliness but disdained any religious obligations; he loosely denied the existence of hell, heaven, and the human soul and gleefully admitted faking miracles for the money.

Giacomo is an extreme example, but the cosmopolitan world of thirteenth-century towns must have fostered skepticism and debate.[56] Some of the tales told in sentences from the Orvietan judicial records suggest popular irreligiosity, a lack of respect for the sacrament. One is the clever jailbreak of a fellow named Petruccio, nicknamed Pazzo, or Crazy, who was imprisoned for theft. Presumably he was in jail because he was unable to pay the hefty fine and would therefore suffer the penalty for theft, the loss of an eye. A woman smuggled in a rope wrapped in a piece of cloth. Then "Petruccio made himself ill so that he seemed about to die." He was given the chance to do penance and receive the Corpus Christi. "Asking the guard that for God's sake he be placed in the upper part of the prison, by false blandishments, persuasions, and deceptions" he used the rope and escaped.[57] Presumably, like the wicked man in the first story of Boccaccio's *Decameron* whose phony confession led to his post-mortem veneration as a saint, Crazy Petruccio lied to the priest when he confessed and received the sacrament.[58]

As Grado Merlo has suggested, unorthodox ideas in the thirteenth and fourteenth centuries spread along the roads. Non-Catholic and even non-Christian practices were certainly available.[59] Two Orvietan texts briefly mention magical practices, ascribing them to disreputable women. Among the miraculous cures of Ambrose of Massa was that of a woman named

Palmeria who had suffered a miscarriage and demonic possession as a result of a prostitute's curse.[60] The civic judicial records include a woman who was sentenced for using *fatias*, enchantments, to seduce a married man.[61] Some magic was grounded in Catholic Christianity, like the use of the consecrated host in a love potion.[62] Other magic cases had little to do with Christian belief. In Bologna in 1286, a doctor was accused by his goldsmith neighbor of making love potions and a wax image of a woman with a pin stuck through its heart. Buried under the goldsmith's threshhold, the image caused the man's wife to lose her "good sense," desperately long to be with the doctor, and give him valuable property.[63]

The best single collection of evidence for late medieval popular belief and speculation is the Fournier Register, depositions heard by the bishop of Pamiers in southern France between 1318 and 1325. People questioned about knowledge of non-Catholic beliefs often mentioned not only magical ideas but forms of materialism. Their answers recall Bonigrino's insistence that bodies come from a process of generation, though he, of course, also believed in the soul. Jacotte Carot of Ax asserted to a group of women waiting at the mill for their wheat to be ground that there is no resurrection of the flesh and future life. In what must have been an extraordinary moment, she swore by the flour to the finality of death.[64] Guillemette Benet of Ornolac considered that the soul is only blood, a belief based on direct observation: she had watched a child die, and no soul escaped its lips, nothing but wind.[65] A stonemason from Tarascon argued what amounted to the Aristotelian view that the world and its cycles of generation and corruption are eternal.[66] Emmanuel Le Roy Ladurie, in a popular study based on the register, has argued that these beliefs surfaced because of doubt created by Catharism. This causal order seems to me reversed: Cathar teaching enjoyed success because of a climate of doubt and independent speculation.

Skepticism was not only a matter of popular non-Christian ideas, but also was a reaction to the changing nature of the Catholic church. Some of the practices emphasized at the Lateran Council in 1215 became special targets of doubt: the sacrament of marriage and enhanced clerical authority, especially as exercised in confession, penance, and the other sacraments. The Mass became the center of lay worship, and transubstatiation—the transformation of the bread and wine into the body and blood of Christ—was emphasized. The Mass also became a ritual form for the expression of the elevated status of the clergy.[67] And, as discussed earlier,

clerical authority and the Mass became very common foci of doubt.[68] A
man called Bartolomeo "Speçabrage" from Sandrigo was sentenced by the
Inquisitor in Vicenza in 1292 for "speaking evil of the body of Christ."
Speçabrage had raised a large *lasagna* on high and pointed out, "Could I
not say that this *lasagna* is the body of Christ, as the priests say when
when they raise their *calesetas* [wafers] when they celebrate [Mass]?"[69]
(This lasagna was not of course a modern one but some form of baked
dough, perhaps layered with cheese.) The action exactly parodied the ritual gesture that linked the miracle of transubstantiation with priestly authority. The sentence was clever as well: Speçabrage was not only fined
and made to wear the cross but required to venerate the consecration of
the Host. He was to attend every Sunday and festival mass in the church
in Sandrigo until Easter and to hold a lit candle from the moment of the
elevation of the Host until the priest began the Pater Noster. The required
gesture would honor not only Christ 's body but the authority and sacramental power of the priest. This lesson was a clear and very public one.
The gesture of respect was to be repeatedly performed in the local church,
where Speçabrage's actions would be seen by his friends and neighbors.
The people who had heard him criticize the clergy and the sacrament
would now watch him honor their authority.

In 1302 the inquisitor in Bologna sentenced a Florentine moneylender,
Ser Bonacursio di Neri Bonelle, for denying the Mass and the need for
divine grace. Bonacursio denied that the Host was the body of Christ,
repeating the familiar point that even if Christ's body had been as big as
a mountain the priests would already have eaten it up. He also argued
that those who have wealth in this life lack no other grace or gift of God,
saying, "When have you seen a dying man return to us who from another
life brings to us new life?"[70] The inquisitor, Manfred of Parma, interpreted this view as a denial of the afterlife.

Skepticism and anticlericalism went together: the Fournier Register includes Raimond de l'Aire, who believed that the soul is only blood and
there is no afterlife and concluded that clerical efforts to encourage chari-
table donations for the souls of the dead were a trick.[71] An acquaintance,
when asked about the annual lamb tithe, responded that rather than pay,
they should give one hundred libre to two men to kill the bishop.[72]

One of the great accomplishments of the Lateran Council was a careful
definition of what it meant to be a Christian and to have some expectation
of Christian salvation. It is startling to find contemporary evidence of

more relativist ideas, like Bonigrino's seventy-two faiths. Some believed in the extension of Christian salvation to the unbaptized. The priest Arnaud de Monesple believed that in the end Mary would intercede with God and not only all Christians but all Jews would be saved, rendering baptism in the end irrelevant.[73]

Thirteenth-century popular exempla and miracle stories emphasized penalties for doubt. Doubt is a central theme in the tales contained in Jacopo da Voragine's *Legenda Aurea*, the *Golden Legend*, a "medieval best-seller" among the collections of lives of the saints.[74] Jacopo (d. 1298), the compiler of the tales, was a Dominican provincial for Lombardy and (at the end of his life) became the archbishop of Genoa; he collected what has been aptly called the popular folklore of the saints. Jacopo intended the compilation as a sourcebook for clerics, who could use the anecdotes in their sermons, and he emphasized tales that reinforced social order and hierarchy.[75] The *Golden Legend* is full of stories about doubters threatened with supernatural punishment or somehow confounded. Expressions of doubt served in part to set the stage for the ensuing miracle. But this strategy was not purely a rhetorical device. Jacopo believed that simple folk are best convinced by miracles; the tales provided anecdotes for preachers seeking to castigate religious doubt.[76] Some doubts concerned older religious forms, like the authenticity of a relic. When Venetian merchants were carrying off the relics of Saint Mark to Venice, and passing sailors doubted that it was truly Mark's body, they were threatened with shipwreck until they proclaimed the truth. One very skeptical sailor was possessed by the devil and tortured until he was brought before the saint's body and declared his belief.

Other tales spoke to contemporary concerns, with an emphasis not on doctrine but on clerical motives, particularly doubts of the spirituality of the mendicants. Many of the miracles of Saint Peter Martyr, the Dominican inquisitor, punish doubt as well as confound heretics. Doubt of the purity of Dominican motives was very unwise. In Utrecht, a group of women sitting spinning in the marketplace watched a celebration honoring Peter Martyr. "You see?" they said to the people standing around, "those friars know all about raising money! Now they want to pile up a lot of money to build big palaces, so they've invented a new martyr." The thread they were spinning and their fingers became covered with blood, which they interpreted to mean that they had "said bad things about the blood of the precious martyr." When the repentant women told all to the Dominican prior, he called everyone together and announced what had happened. A master of arts "began to make fun of the whole story, saying . . . 'Just look at the way these friars beguile the hearts of simple people! Here they've got together some nice little neighbor women and had them dip thread into some blood and then pretend that a miracle had happened.'" His educated skepticism of the miracle attracted the wrath of God, Jacopo tells us. He was seized with a fever and was at the point of death, when he confessed his misdeed to the Dominican prior and his sin to God, and promised special devotion to Peter Martyr if only he were cured. He was immediately made well.[77] Miracles could punish doubt and compel belief, at least in Jacopo's tales.

The most common point of doctrine doubted in these cautionary tales and exempla is transubstantiation. And often, doubt of this teaching is ascribed to women: many stories tell of a doubting woman given a miraculous demonstration of the truth of the Real Presence. In a famous miracle attributed to Gregory the Great, a woman laughed as Gregory consecrated the Host and began to place it on her tongue. The saint placed the Host instead on the altar and asked why she laughed. "Because you called this bread, which I made with my own hands, the 'Body of the Lord.'" Gregory "prostrated himself in prayer, and when he rose, he found the particle of bread changed into flesh in the shape of a finger. Seeing this, the woman recovered her faith." The saint "prayed again, saw the flesh return to the form of bread, and gave communion to the woman."[78] This version is mild: in many tales the Host at the moment of elevation becomes an infant.

These tales are filled with a skeptical population, dubious that the bones are really Saint Mark's, suspicious that the Dominicans faked the blood on the thread and the cult of the new saint, extremely doubtful that the bread on the altar really somehow becomes the flesh of Christ. Enhanced claims for clerical authority and power invited critical scrutiny of the clergy. People who were sharply aware of the ways in which religious claims could bolster clerical wealth and authority might well doubt those claims. Ser Cursio, the Florentine sentenced by the inquisitor in Bologna in 1301, was denounced for saying that everything done by priests, prelates, and friars was intended to extort money from the simple folk of the world and to keep them under the feet of the clergy.[79] This belief led him to question the Eucharist as well, stating that "the sacrament, which is publicly said to be the body of Christ, which should be in the host, is a fraud, or rather a delusion, and that it should not be believed that the body of Christ could be consecrated in the hands of such sinners."[80] Skepticism of the purity of clerical lives led easily to doubts of their teaching.

Doubt and Authority in Orvieto

I have suggested, then, that popular Cathar beliefs in the thirteenth century were not as anomalous as one might suspect. The scanty evidence for the views of Italian believers suggests not a clear Cathar orthodoxy, but a vaguer, more independent-minded acceptance of aspects of Cathar and Catholic teaching, like the Cathars with godparents in Ferrara or the Bolognese artisan Bompietro who venerated the Eucharist. Some Cathar believers were deeply committed to belief in the absolute goodness of God and his lack of responsibility for pain and suffering; this idea had more resonance than metaphysical dualism and the abstract condemnation of matter. Not surprisingly, they stressed ideas that were very common points of skepticism, particularly transubstantiation and the Eucharist, and the morality of the Catholic clergy. Skepticism of Catholic teachings and of clerical authority were closely intertwined.

Currents of anticlericalism and religious skepticism were very much present in Orvieto in the early decades of the century. Some local clergy were in disrepute: the Benedictines were thought to ignore their Rule, the shabby bishop to squabble endlessly over property with petty nobles and the canons of San Costanzo, the cathedral to be "a den of thieves."[81] And again, the emphasis was on practice: people with little respect for the lives of the local clergy were skeptical about their religious claims. The evidence that does survive derives from the efforts of the Catholic clergy to castigate skepticism and reinforce their authority: tales of doubt confounded by miracles. Master John, the cathedral canon who wrote Parenzo's passion, was preoccupied with doubters and critics. He speaks with bitterness of attacks on Parenzo's cult and with great satisfaction of heretics and skeptics confounded, silenced, and even converted when they witnessed the power of Parenzo's corpse and tomb. On the day of Parenzo's death, a woman of Sermognano, in the diocese of Bagnoregio, who had

had an heretical friend punished by Parenzo, exulted at the death. "With bent knees and raised hands she began to blaspheme against the martyr, saying, 'Blessed be God, because the worst of men is dead, a man who unjustly punished many people.'" She suffered an instantaneous injury to her mouth and was only cured after a penitent visit to the tomb.[82] The woman had accused Parenzo of the unjust exercise of power and judicial authority and was dramatically silenced. Her penance at his tomb under-scored his justice, as well as the bishop's and clergy's power to hear confession, exact penance, and grant absolution.

A castellan from Allerona questioned not Parenzo's justice but his sanctity and the veracity of the tales of his miracles. He "said that the martyr had been a sinner and that no blind person could possibly be healed by him." A nobleman from Bagnoregio openly mocked the new cult: he "did not believe any of it, but rather in contempt and derision of the martyr said that he had a blind donkey and wanted to take him to the tomb of the martyr and use the donkey to test the martyr's power and learn whether he could illuminate the blind."[83] Both men instantly were themselves struck blind. Their skepticism and derision were seen as slights to the bishop, who was closely linked to Parenzo: the men had not to prostrate themselves at the tomb but to confess the sin to the bishop to regain the saint's favor. Even that did not suffice. The contemptuous nobleman with the blind donkey, despite his confession, remains blind at this writing, Master John wrote, although at least the burning and pain in his eyes went away.

The *Leggenda* suggests, then, that Cathar ideas spread in Orvieto in an atmosphere of skepticism of miraculous claims. These points of doubt were familiar: the purity of clerical lives and motives and the veracity of their miracles, particularly transubstantiation. And the episcopal response in Orvieto, as elsewhere, stressed displays of supernatural power that answered doubt and proved authority. The most effective was the tale of the miracle at Bolsena, which became central to the definition of Orvietan catholic belief. The miracle at Bolsena is a tale of a priest who doubted transubstantiation and the Eucharist. While on a penitential pilgrimage to Rome, his doubts were answered by a miracle as he consecrated the Host. As I discuss later, this miraculous answer to doubt—by implication an answer to Catharism—came to be lavishly celebrated in Orvieto. The universal Corpus Christi feast was established in Orvieto and came, with time, to be celebrated there with a large civic and ecclesiastical procession.

The new cathedral was built with a chapel dedicated to the relics of the miracle and frescoed with Eucharistic miracles. At the center of late medieval Orvietan Catholic piety, then, was the refutation of doubt and the miraculous affirmation of transubstantiation, the sanctification of physical food and of the human body.

SIX

$\int$exed Bodies, Married Bodies, and Dead Bodies

MIRACULOUS DISPLAYS OF power that answered doubt and proved sanctity very often took the form of a change to someone's body, a change that could shock even the skeptics who only believed the evidence of their eyes and ears. Physical bodies were at the center of the debate between Cathar and Catholic: their origins and their potential for sanctity and corruption. In the thirteenth century the human body was, to use Levi-Strauss's familiar phrase, one of the things that is "good to think with," a vehicle for discussion of the origins and nature of good and evil and of human potentiality. Cathar dualists identified evil with the material body in various ways, understanding it to be the source of pain and suffering and as an alien imposition on true natures that are pure spirit. This denied the late-twelfth- and thirteenth-century Catholic emphasis on the potential of bodies for sanctity and on the body as inseparable from the spirit and integral to a person's identity. In late medieval Catholic piety, religious values were often expressed through bodies, and a person's spiritual state evident in their physical condition, as Saint Francis's identification with Christ was evidenced by his stigmata, the Crucifixion wounds that opened in his body. Sanctity and sin were best revealed by the state of one's body, both in life and even after death.

This chapter explores three topics in Cathar understandings of male and female bodies, set against the background of contemporary Catholic belief. The first is sexual difference and lust. The dualist explanations of human nature in Cathar creation stories opened up the question of the origins of human sexual difference and concupiscence. As in chapter 5, I focus on popular belief, examining whether these radical ideas were taken up by Cathar believers. The section explores ideas about sexual difference as stated and as practiced by Cathars. How did Italian Cathars describe the creation of sexual difference, and to what extent did Italian Cathar women break with contemporary gender norms in practice?

The second topic is marriage. One teaching common to virtually all Cathar texts is the condemnation of marriage and the procreation of children. The Catholic Church at the end of the twelfth century redefined the sacrament of matrimony in terms not of sexual consummation but of free choice, and some scholars have argued that this shift was an effort to vindicate marriage in response to the Cathar attack. The redefinition also served to strengthen clerical authority over marriages, and it may be that some people were attracted to Cathar teaching because they disliked what they perceived as episcopal and papal use of the doctrine of consensual marriage for political ends. A 1212 dispute in the Orvietan bishop's court suggests this possibility, as I will show: it reveals men from Cathar houses who lost a marriage case adjudicated by the bishop on consensual grounds.

Finally, the chapter turns from sexuality and marriage to a third focus of debate over the body: corpses. Catholic clerics did not directly attack dualist heresy by emphasizing the divine origins of human sexuality and consummation as the perfection of the sacrament of marriage. Instead, they answered heresy by stressing the ways in which corpses revealed sanctity or sin. For Cathars, dead bodies were putrid meat, unconnected with the spirit that after death either entered another body or returned, freed from matter, to the celestial kingdom. For Catholics who believed in the resurrection of the flesh, a corpse was still integral to the identity of the dead person and retained that person's characteristics. When dead bodies like Pietro Parenzo's mangled corpse miraculously displayed saintly attributes, this supernatural show of force proved dualism to be wrong. Ultimately, this conflict over the qualities of bodies was a debate over the

meaning of pain and illness; the chapter turns finally to Orvietan understandings of illness as expressed in their testimony to the healing miracles
of a local Franciscan saint, Ambrose of Massa.

Creation and Sexual Difference

The most radical social teachings of the Cathars concerned sexual difference, sin, and authority. The dualist idea that the physical world is diabolic in origin and not a divine creation opened up questions about human identity and the division of humankind into two sexes, male and
female. A Bogomil treatise that circulated widely in western Europe, the
Interrogatio Iohannis, depicted lust and sexual difference itself as alien to
identity, imposed by the devil. This idea was a radical break with the
Catholic teaching that sexual difference was instituted by God and concupiscence—the loss of perfect rational control of the body—the result of
an act of human will.

The implications for the social order were dramatic. First, this understanding of human nature contradicted contemporary justifications for political authority: the idea that authority is necessary because of human
weakness that is the consequence of original sin. Because Adam chose to
disobey, his descendants suffer a lack of just order and a need for rational
control, in the body and in society. In Cathar teaching, Adam never chose
to sin: humans are essentially angels. Capable of rational control, they can
purify themselves of matter and again become perfect. Do they then need
control by outside authorities? Second, Cathar beliefs challenged established gender roles: a teaching common to virtually all Cathar texts is the
condemnation of marriage and procreation. A woman's role as wife and
mother has no value, since giving birth and nurturing children only perpetuates the evil of existence in the body. The body could not define
people's roles in the Cathar faith: both sexes could become perfects,
preach, and administer the sacrament. Thus, what of the structure of
patriarchal authority, in the household and in society?

The focus of this section is on identity and sexual difference in the
belief and practice of Italian Cathars. It first examines ideas of sexual
difference and of lust in Cathar accounts of creation and in the statements
of accused Cathar believers. Cathar theology opened up the possibility of
radical critiques of the social order, but what aspects of these ideas did

Italian Cathars actually take up when they described their beliefs? I turn next to the complex question of practice and the actions of Cathar women. One common argument in the social history of European Catharism has been that women were especially drawn to the faith because it offered them opportunities that did not exist within the Catholic Church. The practice of Cathar women differed in Orvieto and in Florence; however, to some degree in both towns, a denial of sexual difference was expressed and taught through the actions of women who became perfects.

Cathar preachers taught their faith by telling a creation story, a tale that explained how the physical world came to be, despite God's absolute goodness, through diabolic evil. Creation accounts that were perhaps intended by theologians as myths to be understood allegorically were passed on in the form of stories, and there is little evidence to suggest that the people who heard these tales analyzed them as allegories. The most detailed Italian example is the tale told by the captured perfect Andreas to Gregory IX, discussed earlier. In that account, the devil in the form of a great dragon, together with the fallen angel Lucifer, trapped captured angels in bodies, and then Lucifer repented and made humans mortal and thus ultimately able to escape their bodies. Cathar preachers' tales generally agreed on the trapped angel, the diabolic creation of humankind, and the consequent belief that marriage and procreation are evils because they result in a disastrous continuation of the devil's scheme in the form of children, spirits again trapped in flesh. The tales differed, however, in their analysis of human identity. The idea of dualist creation opened up the possibility of rethinking concupiscence and sexual difference itself.

The *Interrogatio Iohannis,* a Bogomil text reportedly carried by Nazarius to Italy and circulated from about 1190, sets out absolute dualist teaching on sex.[1] This text emphasizes the view that sexual desire and sexual difference itself are impositions and alien to identity. This point of view is radically different from the Catholic understanding of sexual difference as instituted by God and eternal. The text describes in detail Satan's creation of human sexuality.[2] Satan formed a male and a female body out of clay and then told two angels to enter into the bodies. The two angels differed in status but not in gender: the angel that became Adam outranked the angel that became Eve, since he came from the second rather than the first heaven. After they entered into the bodies, "the angels grieved deeply that they thus had a mortal form imposed upon them and that they now existed in different forms."[3] In other words, they wept to find that they had bodies that were sexually differentiated, male and female.

When Satan commanded them to "perform the works of the flesh in their bodies of clay," the newly corporeal angels did not know how, and Satan had to find a way to endow them not only with materiality but with lust. His scheme included the creation of Paradise, where he literally dumped lust into their heads. "Entering into the form of the serpent he deceived the angel who was in the form of a woman and poured out lust for sin upon her head, and the lust of Eve was like a burning oven." He "made his lust with Eve with the serpent's tail."[4] Then Adam was endowed with concupiscence as well. In this account, then, sexual desire and sexual difference were entirely alien to Adam and Eve's true natures and identities, imposed upon them by Satan to their great sorrow. Further, material bodies and concupiscence were quite distinct: the angels, given bodies, did not know what to do with them until Satan added lust as well.

The *Interrogatio Iohannis* is a powerful dualist account of sexual difference as a Satanic invention imposed on angelic spirits that were bodiless and so had neither sexual characteristics nor lust. Angelic spirits differ in rank but not in gender; when they return to the realm of pure spirit they will shed their sex with their bodies.[5] This concept directly challenges the Catholic understanding of sexual difference as a divine creation: at least from the time of Augustine, western European Catholics were taught that humans were originally created with bodies that were sexually differentiated but entirely free of lust, able to do their duty and propagate the human species without any loss of perfect, rational control. Resurrection would, of course, take place in sexed bodies as well.[6] Sexual difference is instituted by God and essential to human nature. Sexual concupiscence, on the other hand, is not a divine creation but is the result of the human choice to disobey, transmitted as original sin.[7] That sin is expressed by a bodily change, the loss with the fall of Adam of man's perfect control of the movements of his genitals. For Bogomil dualists, then, lust is a diabolic imposition on natures that are essentially pure; for western European Catholics, lust is a part of human nature but the result of their corruption due to a tragic choice of the human will.

Did Italian Cathars take up the idea that sexual difference was a diabolical invention? The *Interrogatio Iohannis* was available in northern Italy. The inquisitor Anselm of Alexandria mentioned that the text was repudiated by one faction in Lombardy, over the issue of the incarnation of Christ and Mary, but believed by others.[8] The text was probably influential in Languedoc after 1220.[9] However, most contemporary Italian Cathar versions of the creation story did not take up and develop this understanding, and they tend to be closer to a Catholic condemnation not of sexual difference itself but of the sexual act and concupiscence. The 1229 statement of Cathar beliefs by Andreas touched on the creation of sex only briefly, and treated sexual difference as a given, not an aspect of creation to be explained. Adam was created male, since Eve was made afterward as his "woman associate." Lucifer, concerned to undo the damage caused by the creation of humankind, ordered them not to eat of the tree of the knowledge of good, which meant not to "commingle themselves," but the devil in the form of the great dragon made them do so.[10] Procreation was not their choice but part of the diabolic plot; they were moved not by lust but by an outside agency, the devil's orders.

An account of creation in an imaginary debate between a Catholic and a Cathar, written by a Florentine around 1240, again treats sexual difference as a given, and the male as normative when it condemns the sexual act and procreation. The Cathar in the debate calls the tree of the knowledge of good and evil in Paradise a woman's womb, so that the prohibition on eating of the fruit of the tree meant do not fornicate with a woman. It is again the serpent, that is the devil, who first fornicates with Eve.[11] The Cathar goes on to state that the Cathars condemn not marriage but adultery: marriage is between Christ and his Church, but "that foul business which a man does with a woman when he carnally commingles with her, it is that adultery which we forbid."[12] Marriage is a spiritual relationship, and since sexual relations pollute it they are considered adultery. This understanding is close to some contemporary Catholic ideas of spiritual marriage, as Dyan Elliott has pointed out.[13] In the twelfth century, the marriage of Mary and Joseph was discussed as an exemplar of a perfect union because it was believed to have been chaste.[14] Of course, the underlying rationale differed: Cathar and Catholic shared an emphasis on the condemnation of lust, but not the condemnation of procreation itself.

The Dominican Moneta of Cremona in his 1241 treatise against the Cathars does report the idea that sexual difference is diabolical in origin. Moneta writes that Cathars "believe that the bodies of men and women were made by the devil, and the difference of shameful members, whence they say comes all damnable carnal coition." [15] He repeats a Cathar version of original sin:

> Satan shut another angel into the body of a woman made from Adam's side while he slept. With her Adam sinned. Adam's sin, they declare, was carnal fornication, for they say that the serpent came to the woman and corrupted her with his tail; and from that coition Cain was born, they say. . . . They also say that the woman, accustomed to concupiscence, went to Adam and showed him how to copulate with her, and persuaded him, and just as Eve persuaded him, so Adam committed the act; and this, they declare, is the eating of the tree of the knowledge of good and evil.

Again, original sin is not a voluntary choice but a diabolic imposition. The tale explains first the creation of sexual difference and then the creation of lustful female nature. When Adam and Eve began to cover their genitals with clothing, "this was done, not because they had sinned with these members, but because they were rebels against their superior, the true God; their baser part, the flesh, rebelled against its superior, the spirit." [16]

This view is similar to thirteenth-century Catholic understandings of original sin—derived from Anselm of Canterbury and developed by Alexander of Hales and then Thomas Aquinas—in terms of a loss of original justice, understood as just order within the body. This idea of the body politic—the identification of political hierarchy with the hierarchical ordering of the body—was developed in medieval political medical theory: lust is the loss of the control that originally constituted just order, the rebellion of the subordinate parts. [17]

These accounts of Adam and Eve share the idea that it was the serpent who was ultimately responsible for human concupiscence. The serpent represented diabolic masculine lust: his tail became the devil's phallus. He corrupted Eve and taught her the sexual act; she then corrupted Adam. Sexual concupiscence, the impulse that for Augustine both expresses and transmits original sin, is imposed on Adam and Eve from without in these Cathar accounts. [18] The newly created humans have no agency: like God, they are pure and innocent. They are victims in no way responsible for their loss of control and consequent suffering. The Catholic understanding of original sin in terms of an act of will, disobedience freely chosen, is absent. [19]

And yet, there is a long tradition of ambivalence about marital sexuality and condemnation of pleasure in Catholic teaching. Eve's role in first acquiring lust and then seducing Adam in Italian Cathar texts is close to Catholic views of female nature, particularly the Augustinian view that Eve represented the desire for sin and Adam rational consent.[20] Medieval Catholic theologians were at times close to a dualist condemnation of physical functions themselves. Probably there was some dualist influence on Augustine of Hippo's understanding of the consequences of original sin in terms of concupiscence, in which sexual pleasure and the loss of perfect control of the genitals is a consequence of the Fall. This understanding resembles the Manichee view of matter as characterized by random motion, as Johannes van Oort has shown. The late twelfth century saw severe condemnations of physical pleasure by some Catholic theologians. The canonist Huguccio, teacher of Innocent III, argued, as Thomas Tentler explains, that "every act of sexual intercourse, even in marriage, involves guilt and sin [*culpa et peccatum*] because every time a man experiences sexual pleasure he is guilty of at least a small venial sin." He differentiated his view from dualist heresy by distinguishing between heretical condemnation of sexual intercourse as mortal sin; he considered it only venial.[21]

Other versions of creation reportedly told by perfects were far from any Catholic or dualist understanding. The *Brevis summula* was a collection of Cathar teachings put together by an Italian Franciscan around 1250.[22] He got the material, he tells us, from two Cathar preachers: "That they believe and understand all this I have gathered and learned from the words of John of Bergamo, one of their preachers and teachers, who told me he had been a Cathar perfect for forty years, and from the words of John de Cucullio, who, as he told me, was likewise a teacher and preacher among them for twenty-five years."[23] The author reports that, according to these preachers, Albigensians explain the incarnation of Christ through a celestial adultery story.

> [T]hey say that Lucifer was the son of the evil god and that he ascended into heaven and found the wife of the celestial king without her husband, that is, God. There he went so far as to lie with her. As she at first defended herself, Lucifer said to her that if he should beget a son he would make him god in his kingdom and have him worshipped as a god. And so she yielded to him.

The story is worthy of Homer. It would be difficult to fit it into any dualist theological scheme, since the picture of a married God hardly implies a spiritual realm without sexual difference, or even for that matter a condemnation of matrimony. One wonders who performed the ceremony. "It was in this way," the author continues, "that the Albigensians say Christ was born and brought his flesh from heaven, and this is their great secret. They want to say that he was not truly man, but an angel incarnate and that he was not the son of the Blessed Mary and thus did not assume his flesh from her, and that he neither ate not drank corporeally."[24] The queen of heaven had a spiritual rather than corporeal body, but could be seduced nevertheless. The tale evokes the promises in seduction stories as they are represented in contemporary court records, as when a man in Bologna in 1285 coaxed a young woman to become his concubine with the promise that if she bore children his father would allow him to marry her.[25]

The tale also recalls a perfect in France who considered the angels sexual, and even lustful, but all male. In the cosmological tale told to Jean Maury and preserved in the Fournier Register, the devil first tempted the angels in Paradise by showing them a beautiful woman and promising them similar wives. Pressed by his questioners, Maury admitted hearing that in consequence, the good God had ruled that no woman could enter Paradise without first being transformed into a man.[26] A heretic had also told him that carnal knowledge of any woman, even one's wife, was a great sin. "When someone knows a woman carnally," the heretics said, "the stink of the sin rises up to the top of heaven and spreads out over the whole cosmos."[27] Angelic natures have male sexual attributes; it is their lust for beautiful wives that brings about their fall.

The perfects who recounted these versions of the creation of sex were quick to blame the devil for physicality and evil, and to tell a story that absolved God and humankind of any responsibility for evil. Their concern with divine and human purity was the crucial point of difference: the Catholic tradition emphasized not human innocence and diabolic victimization but human volition and human culpability.

What about the depositions of Cathar believers? As shown earlier, the passionate Toulousan Cathar Peter Garcias urged the condemnation of sex and marriage with enthusiasm in his conversation with Friar William. His wife, Ayma, was an uncomprehending beast, and he had abstained from sexual relations with her for two years, since sexual abstinence was necessary to purify the spirit. This statement is a clear acceptance of a dualist condemnation of sexuality; Garcias also utterly denied any bodily resurrection. When he called his wife an uncomprehending beast, he struck a note of disdain for women, or at least disgust with Ayma, that suggests not a denial of sexual difference but rather an acceptance of the common medieval identification of woman with physicality and the body.[28]

Unfortunately, while Italians may have spoken eloquently about sex and marriage to the inquisition, their testimony, to my knowledge, does not survive. Two depositions mention marriage only briefly. Bonigrino argued that Christ did not institute it and defended his position by explaining Christ's presence at the wedding at Cana in terms of consolation. Human beings come into existence through a process of generation and corruption that he did not characterize as evil, though he believed that some souls destined for salvation were trapped angelic spirits.

In Florence in 1244, the consoled Cathar Andreas was questioned about his beliefs and then condemned to be handed over to the secular arm and burned. Of the fourteen statements he made, only three were explicitly recorded as responses to questions: denials of the Eucharist, the resurrection of the flesh, and marriage.[29] It may well have been not Andreas but his questioners who were concerned about marriage. Significantly, the notary's text was corrected to make the belief statements more precise, in accordance with inquisitorial procedure. Presumably, it was read back to Andreas and he was allowed to make changes. Two changes were made, and both concerned Cathar beliefs about materiality and the body. The statement that it is a mortal sin to eat meat was crossed out in favor of the statement that Christ prohibited the eating of meat.[30] The concept of mortal sin is, of course, Catholic and not Cathar. The word "carnal" was inserted to modify marriage: it was not simply marriage but carnal marriage that was condemned.[31] Valid marriage was spiritual.

Andreas did not believe in the resurrection of the body and did not wish his body to rise again. But despite his dualist condemnation of the physical body, like Peter Garcias he assumed a normative maleness: he told his questioners that Christ came only for the salvation of the brothers and that they alone would be saved if they did penance. The angels are the brothers of Christ, somehow male before they were trapped in the body. When Andreas condemned marriage, it was the salvation of the husband that was at issue: he stated in response to a question that he did not believe that a man who was with his wife in carnal marriage can be saved. In effect, Andreas assumed a normative maleness, and by implication identified woman with the body: a person could not be saved unless he avoided sex, understood as carnal relations with a wife. Andreas recalls the perfect in the Fournier register who explicitly pictured the angels as male.

These statements of belief probably all derived from men. What about the beliefs of Italian women? One does not have to adopt the idea that there is such a thing as an essential female nature to agree that many thirteenth-century women, because of their life experience, might have understood the implications of dualism rather differently from men of their status. Sadly, little evidence survives: I know of no extended depositions from Italian women that speak of marriage, let alone sexual difference. Cathar women demonstrably did preach and teach their faith but few of their words survive.

Sexual Difference in Cathar Practice

An alternative way to explore Cathar understandings of sexual difference is through examining their practice. Historians of religion have learned in recent decades from sociologists and anthropologists—notably Pierre Bourdieu—that belief systems are taught through practice. That is, people learn understandings of the social order, authority, and even cosmology through models of behavior, repeated gestures, and practices.[32] Not only inquisitors but people accused of heresy in the thirteenth century were quick to insist that practice implied belief. Some defended themselves or family members against a charge of Cathar heresy by pointing to marriages and offspring. In Vicenza in 1287, the heirs of the long-dead Marco Gallo sought to avoid a post-mortem condemnation for heresy that would strip them of their property. They produced witnesses to prove that he had not been a heretic: he had a wife, "stayed with her in marriage while he lived, according to the custom of the Roman church and by her had many sons and daughters." He also received the sacrament at death.[33] As Francesca Tognato points out, this defense the passionate cry of the weaver in Toulouse accused of heresy: "I am not a heretic, for I have a wife and I sleep with her. I have sons, I eat meat, and I lie and swear, and I am a faithful Christian."[34] Belief and practice were bound up together.

What was the practice of Italian Cathar women? Were there many female perfects, and to what extent did they actually play sacerdotal roles, roles that violated contemporary gender norms? The answers, not surprisingly, are mixed, and it may well be that the extent of women's active involvement varied by town and by social status.[35] Master John, author of Pietro Parenzo's *Leggenda*, tells us that it was two female missionaries who succeeded in spreading the Cathar faith in Orvieto at the end of the twelfth century, and a group of pious matrons who were first persuaded by them. Thus, he described a special initial impetus from female preachers. There is some evidence that this pattern persisted. Some Orvietan women were of course very religious, like Bonadimane, who testified to a healing miracle of the Franciscan Ambrose in 1240 and then was convicted post mortem of Catharism in 1268.[36] Little informal clusters of female penitents existed in Orvieto as in other Tuscan and Umbrian towns. A hint of a circle of religious women appears in a benefaction in the 1251 will of Gastia, daughter of Stefano di Falko: she left four libre on behalf of her soul, with forty soldi to be given "to those women whom her mother knows," and her heir was termed her friend, Madonna Tedora.[37]

In 1268, one-third of the Orvietans sentenced for heresy were women: twenty-eight out of eighty-five. At least fourteen were widows, and most of these were the widows of convicted Cathars. At times, as in the case of Domenico Toncelle, the inquisitors targeted the female relatives of important dead men but not the men themselves. There were close ties between some of the women sentenced, like Bellapratu and her daughter-in-law Grana, furriers' wives who lived in the same household, and the three Guidutie sisters. Small groups of women were sentenced together, perhaps reflecting their close association.[38]

Female perfects were uncommon in Orvieto: five are mentioned in the 1268 sentences, compared to at least thirty-two male perfects, or about 15 percent.[39] However, one active female perfect was at the center of a little network of women, all from interconnected families of the merchant elite: the perfect Ricca is mentioned in the sentences of all three Guidutie sisters, as well as those of Vianese, the wife of the merchant Giovanni Claruvisi, and Camera, the widow of the early popular leader Rainucci de Arari.[40] It was Ricca who came at the summons of Verdenovella to console the dying servant woman Dyambra.[41] Her active role may have been more acceptable in merchant houses than in those of the nobility. The

Toste, who lived in the style of the minor nobility despite their lack of titles, had little contact with female Cathars: no Toste sentence mentions Ricca or any other perfecta.

In Florence, it is clear that in the 1240s, clusters of women were at the center of the faith. Evidence survives from the depositions of thirty-one people who were questioned by the Dominican inquisitor in the 1240s. The inquisitors were not obviously targeting women: the dossier was assembled in order to obtain a heresy condemnation of two powerful and defiant brothers, Pace and Barone del Baroni. Two of the documents are, in fact, summaries of testimony that list what could be proved against the Baroni and leave out information about other possible Cathars. Despite the fact that the targets were two men, over half of the witnesses were female: seventeen of thirty-one witnesses. Furthermore, the number of convinced Cathars who were female was significantly higher. The witnesses named at least fifty-three perfects, or people who received the consolation. Of that group, at least twenty-three were women—over 40 percent.

The stories in the depositions suggest the special involvement of women from minor elite families. When the inquisitors adduced evidence against Rinaldo de Pulci, they drew entirely on women. First, they cited three female perfects, Biatrice de Sizis, Albense of Siena, and Contelda, who admitted that they had been consoled in his house and had stayed there for a time. Furthermore, "noble ladies and other women worthy of faith" claimed "that they saw Torsello and other consoled heretics often perform the imposition of hands in his house." Finally, it was proved by "other women who were believers and have returned to the faith and by a certain female servant of his house, that they often saw heretics in the house."[42]

Cathar practice in Florence did break with contemporary gender expectations, though within limits. Elite men like Barone del Baroni made the formal bow of reverence to perfected women. No Florentine source mentions women administering the consolation, as Ricca did in Orvieto for the servant woman Dyambra. But women did teach and even preach. There are striking Florentine references to women teaching the Cathar faith. The Baroni brothers admitted that they learned heresy from their mother, the consoled Cathar Belliotta.[43] Five times, people mentioned women teaching other women. For example, before Albense became a perfect, she stayed in a hospice for four months to learn Cathar doctrine from two female perfects, Fioretta and Meliorata. Johanna, the wife of Locteringhi, testified that she was first taught by a woman named Aspecta.

Madonna Adalina, wife of Albizo Tribaldi, described the preaching of a Sienese woman who was a Cathar visionary. She saw Madonna Tedora "with a certain Sienese woman who closed her eyes like a person who is sleeping and raised up her voice on high and began to speak and preached, and [Adalina] stated that [the Sienese woman] said that Torsello and Marco and others stood at the feet of majesty dressed in clothing ornamented with precious stones."[44] Torsello had been the Cathar bishop of Florence, Marco perhaps the perfect called Marco of Montefiascone in several sentences. The unnamed woman lifted up her voice to preach of a vision depicting an afterlife that rewarded and justified Cathar perfects.

In sum, the practice of Cathar women in Orvieto and Florence did deny contemporary gender roles: female perfects broke with familial expectations and rejected dowry, marriage, and childbirth to pursue autonomous religious careers, and at times played a sacerdotal role. Richard Abels and Ellen Harrison in an extensive study of inquisitorial records from southern France argued that this role was very limited: female perfects were less apt than males to travel and preach, more apt to remain enclosed in a hospice. It was only during the period of active inquisitorial persecution that women played a more active role.[45] We need a thorough study of the Italian female perfects, but the evidence examined here suggests more independent lives. They did not live quietly in houses like Catholic convents. Instead, pairs of women stayed for a few months in a particular house, perhaps to instruct a new perfecta, and then moved on. Women did administer the consolation, at least to other women, and not only taught but preached. Their actions did challenge patriarchal authority in the household and in the larger society.

At the same time, the practice of female Cathars was not altogether anomalous, since religious women who remained within the Catholic Church in the early thirteenth century broke with gender expectations in similar ways.[46] The repudiation of marriage and family became a standard element in the lives of the saints, far more important to Catholic than to Cathar piety. The Florentine noblewoman Umiliana dei Cerchi was a contemporary of the Cathar women discussed here, and she probably knew them. Her vita includes episodes in which she vividly repudiated her roles as wife, sister, and daughter.[47] Women like the Franciscan Angela of Foligno shaped their piety in opposition to expected gender roles: Angela actually prayed for the deaths of her family members and believed that her husband, children and mother died by God's will because they were obstacles to her religious vocation.[48] In the early thirteenth century, some Italian religious women enjoyed considerable independence. Clare and the early Franciscan women, for example, were not enclosed in convents, and Clara Gennaro speaks of female followers of Clare wandering barefoot all over northern Italy. Clare herself at times came close to a sacerdotal role, as in a miracle story in which she deployed the Eucharist against Muslim troops.[49] Clusters of female penitents also enjoyed lives that were not constrained by a rule.

The papacy and bishops moved energetically to control and define these female religious movements, imposing Benedictine monasticism, thus enclosure, on Clare and her followers, and institutional order, in the form of rules under the aegis of the mendicants, on the penitents.[50] As Anna Benvenuti Papi has shown, marginal, irregular religious women in Tuscany came to be constrained by the mendicant orders. The Franciscan and Dominican hagiographers who recorded their lives and miracles shaped the texts to embody specific models of female piety.[51] From this perspective, efforts to repress Catharism as heresy and to place female piety under institutional controls were parallel: both normalized gender, defining and narrowing the roles acceptable for women.

Marriage

Another battleground between Cathar and Catholic was marriage. The Catholic Church at the end of the twelfth century redefined the sacrament of matrimony in terms not of sexual consummation but of free choice, and some scholars have argued that this shift was an effort to vindicate marriage in response to the Cathar attack. I suggest that the accusation that Cathars deny marriage was important to Catholic diatribe because it helped to justify the extension of clerical control over marriages. It may be that some people were attracted to Cathar teaching because they disliked what they perceived as episcopal and papal manipulation of marriage for political ends.

The great period of legal and bureaucratic creativity in the twelfth century brought about a fundamental reexamination of marriage. The central issue was the potential sanctity of matrimony and its inclusion in the list of sacraments.[52] Marriage and conjugal relations were understood, beginning with Augustine, to produce three goods: offspring, faith, and indissolubility. These goods outweighed the evil of sensual pleasure in intercourse and justified marriage and conjugal relations, though only insofar as they were intended to produce children. The idea that marriage is a *sacramentum* also derived from Augustine. From the twelfth century on, as the definition of the sacraments became more precise, there was considerable discussion of exactly what in marriage constituted the sacrament, and many theologians believed that consummation, the sexual union of man and woman, was required for a marriage to be perfected, and thus sacramental. As Seamus Heaney demonstrates, Roland Bandinelli first argued, in his *Summa* of 1143, that the visual sign of marriage was sexual union, signifying the invisible union of Christ and the Church.[53] This understanding of marital sexuality conflicted with the long tradition of condemnation of sexual pleasure. The canonist Huguccio made the extreme argument that sex was only without sin if without pleasure, a view that was not easily reconciled with the idea that sexual union in practice could perfect a sacrament.[54] The debate over the status of marital sexuality and the relationship betweeen sexual consummation and the sacrament led to a new spiritual valuation of marriage, viewed in terms not of physical consummation but of consent and the will. With Alexander III, and then Innocent III, free choice came to define the sacrament of matrimony: present consent between legitimate parties made a marriage, regardless of consummation.[55]

Scholars have suggested that this rethinking of Christian marriage was in part a response to Catharism.[56] Theologians vindicated marriage by emphasizing its spiritual potential rather than its procreative purpose. It is also the case that the Cathars were useful opponents: the exclusion of Catharism aided in the definition of marriage and the normalization of gender. Some anti-Cathar polemicists stressed the idea that the dualist condemnation of marriage led to practices against nature. As we saw, authors included in their attacks on the Cathars the charge that they advocated sodomy and incest. Raineri Sacconi, in his 1250 *Summa*, wrote that "a belief common to all Cathars is that carnal matrimony has always been a mortal sin and that in the future life one incurs no heavier penalty for adultery or incest than for legitimate marriage, nor indeed among them should anyone be more severely punished on this account."[57] Raineri surely knew better: he was, he tells us, a "former heresiarch, now by God's grace a priest in the Order of Preachers, although unworthy."[58] The charge made little sense, as Cathars did not believe in degrees of punishment. As Raineri himself explained, "Not even Judas the traitor will be punished more severely than a one-day-old child, but all will be equal in glory and equal in punishment."[59] James Capelli, who took pains to be accurate and defended the perfects from the charge of sexual debauchery, insisted on their denial of all marriage: "They babble that no one can ever be saved in matrimony. Indeed, these most stupid of people, seeking the purity of virginity and chastity, say that all carnal coition is shameful, base, and odious and thus damnable."[60] When these preachers emphasized the attack on marriage and childbirth as heretical, they were building a Catholic view of sexual and marital normalcy that reinforced a specific understanding of sexual difference as well as their own authority.

Clearly, some townsfolk were alienated by the exercise of jurisdiction over marriage by Catholic clergy, and surely Catharism was appealing in part because the perfects did not interfere with marriages except to condemn them.[61] As Duby has argued, for the laity the purposes of marriage and codes governing it were very different from those of reform-minded clerics who defined the sacrament in terms of present consent.[62] Marriage concerned children, property, and inheritance. It was not possible for everyone because of the expense: a marriage required a dowry, and might produce offspring with claims to property. As a result, concubinage was common, judging from the recurring presence in civic court records of women termed the concubine of so-and-so. Thus, in the seduction case mentioned earlier, the man told the woman he wanted to live with him that if she bore children then his father could be persuaded to allow them to marry, despite her lack of a dowry. She apparently was not convinced. The story suggests the gap between their understanding of what marriage meant, in terms of heirs and property, and the canonical definition: in law, the two had only to exchange words of present consent and they would have been married.

There is evidence to suggest that theologians' definitions of matrimony nevertheless affected Orvietans, in that the local bishop and the papal curia did step in and adjudicate their marriages. In 1205, an Orvietan marriage case was appealed to Innocent III. A knight sought to annul his marriage, claiming consanguinity in the fourth and fifth degree. His wife demonstrated, in response, that they had been married at least eighteen years and had at least three children. Innocent wrote to Bishop Matteo to uphold the marriage. The knight's motives are not clear from the let-ter—whether or not the heirs were living, for example—but he presum-ably wanted a new marriage. Innocent, in this case, closed the loophole that would have allowed the knight to repudiate his wife and take an-other.[63]

In this period of sharp antagonism between the Orvietan bishop and some local elites, the bishop put the new definition of marriage in terms of present consent into practice and used it to exercise authority. A cluster of texts in the episcopal registers reveals the bishop adjudicating mar-riages—in at least one case, on the grounds of present consent. A list of excommunications and absolutions by Bishop Ranerio (1228–48) in-cludes two "pro uxore," on behalf of or because of a wife, though the exact nature of the disputes are unstated.[64]

The record of one marriage case, heard in 1212 by Bishop Giovanni, was copied and preserved in the register, perhaps at Bishop Ranerio's instance. It is an important early example of an Italian episcopal marriage case; because it has not been published in full, I have included the Latin text and a translation in appendix B. Significantly, at least one man from a Cathar house was present. The plaintiff, a man called Oderisio de Celle, claimed as his wife a noblewoman named Riciadonna, arguing that she had consented to the union. The simple exchange of *verba de presenti*, pres-ent consent, between two eligible people was enough in 1212 to contract a legitimate marriage.[65] The case followed canon law procedure. Oderisio, after his oath of speaking the truth, stated that he was married to Ricia-donna: he had sworn to accept her as his wife and given her a ring, and she had consented and sworn just as he did, in the house of Gerardini near Bagno, on the sack near the hearth. This was done in the presence of three witnesses. Riciadonna after her oath of speaking the truth stated that she had never consented to him: neither had she first consented, nor first touched the book; she never kissed him to indicate that she accepted him as her man. He had used force to place her hand on the book, but she had not sworn; he gave her two rings but she rejected them both.

Legal proof required at least two witnesses. Oderisio produced three; each was sworn, testified to these points, and then was questioned. Palto-nario—a cleric, although he was a subdeacon and had neither tonsure nor clerical habit—reported the marriage vow: when Oderisio placed the ring on Riciadonna's finger, he said, "By this ring which I place on your finger, you are my wife, and I am your husband." Paltonario insisted that he knew Riciadonna consented because she had extended her finger and accepted the ring, although he did not hear what she said. A layman named Angelo also testified that she consented. Asked whether Oderisio had been joking, he responded that he saw him kissing her many times. In the disputation that followed the witnesses' testimony, the discussion concerned whether the exchange of rings had been in jest. One of the witnesses, Ildebrandino Canuti, claimed it had, and Oderisio responded that there had been two exchanges of rings, the joking one witnessed by Ildebrandino, and another one, witnessed by the others. Bishop Giovanni then cut the proceedings short: he forestalled Riciadonna's production of witnesses disproving Oderisio's witnesses' testimony, and ruled that there was no marriage, and that Riciadonna was absolved and given license to marry.

Without more context, it is impossible to know whether Bishop Giovanni was rescuing a young woman and her family from being trapped into an unwanted marriage or, more cynically, doing her family a favor by using consent effectively to annul one marriage and make another possible; perhaps both. The testimony certainly suggests joking and flirtation, but that does not mean that Riciadonna did not actually consent. John T. Noonan has made a powerful and convincing general argument that consensual marriage strengthened the ability of individuals to choose their spouses.[66] This particular case does not support that view, because it does not suggest that Ricciadonna was acting in opposition to her family in voiding the marriage. If Ricciadonna's kinsmen had approved of the marriage with Oderisio, presumably some of them would have been present at the ceremony. Her recourse to consensual marriage in the bishop's court probably was not an effort to obtain her own choice in opposition to her kin, but could represent her kin forcing her to repudiate a marriage she in fact had sought. In any case, the bishop was using his power over marriage in ways that enabled him to intervene and manipulate local families' alliances.

The participants can be partially identified: one belonged to a Cathar house, and two others may have as well. Riciadonna is called a freeborn noblewoman, but there are no direct clues to her natal family. The startlingly casual ceremony took place in the house of the late Ranieri Tiniosi, now (in 1212) the house of Gerardino. His status is best evidenced by his relations with the woman present, Algina. She was at times called his servant and at times his *amasia*, concubine, implying that he was living with a housekeeper/concubine rather than a wife. This arrangement suggests that he lacked the wealth and independence to marry. Gerardino was apparently the heir of Ranieri Tiniosi, and may well have belonged to a family of merchants who by the 1260s were using Tignosi as their surname. One of them, called Ingilbert the merchant, was sentenced for Catharism in 1268.[67] There may also be a link to the Tignosi family in Viterbo and the heretical leader "J. Tiniosi" whose political success, despite his excommunication, troubled Innocent III in 1205.[68]

The Miscinelli, a family of Orvietan moneylenders who became well-known for Catharism, were directly involved. Oderisio, the groom, was an elite, since the witnesses referred to his squire. One of the witnesses called him Oderisio de Celle, suggesting his patronymic may have been Miscinello or the nickname Celle. One witness who can be clearly identified was Benedicto Miscinelli. His presence strengthens the possibility that Oderisio was another Miscinelli, a man mentioned in other records with the nickname of Ricco, the son of Miscinello.[69] If correct, this fact is significant, since three of the direct descendants of Ricco Miscinelli were sentenced for heresy in 1268. It is certain, then, that Benedicto Miscinelli was present, and possible that he was there because Oderisio was his kinsman. It is also possible that the events took place in a Tiniosi house. These were families long associated with Catharism.

It may be, then, that Miscinelli disaffection from the Catholic Church was linked to this episode, which—for many elites—showed the ambitious bishop using spiritual claims to grab power. Another marriage case involved a Lupicino, probably a member of the Lupicini, another house with Cathar sympathies. Thus several members of Cathar houses can be located in the episcopal court in the early decades of the century, at odds with the bishop over the nature and politics of marriage. These circumstantial bits of evidence do support the theory that some Orvietans were angered by episcopal and papal claims of authority over their marriages and that perhaps the politics of marriage had some effect on Cathar popular belief.

The Bodies of the Dead

Catholic clerics responded to the Cathar condemnation of the body and to more widespread skepticism of Catholic claims by underscoring miraculous bodily changes that demonstrated sanctity. Very often, the miracles that proved sanctity involved the physical state of the dead. Cadavers are ubiquitous in thirteenth-century Orvietan texts. Caroline Bynum has suggested that "to the Cathars (at least as they appeared to orthodox eyes) the paradigmatic body was the cadaver."[70] In fact, the orthodox were wrong: the paradigmatic body for a Cathar was all too alive. Cathars, at least in principle, paid little attention to corpses, except perhaps to use rotten meat to mock the cult of Parenzo. A corpse did not retain the identity it had when living, and it could be discarded.[71] Preoccupation with the characteristics of the bodies of the dead, like the elaborate mortification of the flesh, was profoundly Catholic.[72] Two holy men became venerated as saints in early thirteenth-century Orvieto: Pietro Parenzo and Ambrose of Massa. In both cases, veneration focused not on their careers while living but on their miraculous corpses. Both texts begin when the men arrive in Orvieto at the end of their lives. They die, and their bodies quickly demonstrate their supernatural power.

To understand this emphasis on miraculous corpses it is important to remember that people in the thirteenth century had contact with the bodies of the dead in a way that most moderns do not. They prepared their own dead for burial. Corpses were usually not permanently interred but moved around, buried for a time, and then reburied. The dead might first be placed in the cemetery, or—if the deceased had been important and had made the right benefactions—in the cathedral, but after a few years, because of a need for space for new burials, they might be moved to an ossarium. The jumble of bones in the cemetery was familiar to townsfolk. When the corpse of a woman named Rosafiore was exhumed from a cemetery to be burned for heresy in Bologna in 1299, Madonna Azzolina Marchi commented, "How do they know which are her bones?"[73] Burial space problems were especially acute in Orvieto because the town sits on a rock of limited area, and its cemeteries could not easily be expanded. A statute of 1315 actually mentions problems with the stench from burials.[74] The claim that a corpse smelled not foul but sweet was a vivid one. A sweet odor proved that the person was a saint, victorious over death, awaiting triumphant resurrection.

This familiarity with the dead is the background of the emphasis on the qualities of dead bodies in thirteenth-century Catholic piety. Corpses figure prominently in the *Leggenda* of Parenzo, as does the idea that the state of a person's corpse and its place of burial are an index of the person's spiritual condition. Thus, when the bishop punished heretics before Parenzo's arrival, those who died "in error" "received a foul burial outside the cemetery of the church."[75] In the *Leggenda*, not only do saintly bodies give off a miraculous sweetness, heretical bodies give off a miraculously foul stink. When one of Parenzo's killers fled to a castello and then died there, his corpse was at first given a church burial. However, the author tells us, it swelled up so that it could scarcely be contained in the grave, and fouled the air so greatly that the locals began to sicken and die. In effect, the man's moral impurity found expression in the way his body rotted, and his inappropriate burial in holy ground threatened to poison the living. So they dug up the fetid corpse and buried it outside the castello, in a foul place. With the cause ended, the author states, the effect ceased as well.[76]

Parenzo's corpse, in contrast, was miraculously incorrupt and did not even appear dead. Despite the many gory wounds, Master John writes, the body gave off not foulness but an aromatic odor. All were astounded and wondered even more that when the heat was greatest, it gave off no foulness but had a color more lifelike than when it had been alive. "The corpse did not pale, and the limbs did not stiffen, deprived of living spirit."[77] Master John, who, after all, was an eyewitness, described local elites checking the corpse, reassuring themselves of its sanctity: "priests and knights frequently touched the fingers and found them pliable, as if the body's vital spirit and soul remained."[78] And miraculous healings began to take place at the shrine where the body lay. The picture of knights and priests continually manipulating the fingers of Parenzo's corpse is a revealing one: perhaps a bit dubious, they were checking for the miracle, testing the body's physical state as an index of the truth of Parenzo's spiritual condition.

The meat-throwing vignette in the passion offers a glimpse of Orvietan disbelief and a lurid rebuttal of the idea that Parenzo's corpse was incorrupt and was healing the sick. Master John writes that it was certain malicious spirits who wished to hinder the gathering of men at the tomb who tossed the putrid meat from a nearby window.[79] The corpse, the gesture implies, was just another stinking piece of dead flesh. The action was a powerful evocation of doubt, an attack on the idea of a sacred, incorrupt dead body. It encapsulates the Cathar understanding of the body as alien to the self, a piece of foul corruption and source of pain and suffering.

The *Leggenda* drew on beliefs that associated honor and dishonor with place of burial: burial in a foul place rather than the church cemetery was a foul punishment that signified exclusion from the Christian community in death, thus in the afterlife. In theory, a well-informed Cathar would deny this, believing that the body in whatever location is itself foul. But not everyone who heard and sympathized with the perfects understood or shared this view. One Orvietan artisan was sentenced for an ironic and touching crime: apparently troubled by the sight of the body of the perfect Josep hanging on the scaffold, he took it down and "buried it with devotion." Josep himself probably would not have seen the need. A curious line in the *Leggenda* mentions a person who dishonored Parenzo's blood by putting it in a foul place, again a very un-Cathar gesture because it implied belief in relics. Master John writes that someone took Parenzo's tunic out of the tomb, washed blood out of it and threw it in the place designated for putrid things; they suffered, he added, divine punishment for it later.[80] The anecdote is incredible: it is hard to imagine that anyone bent on dishonoring Parenzo would choose this complicated modus operandi. To sneak into the church, rob the tomb, and rinse the blood from the tunic in hopes of a relic is plausible. But to do so in order to discard the blood somewhere dishonorable seems complicated and risky: easier just to pitch rotten meat out the window. The anecdote underscores contemporary Catholic sensitivity to the dishonor of filthy burial.

The idea that the state of a person's corpse was an index of that person's spiritual condition derived perhaps from ancient ideas about burial, and the notion that the state of one's corpse will influence one's chances in the afterlife—an idea challenged by the gory martyrs of the Christian tradition.[81] Jacopo da Voragine included, somewhat dubiously, in the *Golden Legend* the tale that the corpse of Pontius Pilate attracted devils and disasters. Pilate killed himself in Rome, and his body was weighted with a stone and thrown into the Tiber. But "wicked, foul spirits made sport of the wicked, foul body, plunging it into the water, and snatching it up into the air. This caused awesome floods in the water and lightning, tempests, and hailstorms in the air, and a widespread panic broke out among the people." The Romans hauled the corpse out of their river and sent it to Vienne (because, perhaps, the name comes from *Via Gehennae*, the road to hell). When the same horrid problems occurred, the people of Vienne buried it near Lausanne. "There the populace, harried to excess by the aforesaid upheavals, took the body away and sank it into a pit surrounded by mountains, where, according to some accounts, diabolical machinations still make themselves felt."[82] Pilate's foul corpse became a demonic playtoy, so disturbing to the elements that it caused bad weather.

A Franciscan cult in Orvieto, dating from 1240, centered on another powerful corpse: the text contains local testimony to the miracles of Ambrose of Massa that offers a very moving look at Orvietan perceptions of the body and its potential for sanctity in 1240. Again, the focus was on a dead man's hand. Ambrose, a Franciscan friar who ended his career in Orvieto, was a modest man who worked in the friars' kitchen and had a reputation as a zealous healer. Other friars, including his saintly mentor Fra Morico, testified that Ambrose not only cared for his ailing brothers but devoted himself to poor people who suffered illnesses: carrying his medicines, he went out to their houses "in order to bind up their wounds."[83] At his death a cult developed in which his corpse and tomb performed miraculous cures: he was a far more successful healer dead than he had been alive. The source is an immediate one: shortly after Ambrose's death, Gregory IX asked Orvietans to testify to his miracles, in order to compile evidence for his canonization. The papal edict was read in all the city's churches, and a notary recorded in Latin the testimony of over two hundred witnesses, on twelve days spread over a period of seven months.[84] The growing cult was, of course, a great boon to Franciscan efforts to establish themselves in the town. Perhaps it was also an effective way to campaign against Catharism, though apparently results were mixed.

Ambrose began to achieve healing miracles as his death approached. A woman called Iacoba, married to a smith, saw the friar pass on the street, eight days before his death, and called to him to advise her on the affliction of her daughter Claruvisa. The friar made the sign of the cross on the child. The following morning the mother found the mark of the cross on the child, and a day later she was "fully freed" (plenissime liberata). On the day of Ambrose's death, Madonna Sclaraldia brought her son Barthuctio to the crowded house where the friar lay dying and asked him to touch the child's eyes, which could not tolerate light. Ambrose had her take his dying hand, touch the eyes with it, and make the sign of the cross. The child was healed. Another woman brought a daughter with growths in her throat and asked Ambrose to make the sign of the cross on the child's throat; the friar did so, and the girl was healed by the following morning. At some point the dying Ambrose was moved to a church, perhaps the new church under construction.[85] When Madonna Gratia, wife of the smith Spinello, approached the saint before his death and had his hand placed on her head to cure her terrible headaches, the encounter took place in a church packed with people. People came to witness the saintly death and miraculous healings, and to be healed.

After death, the friar's corpse continued to perform similar healings. Ambrogio's body was washed and at some point placed on a bier, and people with desperate illnesses packed into the room hoping to be healed. Luca Tancredi Brance suffered great pain from a malformed, inflamed testicle and an inflammation in his thigh: his cries of pain were as agonized as those of a woman giving birth, and he had been heard to say that he would rather be dead. He had often consulted Brother Ambrose in the past. Just after his death, Ambrose gave Luca the cure he had been unable to effect in life. Luca came to the place where the friar lay, took up his dead hand, and placed it on his femur, making the sign of the cross. He was immediately *liberatus*, freed.[86] Similarly, Margarita, the wife of Albonecto di Pietro Martini, took her two-year-old son Dainello (who suffered from a grotesque hernia) up to the bier where the corpse lay, took up the dead hand, and made the sign of the cross on the boy's body. The child was cured, and the bandages that had wrapped him were thrown away.[87] The day after the death, Madonna Balseverina went to the church with her son Nicola, who suffered a life-threatening tumor. Unable to approach the sepulcher because of the crowd of people in the church, Balseverina asked a friar to show her the ground where the saint's body had been washed. Friar Thomas did so, she took some earth and suspended it around the child's neck, and he also was *liberatus*, freed.[88]

The theme of doubt confounded is again important to the text. Ambrose of Massa, like Parenzo, imposed sanctions on doubters and those who broke faith with him. Three miracle stories tell of skeptics confounded, all of them doubters from high social levels. Madonna Giugla, wife of a noble, Messer Franco Zanponis, admitted that when she heard stories of Ambrogio from other people she lacked faith and derided the miracles. After she returned home, she lost her sight, and her health was restored only after she called out to the saint and promised to testify to his miracle.[89] Frederico Pepi Prudentii, no less than the nephew of Bishop Raineri, stated that he had doubted the miracles of Saint Ambrose. Then, when his infant was seriously ill for four days and seemed near death, Frederico and his wife Verdenovella spent the night on their knees praying to God and to Ambrose for the child. "Now he says that he believes everything that is said of the saint, because he saw and sees these things daily."[90] A third skeptic, Ianne Ranucti Zenti, similarly said that he had no faith in the things he heard of Saint Ambrose from others, until his grandson was near death, and a vision led him to carry the dying boy to the tomb, along with a wax image; again, the child was healed.[91] The emphasis is on the saint's power, as in the story of the doubting woman whose sight returned when she agreed to testify.

The cult was an overnight success. It directly aided the construction of a new church. Ambrose had been visited in life by an angel who instructed him to become ill and then go to Orvieto where the friars hoped to build a church. It is clear, from an indulgence of Gregory IX dated a month before the friar's death, that the Franciscans were planning a new church, since contributors were offered a forty-day indulgence.[92] A contemporary chronicle states that the Franciscan church was founded in 1240.[93] In 1243 the Franciscans were able to move there.

The cult of Ambrose focused on bodies, both on the pain-ridden bodies of the sick and on the corpse with its miracle-working powers. Even long after death, the body effected miracles: a tradition developed in which ill people passed the night on Ambrose's tomb, in hopes of a cure. Unlike many contemporary saint's lives, including that of Parenzo, the stress is not on the physical qualities of the corpse itself—sweet smell, or lack of corruption—but on thaumaturgical power. Perhaps Ambrose's Franciscan colleagues fostered this intense physicality as a conscious answer to the Cathars. But the popular testimony in the register has real force: it would be unjust to view these miracle stories as simple political concoctions. The cures, after all, began when Ambrose made the sign of the cross on a sick child in the street. The story of her cure apparently spread, and more people came to the friar for similar aid, even after his death. It seems to have been the Orvietans who perceived this power to reside in his dead hand. The brothers made his corpse available, encouraged the crowds, and benefited from the cult, but it is doubtful that they somehow concocted it.

The miracle stories told of Ambrose are a reminder that pain and suffering lay behind debates over the flesh. Most of the miracles saved children from crippling disease or accidental tragedy: a toddler who fell from a high window and a boy who drowned in the river were restored to life. Or they saved people from intractable pain. Some stories are very intimate: one woman who—after many days of labor—had been unable to expel the dead fetus within her, was rescued by Ambrose from an agonizing death. The word *liberatus* is used repeatedly: Ambrose through healing made people free. The sufferers were freed from pain—from the constraints and weakness of their bodies—through physicality, the touch of a dead man's hand. Again, often the most evident motive for Cathar faith was a belief that God is in no way responsible for pain and grief: conflict over the body was a debate over the meaning of pain and illness. The cult of Ambrose did answer the Cathars in a very satisfying way. Perfects, after all, could offer no compassion, no miracles or aid in this life, but only a remote and austere afterlife. Ambrose was a saintly man who also could provide compassion and healing, liberate a suffering child from pain.

There is thus a wide gulf between the dualist condemnation of the human body and the Franciscan emphasis on sanctity expressed through physical transformations, including the saint's incorrupt, miracle-working corpse and the healing of the sick. Nevertheless, the two seemed less distinct to some contemporaries. The view of evil depicted in these miracles in a curious way recalls Cathar teaching. Illness is understood here as an external force, something that makes a person captive, like demonic possession. The saint could free people from illness just as he freed them from demons. Marie-Christine Pouchelle, in a study of the *Golden Legend*, shows that its author similarly understood sin as an external force.[94] Evil is not something within, the result of a human choice and human failure, but rather something from outside that takes a person prisoner. This concept is very close to a Cathar understanding of evil as something imposed on true, angelic natures, as contamination.

Furthermore, contemporaries did blur the distinction between Cathar and Catholic saintliness. The cult of Armanno Punzilupo in Ferrara was not so different from that of Ambrose: there was the same fascination with the corpse, and again a crowd gathered at the church to gaze at it before it was interred. The miracles also are similar, including the same style of saintly patronage: the exchange of a wax offering and promised devotion for a cure. There was, in both cases, a continuing focus on the saint's tomb. People were outraged at Armanno's disinterment: in Bologna in 1301 Francisco Guidecti, formerly of Ferrara, was still saying that Armanno Punzilupo had been a good man and had performed many miracles, and that it was unjust and evil to condemn him and burn his corpse. The inquisitor in Bologna perceived this statement as a serious threat and imposed a stiff penance and a gag order: Francisco was to say that Armanno had been an evil heretic, not a good man.[95]

These cults reflected contemporary religious attitudes and needs. Some individuals venerated both Cathar and Catholic holy men. The Orvietan Dominico Petri Rossi, sentenced for Catharism in 1269, was a Franciscan tertiary.[96] Another convicted Cathar, the young nobleman Messer Rainerio Munaldi Rainerii Stephani, first testified to Fra Jordano that he travelled to Castellonchio to consult with perfects concerning "his infirmity," suggesting, curiously enough, that he looked to the perfects for healing.[97] Bonadimane, the wife of the late Messer Accitane, was convicted post mortem of Catharism in 1268.[98] Bonadimane also testified for Ambrose: when her nephew or grandson, the son of Pietro Leonardi, was so ill that the family had candles prepared for his funeral, she made a vow to Ambrose that she would carry a wax image to his tomb if he healed the boy.[99] Again, the child was healed and she fulfilled her vow. The story does not mention the saint's corpse. Her trajectory seems reversed: one expects her to reconvert from Catharism to Catholic piety because of the efforts of the Franciscans. Bonadimane may have moved in the opposite direction, from acceptance of the healing miracles of an Ambrose to a greater skepticism and sympathy for Cathar repudiation of the physical. But my guess is that she did not consider Ambrose and the Cathar perfects to be so far apart. Concerned not with doctrine but with practice, she simply reverenced them all as powerful, saintly ascetics.

Cultic emphasis on the sacred properties of dead bodies flourished in Orvieto into the fourteenth century, judging from the career of the Blessed Vanna, an Orvietan seamstress who became a Dominican tertiary and died at age forty-two, in 1306. Her vita includes the stress on sanctity through physicality, feeding, and the body characteristic of accounts of many late medieval holy women, including starvation, illness, and Eucharistic piety.[100] When Vanna was too ill to attend the Mass one Christmas, for example, she was miraculously fed communion at home, receiving in her mouth the Host in the form of a miraculous light. There is an intense preoccupation in her *Leggenda* with the physical attributes of death. When Vanna meditated on the martyrdoms of the apostles Peter and Paul, her body took on the postures of their martyrdoms and seemed a cadaver; when she meditated on the passion of Christ, her body took on the form and stiffness of the cross. The sweet scent of her corpse after her death is elaborately detailed: she gave off the perfumes of various flowers, which were associated with her virtues.[101] Vanna exemplifies the triumph of Catholic orthodoxy with its identification of sanctity with the physical attributes of bodies, particularly the bodies of women. In her case, no one responded with the scornful toss of a piece of rotten meat, the Cathar comment on the cult of Parenzo a century before.

This chapter has examined three topics in the debates between Cathar and Catholic understandings of the human body: sexual difference, marriage, and corpses. All three concern not only understandings of purity—whether bodily attributes can be sacred—but understandings of power and the nature of authority. The Cathar denial of an original sexual difference and an original sin implied fundamental questions about the need for hierarchical authority: If humans are intrinsically pure, what justifies the special authority of a king, a priest, or a husband? The question was answered, in part, by Catholic emphasis on marriage and corpses. Marriage cases, like the 1212 dispute in the Orvietan bishop's court, were demonstrations of clerical authority to define and adjudicate marriages. And the miracles of sacred corpses were demonstrations of power as well, proving the claims of bishops and friars. Debates over purity and the sacred were also debates over the legitimacy of authority.

I return in part 3 to the specific case of the Cathars in Orvieto, in order to examine closely the politics of the repression of Catharism as heresy. This approach provides another perspective on contemporary ideas about purity and about power. I will suggest that repression depended on a repeated characterization of Cathars as impure—as dirty heretics—and on a new association of civic authority with Catholic orthodoxy, demonstrated in the Corpus Domini cult.

PART III

ORTHODOXY
& AUTHORITY

The Cathars Become Heretics

*I*nquisition, Repression, and Toleration

IN 1268 AN INQUISTION headed by a Franciscan, Fra Benvenuto, sentenced the Orvietan Cathars. This event was dramatic political theater. On 16 April, with the "full popolo of men and women of the city convoked by order of the inquisitor" in the Piazza San Francesco, in the presence of the podestà, the capitano del popolo, the bishop, three notaries, friars, and other officials, the first sentence was read. Stradigotto the furrier, now an old man, was present in the piazza to be condemned as a relapsed heretic. The notary read out the sentence: he had received in his home six named perfects; he had denied the major sacraments of the Church, including baptism, marriage, and the Eucharist; he had had his wife, Benvenuta, consoled. All of his property was confiscated, to be divided between the inquisition and the commune. Stradigotto received no further sentence, and it may be that he was seriously ill. The old man was dead within four months.

On 14 May, almost a month later, Fra Benvenuto and his fellow inquisitor Fra Bartolomeo of Amelia appeared for a second time on the church steps and in the presence of the populace and civic and church officials sentenced another old man, Cristoforo de Toste, along with his kinsman Raynerio di Stradigotto Ricci. Both were absent. Cristoforo, first questioned by the inquisition thirty years earlier, and one of the men responsible for the attack on the Dominican Fra Ruggiero, was excommunicated, as was his kinsman Raynerio; their houses and tower in Santa Pace were to be destroyed. Six days later, a third old man, Raynerio's father, Stradigotto Ricci—who, like Cristoforo, was first questioned by Fra Ruggiero in 1239—was sentenced and deprived of his property as well. Two brothers from Lombardy, men of much lower status, were sentenced on the same day; unlike the Toste, they were actually present. The following day, two more men were sentenced. Two weeks later, on 30 May, eleven people were sentenced, including six Toste males. The first woman and the first dead man were included, Domina Belverde and her dead husband, Bartho Francisci, whose bones were to be dug up and burned if they could be identified. Filippo Busse was present to hear his sentence, and he may have been the source of much of the inquisitor's information, since he had been captured, imprisoned, and repeatedly questioned until he was persuaded to tell all. The sentence does not reveal how long he had been incarcerated.

The spectacle went on intermittently until 22 January. In all, eighty-five people were sentenced, twenty-eight of them women. In eighteen cases—twelve men and six women—the inquisitors convicted the dead. They were to be disinterred, and their ashes were to be scattered, goods taken, and houses destroyed. The inquisitors included not only easy targets, like artisan's widows or immigrant laborers like the brothers from Lombardy, but elites, rich merchants, moneylenders and, in one case, a very well-connected titled noble. On May 21, Messer Raineri Munaldi Raineri Stephani, proven—despite his denials—to have been a believer who made the formal bow of reverence to perfects, was excommunicated and condemned to wear the yellow cross. When Messer Raineri failed to honor the sentence and wear his cross (as discussed later), the inquisitors, in an impressive show of political strength, were able to haul him back in and sentence him again.

This chapter examines the sentences of the 1268 inquisition and the problem of the repression of heresy in thirteenth-century Italy. An Orvietan inquisition had failed in the late 1230s and '40s. Why was a new inquisition successful in 1268–69? I argue that the explanation is a combination of factors. The gradual shift of political power after 1265—

evidenced by a strong Guelf and papal, as well as Angevin, presence in the town—made the new Franciscan inquisition possible. The inquisitors in 1268–69 were two local men who knew the community and whom to pursue. They were politically careful: powerful people were treated delicately, and no one seems to have been punished in a way that outraged local sensibilities. The most effective way the friars punished Cathar families was by confiscating their property: this deprivation, unlike salutory penances or even the requirement that Cathars wear the yellow cross, lowered a family's status over the long term. The inquisitors also sought to stigmatize heretics and gain popular support through the repeated use of language that associated heretics with filthiness and treason. This campaign was less successful: people continued to be tolerant, and those convicted of heresy were not therefore treated badly even by civic authorities. I turn finally to the popular reaction to the punishment of heresy evidenced by the registers of a less cautious inquisitor, Fra Guido of Vicenza, whose execution of heretics in Bologna provoked a major outburst.

Guelf Dominance and the Sentences of the Inquisitors

The success of the 1268 inquisition in Orvieto was made possible by a shift of power that was connected with the larger factional wars of the Italian peninsula. By the end of the 1250s, Orvieto was allied with the Guelf party: at the bloody 1260 Battle of Montaperti between Guelf Florence and Ghibelline Siena, Orvietan troops fighting on the Guelf side suffered terrible losses. It was after the battle that one of the Toste, traditionally considered not only Cathar but Ghibelline, actually held office, evidence perhaps of a brief Ghibelline resurgence. In the fall of 1262 Urban IV began a visit to Orvieto that was to last two years.[1] The huge presence of the papal curia itself altered Orvieto's cultural and political climate. By 1300, the curia included a staggering five to six hundred people: cardinals, courtiers, and armies of clerks and domestics, as well as actual troops. In the summer of 1264 King Manfred of Naples and Sicily waged a military campaign intended to capture Orvieto and the pope within it. The effort was unsuccessful, and Manfred and the Ghibelline alliance ultimately were trounced by Charles of Anjou at Benevento in February 1266.[2]

Orvieto for a time became a focus of Guelf and Angevin power. The city's internal politics during the period suggest not a sudden break but a gradual shift to a more aristocratic regime closely linked to Catholic authority. Popular offices remained in place but often were held by Guelf nobles. The Monaldeschi gained power. Messer Cittadino Bertrami served as prior of the arts and società in 1259, and official acts took place in the Monaldeschi palace.[3] In 1262 Messer Pietro Raineri Munaldi served as podestà of the castrum of Lugnano and was instrumental in the donation of the castle of Ramici to Orvieto, represented by the capitano del popolo, Messer Matteo Toncelle.[4]

In the 1260s, factional antagonisms were muted and did not obviously determine political decisions. Pope Urban himself thought the local Ghibellines too powerful, and he grumbled about them at his departure. The Filippeschi lineage, who were considered the Ghibelline leadership, were treated equitably: a list of quitclaims from the creditors of the commune in 1259 includes Stephano Henrici Phylippi as well as Ildibrandino Hermanni Nigri.[5] In 1262 Ranuctio di Messer Filippo Bartholomei Filippi, acting explicitly on behalf of "the other men of his house and consortum" petitioned the commune for the right to build a structure over the vault of their shop, which was currently unusable because the rain poured in. The shop adjoined the piazza, tower, and other shops of the commune, and possibly was one of the shops that belonged to the city, and was being used by the family.[6] The Filippeschi promised that they did not seek to acquire any rights in the new structure, which would belong to the commune; they simply wanted to keep the rain out. Their petition was granted.[7] After Benevento, many Orvietans were nervous about their great Guelf ally, Charles of Anjou, and when he planned a visit in 1268 the town actually contemplated opposing his entry by force of arms. The Guelfs initially closed the city gates and encouraged their Ghibelline neighbors to remain in the town, suggesting a greater concern for internal stability than for loyalty to the international Guelf faction. Ultimately, they were persuaded to admit Charles.[8] It was in this period of Guelf success and the fading of popular rule that the Orvietan inquisition was revived.

In 1265, the year between Urban IV's departure and the Angevin victory at Benevento, a new Franciscan inquisition, headed by Fra Jordano, convicted a number of Orvietans.[9] We have only indirect references in the 1268 sentences: in eight cases, the sentence refers to earlier questioning or a sentence by Fra Jordano. In most cases, people recanted to Fra Jordano and then relapsed and continued to aid the perfects and practice Catharism.[10]

In 1268 the inquisitors were two locals, Fra Bartolomeo of Amelia and Fra Benvenuto of Orvieto. Surely their local knowledge aided them: they knew not only the right questions, but whom to ask. They also acted with some delicacy, and the politics of the sentences are complex. The assumption in some of the literature on Italian Catharism is that the new political climate enabled Guelf elites to attack their old enemies under cover of accusations of heresy. However, Orvietan factional divisions in the 1260s were muted: the virulent attacks characteristic of towns like Florence were rare. Furthermore, the actual sentences do not clearly sustain the view that they were motivated by faction. A few individuals and families linked to the Ghibellines were sentenced, notably some Miscinelli. But the political actors more obviously targeted were former popular officials. In addition, most of those sentenced were already dead, including Amideo and Provenzano Lupicini, Martino Guidutii, and Pietro Adilascie. Amideo had been a rector of the popolo as late as 1266. It may be that it was easier to convict the dead and that living men of comparable stature escaped. The most important Cathar popular leader, Domenico Toncelle, was not condemned post mortem, but despite the political clout of his brother Matteo—the family was punished: Domenico's living widow, Syginetta, suffered the loss of her dowry, and the Toncelle house where both Domenico's father, Toncella, and his brother Artone had been consoled was slated to be destroyed. The Toncelle tower was left standing.

The sentences emphasize not only prior encounters with the inquisition but specific actions and associations. Heresy was difficult to prove through intangibles like belief—which, as I have shown could be very complex—but was demonstrated through actions. These are detailed in the sentences: trips to hear the perfects preach or gifts to them of advice and aid, charity, or necessities and food and drink—in one case, a salted fish. [11] Encounters with perfects were carefully listed, with individual perfects named.[12]

Most people were not present to hear their sentences read; of course, eighteen of them were already dead. The people who actually could be made to stand in the piazza and hear their sentences read tended to be less wealthy and less important. One way to demonstrate this point is to examine the thirteen cases in which the marginalia of the register of sentences indicate that the commune found no property. One might expect that these people without property were dead and their estates dispersed, or they had fled with their movable goods. In fact, nine of the thirteen were present to hear their sentences. The group for whom no property was found included a furrier and a shoemaker, three men from a nearby village called Castellonchio, and five widows.

The sentences ranged from wearing the yellow cross, performing specific penances like pilgrimages and fasts, and paying monetary fines to excommunication and perpetual imprisonment. Conviction could redefine a person's political status. There was a careful attention in the sentences to legal status: whether a person was a *civis*, or citizen, or merely a *habitator*, or inhabitant, of the town. In many cases, conviction meant a loss of legal capacity: contracts were nullified, wills invalidated, public offices and honors lost. A man's debtors were no longer obligated to repay him, since their contract became meaningless. Heresy conviction also often meant the loss of real property, both through confiscations and because of the fact that in every case in which the inquisitors could show that the Cathar sacrament—the consolation—had taken place in a particular house, they ordered the demolition of the house as a "receptacle of filth."

Some demolition did actually take place. A 1270 donation reveals a woman who was unfortunate enough to buy a house from Filippo Busse and his wife shortly before his capture and their condemnations: Filippo was imprisoned, the property was destroyed, and the buyer was left hopelessly trying to recoup her investment.[13] Another woman, according to her sentence, went voluntarily to the inquisitors to confess that her dying servant woman had begged her mistress to bring a perfect so that she could receive the consolation. The mistress brought two perfects, who administered the sacrament under the solarium of her husband's house. She also received the perfect Ricca in her home for one night and "heard her warnings," and she had once sent the perfects bread and wine.[14] The inquisitors, rather mercilessly, ordered the woman's house destroyed, since the consolation had taken place there.

There was some concern to protect dotal rights. When a woman was convicted, generally her dowry was confiscated, but if women not considered heretics had dotal rights in a confiscated property, those rights were apparently respected. One piece of evidence shows that in 1265 when the confiscated property of a heretic included a widow's dowry, she was somehow paid off or given *alimenta*, support. As shown in chapter 6, after the house of the Cathar furrier Viscardo was destroyed, the building site was given to his widow Bellapratu in payment of her dowry. The 1268 sentence of Adalascia, the wife of Bartho di Pietro Saraceni, slated her property to be confiscated but explicitly stated that goods could be reserved by the Roman Church and the inquisitors to provide for her daughters.[15]

In practice, at least in 1268, the proceeds of all of these confiscations were divided between the Church and the commune. The surviving copy of the register of sentences, judging from the marginalia, was a record used by communal officials to keep track of the confiscations, and it was probably cross-referenced with another volume, perhaps a treasury register. This business was a lucrative one for the town, as well as the Franciscans. In two cases in which the later history of the confiscated property is known, it was resold within a month. It was property confiscation that had a long-term impact on a family, as discussed later. The list of women convicted in 1268–69 may be indicative of the inquisition's interest in property. Of the twenty-eight women, at least fourteen and probably more were widows, most of them the widows of heretics. Their convictions made possible the confiscation of property that had been reserved because of their dotal rights And, as I have mentioned, widows of heretics, like Bellapratu, who feared conviction by the inquisition might make efforts to protect their property by transfers to their families.

Many of the people sentenced, as has been shown, belonged to overlapping circles of popular officials, merchants and moneylenders, and prosperous artisans, associated with the Toste, Lupicini, Miscinelli, Toncelle, and the community of furriers. Who else appeared in the sentences? A very few were identified as residents of the country rather than the town: the group of poor men from Castellonchio. The village must have included a Cathar hospice, since a number of sentences mention people going to Castellonchio to hear the perfects preach. A few nobles were sentenced. One titled noble, Messer Jacobo Arnuldi, was excommunicated for receiving perfects in his palace.[16] There was also a young nobleman, Messer Rainerio Munaldi Rainerii Stephani.[17] He came from a family with a long and distinguished tradition of public office; the family was quite wealthy. His father, Munaldo, at one point lent funds to the commune, to pay the podestà's salary, and in fact he was serving as capitano del popolo in 1268, when his son was convicted of heresy. Rainerio had an illness or physical disability: he confessed to Fra Jordano that he had consulted with perfects in Monte Marano and Castellonchio concerning his "infirmity," but claimed he had never been a believer. Fra Jordano, moved by mercy, political savvy, or both, absolved him.[18]

Messer Rainerio was probably much more closely involved; it is revealing that he owed a large sum to Gezio and the furrier Stradigotto. In 1268, the inquisitors concluded that Messer Rainerio was in fact an enthusiastic believer who had made reverence to perfects, heard their preaching, and given them aid. Fra Benvenuto nevertheless was cautious. He excommunicated Rainerio and sentenced him to wear a cross but left his goods untouched; a confiscation would have affected his very powerful kinsmen.

Rainerio ignored the sentence and disdained the cross. When, after eighteen days, he still failed to comply, the inquisitors imposed a fine of one thousand libre. This time he turned up to be sentenced and did pay the fine; surely; his family had been embarassed by his actions, feared confiscations, and encouraged his compliance. Still, Messer Rainerio did not suffer any long-term consequences. He kept his title, and he shows up in the 1292 catasto as one of the wealthiest Orvietan proprietors, with over three hundred and twenty hectares of land.[19]

Three men received penitential sentences. Dominico Petri Rosse was a Franciscan tertiary who confessed that he knew several perfects, had heard their preaching and made them reverence, and had conducted several perfects between hospices and met with them in Castellonchio, where he had eaten and drunk with them.[20] The Franciscan inquisitors were concerned because he had dishonored their habit.[21] He was given penitential penalties: he was to wear the cross, to clothe twenty-five paupers, spending forty soldi per pauper, to make the next quarantena at Rome, as instituted by the popes, to fast every Friday for his entire life, to keep the fasts of the Roman Church, eating nothing cooked except bread, to say the Ave Maria and Pater Noster fifty times a day, and to confess three times a year to a Franciscan confessor.[22] Two others received penitential sentences: Locto di Guilelmo Surdi, who came to the inquisitors of his own volition to confess that he had been a believer for two years, and the wealthy and well-connected moneylender Petrutio Ricci Miscinelli.[23]

A young trumpet player was also sentenced: Petrutio Guidi Becci. His father had sent him to the perfects in Castellonchio many times; once he took them bread, wine, and fish. He heard their preaching, and they taught him to reverence them and gave him things to eat and drink. He guided perfects on several occasions and was paid for it. Petrutio was sentenced to wear the cross and fined one hundred libre, which was paid.[24] He was also prohibited from usury and required to repay those from whom he had extorted interest.

Finally, some individuals sentenced in 1268 are simply untraceable. A woman called Benvenuta of the contrata Putei confessed that she had believed in Catharism for twenty-five years. She was present to hear her sentence, which required her to wear the cross and lose her dowry and all of her property. Her lack of husband or patronymic suggests low status. Did she in fact have a dowry? Some property was taken from her, as the marginalia indicate that the commune was satisfied that it had received its share.[25]

Repression and Power

James Given, in a provocative article, wrote of the deployment of what he termed technologies of power by the inquisition in the Languedoc: the use of these techniques of manipulation, he argues, put the inquisitors' methods at the forefront of medieval statebuilding. Given emphasizes four techniques: the systematic imprisonment and isolation of suspects, the judicial *inquisitio,* complex record-keeping used to control information about suspects, and the "construction of a political economy of punishment" to place convicted heretics in "a degraded and permanently marginalized subgroup of penitents."[26] His emphasis on the techniques of governance and coercion is a valuable corrective to an older tradition in which statebuilding was understood in terms of constitutional change and the formation of new governing institutions. However, the argument that these techniques of the inquisitors were both novel and effective does not closely apply to Orvieto or, probably, to the thirteenth-century Italian towns more generally.[27] First, techniques of governance like the judicial inquiry and the careful preservation of records used to make claims based on past events were hardly original with the inquisition, as registers like the papal *Liber Censuum* and the Orvietan survey of the beni comunali suggest. Second, techniques of manipulation were only effective when they could be enforced. Judges could summon witnesses to an inquest forever, but unless they could compel the witnesses actually to appear, the exercise hardly built their power.

Emphasis on "technologies," then, raises questions about the understudied problem of enforcement. How could communities be made to comply? In part, this is a straightforward question about police power, the ability of an inquisitor (or, for that matter, a civic judge) to send armed men who could ensure that a given order was carried out.[28] Nothing is more apparent in the registers of judicial sentences that survive from thirteenth-century Orvieto—including the inquisitorial register—than the lack of significant police power to back up the court. Fumi estimated that the Orvietan podestà had thirty policemen to enforce his decisions, in a district of thirty to forty thousand people. The vast majority of persons sentenced in the podestà's court were contumacious. Whether they fled the area, stayed in the community but in hiding, or simply ignored the court probably depended on the severity of the charge, that is, on how much was at risk if they stayed. The inquisition in 1268–69 produced only sixteen living heretics to hear their sentences, and those actually present tended to be modest artisans, and widows, people without property. Apparently for people with resources worth protecting, the risks of avoiding the court were preferable to the risks of confiscation. At least thirty-seven of the living sentenced in 1268–69 were absent when their sentences were read, many of them explicitly contumacious.[29]

Sentences were very often honored in the breach. Wealthy and powerful people might just ignore them, like the nobleman Rainerio Munaldi Raineri Stephani, sentenced in May. Surely it was because his father was capitano del popolo that he ignored the friars and disdained to wear the yellow cross. In turn, perhaps the inquisitors in his case were able to take action because his family had considerable political capital and even real property at risk and forced him to comply.[30] This situation was probably exceptional. Furthermore, most convicted heretics and their families did not really remain in a "permanently degraded underclass," as Given put it, but over time threw away their yellow crosses and went about their business. In Orvieto, many former heretics prospered. Petrutio or Pietro Guidi Becci, who had been fined one hundred libre, when he was prohibited from lending money and required to wear the yellow cross, went on to enjoy a long career as official *banditor* for the commune, a job in which he blew a trumpet and announced the decisions of the podestà.[31] He appears in that very public role in the judicial records as early as 1272.[32] It is doubtful that he wore the cross of a convicted heretic when he served as civic trumpeter, announcing the decisions of the podestà and the Seven.

The town's leaders were ambivalent about the heresy convictions, at least in 1269, judging from the actions of a popular judicial official called the exgravator, literally the unburdener, to whom people could petition to overturn the sentences of the former podestà. A few convicted heretics turn up in the single extant exgravator register, which dates from 1269, just after the heresy sentences. Frederico Guiscardi, only a few months after the 22 January sentence of his mother and wife for heresy, appealed a fine. He had been unjustly fined forty soldi because of a petition of a laborer for an unspecified offense. The exgravator granted his appeal and lifted the fine.[33] More dramatically, the heirs of Provenzano and Amideo Lupicini appealed a fine for unpaid taxes that was a direct consequence of the family heresy convictions. The Lupicini heirs complained that their assessment for the *cavallata,* or civic cavalry, was unfairly high since, although the inquisition had confiscated much of their property, the assessment that they could supply three horses had not been reduced. The exgravator found this complaint reasonable and lifted the fines.[34] The family—despite the fact that the inquisitor's 1268 sentence explicitly deprived the Lupicini children and grandchildren of legal privileges—deserved a fair tax burden. Thus, while the inquisition used post-mortem sentences to make examples of prominent men like the Lupicini who had served in high office, Orvietan officials hesitated to punish those men's children. The inquisitors themselves also showed restraint: there were no obvious cases in Orvieto in which dead men were convicted of heresy in order to deprive their descendants of property or offices, like the 1313 Florentine trial of Gherardo de Nerli, which stripped his grandson of his benefice.[35]

The most effective way the inquisition did degrade a family's status was probably not by the imposition of the yellow cross, which was difficult to enforce over time, but through the long-term impact of huge fines and the confiscation of real property. As has been shown, the confiscations were not fictive: at least in a few documented cases, the inquisitors and the town government were able to collect the money and take over and sell or demolish the house. A family that lost its wealth lost status as well, and artisan houses were especially vulnerable. The impact on artisans is apparent in the sad career of Frederico, the son of the Cathar furriers Viscardo and Bellapratu. He was never convicted by the inquisition, but he suffered property losses because of the sentences first of his father, and then of his mother and his wife, Grana. He was still called a furrier in 1269, when the exgravator lifted the judicial fine for him, but he had almost certainly lost his shop. In the 1280s, Frederico was in and out of the courts, fined for carrying a knife in town, accused and then absolved of petty theft. He remained rebellious: in 1287 he was fined because he lifted his hand from the judicial tribunal in defiance of the court's order. This was a curious form of incarceration, generally for unpaid debt.[36] He may well have resorted to petty theft, and his son Jacobutio was accused and sentenced for more serious theft as well. Interestingly, when Jacobutio was sentenced, the court protected the interests of the young man's mother, Grana, by providing that she was not to be burdened by his fine.[37] Grana had been sentenced for heresy and condemned to the loss of her goods in 1269, and perhaps they thought she had suffered enough. She lived in a house rented from a Master Alexander. In effect, when the inquisition sentenced Viscardo and demolished his shop in 1265, they destroyed the patrimony that probably would have made prosperous furriers of the son, daughter-in-law, and grandson, Frederico, Grana, and Jacobutio. Instead, they became marginal—renters, debtors, even thieves.

Elites did better. The Toste, the family most strongly identified as heretics, lost much of their property, and after 1269 they suffered continuing discrimination and appropriations.[38] Many remained in the area. Even Rainuccetto, the son of Cristoforo Toste, stayed—though living apparently not in Orvieto but in the nearby village of Ficulle.[39] They did not regain their palaces and status. However, some family members prospered. In 1311, a Toste who was probably Cristoforo's grandson served as one of the Seven.[40] Clearly, the view reiterated in their sentences that they were a brood of vipers did not convince their neighbors.

Houses associated with Ghibellinism and the Filippeschi were further punished, for reasons of political factionalism. The Miscinelli, despite confiscations for heresy, still owned extensive lands in 1292: Celle de Miscinelli was one of the wealthiest Orvietan proprietors. The Miscinelli were heavily penalized as Ghibellines in 1313.[41] Overall, Orvietans continued to be tolerant in practice and slow to treat their Cathar neighbors, even when they were troublemakers, as heretical traitors. Did the 1268–69 inquisition effectively end Catharism in Orvieto? Very little record remains after 1269. Two extant letters of Boniface VIII mention links between heresy sentences and Orvietans, referring to Giovanni Feraloca and the family of the wife of Neri di Turi. Neither letter is clear evidence of continuing Orvietan Catharism.[42] As a result, one can only argue from absence. But probably, given the town's importance to the papacy in the late thirteenth century, if Cathar circles had remained influential another major inquisition would have been launched. My guess is both that the faith was becoming less threatening to authorities as it ceased to attract political leaders like Domenico Toncelle, and that it slowly disappeared in Orvieto.

What made a medieval community comply with the decisions of a tribunal? In Orvieto, the inquisitors were local men, and they acted with restraint. Inquisitors could be on very thin ice, and really unpopular executions did provoke dangerous outbursts and attacks. From this perspective, the most important work of an inquisitorial tribunal was ideological: a matter of convincing the community to view their Cathar neighbors as heretics, with all that the word came to imply, and of defining for the community the Catholic orthodox alternative. Here lies the real limit of Given's analysis: the success of inquisitors in Orvieto and elsewhere depended on what the South African historian John Mason has called "the heavy work of cultural construction."[43]

Catholic attacks on heresy relied on images of heretics as dirty. Some of these images appear in the language of Innocent III and became formulaic.[44] Heresy is not only treason but disease and filth, associated with certain dishonorable animals. The Orvietan sentences of 1268 repeat these formulas: the Toste house where the consolation took place is called a receptacle of filth and a lair of traitors.[45] A person from a family with a tradition of heresy like the Toste is the poisonous progeny of vipers; a relapsed heretic is a dog returning to its vomit.[46] Catharism was driven by a passionate enthusiasm for purity. The perfects led austere, abstinent lives and preached an understanding of spiritual things as utterly uncontaminated by contact with materiality and corruption. People often said that it was because the Cathars were good men that theirs was the way to salvation. The inquisitors opposed the Cathar reputation for unsullied purity with repetitive formulas that stressed heresy as impure: as dirty, dishonorable, and bestial.[47]

Did this strategy work? The linking of heretics and dirtiness gained some credence, judging from contemporary insults. Insults sometimes appear in the civic judicial records, which survive in Orvieto from as early as 1269. The offense was called *verba iniuriosa*, harmful words or verbal defamation. Insulted individuals could go to court, file complaints, and, with luck, see their insulters slapped with a modest fine, though typically, the insulters reponded with a parallel complaint, fines were exchanged and only the court benefited. Often the judicial sentences include the actual insults. Most were sexual, like "son of a whore" or "dirty whore," but in the 1280s and '90s, a few insults did refer to heresy. One man called another a son of a dirty heretic; another fellow was called a thief and a heretic.[48] The first insult, in particular, implies acceptance of the stereotypical association of heresy and dirt. One Orvietan was actually nicknamed Heretic or Patarene, and presumably this was a term of opprobrium. He was a Toste neighbor and just possibly himself a Toste.[49] The term patarene suggests both heresy and treason; however, it may have been the choice of the recording notary and is not necessarily the actual vernacular term used.[50] The implication of these bits of evidence is that heresy and dirt had become linked in some people's minds, at least, and that being called a dirty heretic was offensive and harmful enough to warrant a trip to court and a fine.

While the inquisition and contemporary preachers in thirteenth-century Italy had some success in promulgating ideas associating heresy and dirtiness, they were much less effective in defining heretics as a social category or, as Given put it, a permanently degraded underclass. People in thirteenth-century Italy who were sentenced for Catharism simply were not treated as dirty heretics or treasonous vipers. There were groups of people in the late thirteenth century that were defined as having a special group identity because of a single attribute or activity. The most obvious examples are lepers, who were identified by a somewhat problematic medical diagnosis and then ritually defined and excluded as a special outcast group.[51] Groups defined by a sexual activity—prostitutes and, perhaps, homosexuals—are a more difficult case. Laws in this period spoke of prostitutes as a class of people. References to homosexuality were more typically to the sin of sodomy rather than to a minority group defined by sexual preference. Clearly, there were women who sometimes sold sex, and men who sometimes engaged in sodomy but were probably not defined by that activity by their neighbors. In the case of former Cathars, and probably those who engaged in sodomy or occasional prostitution as well, late thirteenth-century Italians tended to be tolerant. In Orvieto, as I have shown, some people convicted by the inquisition and their descendants prospered. Even when former heretics did not do well, Orvietans could be merciful, as when the officials of the podestà's court provided that a young thief's fine not burden his mother, the convicted heretic Grana.

Protest and Popular Toleration: The Tumult in Bologna

What did people in late-thirteenth-century Italy think of the inquisitors and the idea of heresy? I have suggested that the 1268–69 inquisition in Orvieto enjoyed some success because Fra Benvenuto was a local and because he showed restraint. The people sentenced were genuinely guilty at least of association with Cathar perfects, and were not, as far as we know, treated with terrible brutality. Their later careers also suggest that Orvietans were not persuaded by the rhetoric of the sentences to regard people convicted of heresy as dirty or treasonous. Nevertheless, the Orvietans did comply with the Franciscan inquisition.

In other cases, inquisitors were far more extreme. One chronicler reports that Dominican Giovanni of Vicenza, over a period of three days, had fifty-one people who had been condemned for heresy burned to death in the forum in Verona. They were "from the better among the men and women of Verona."[52] When an inquisition was more extreme, people did, in fact, protest its actions. In Bologna, a Dominican inquisition headed by Fra Guido of Vicenza in the 1290s imposed very heavy fines and remanded a number of people to the secular arm to be executed for heresy, sparking violent community protest. The Bolognese inquisition pursued not only Cathars but the irreligious monk Fra Giacomo Flamenghi and a handful of local supporters of the Colonna family against Pope Boniface. The extant register of the acts of this inquisition has been edited in two parts and extensively analyzed by Lorenzo Paolini and Raniero Orioli, and this discussion draws on Paolini's research on the Bolognese Cathars.

Many Bolognese disapproved of the inquisitor's treatment of heretics, including members of the clergy who had no apparent sympathy for Catharism. Messer Manfredo Mascara, cleric of the church of Sant' Andrea of Padua and an archdeacon, actually took on the role of legal procurator for an accused Cathar, the purser Giuliano. Manfredo had the courage to appear on Giuliano's behalf before the Dominican inquisition, risking, as Paolini has pointed out, the serious charge of aiding heretics. Messer Manfredo explicitly counseled Giuliano to flee if he knew himself to be guilty of heresy, even if he was summoned by the inquisitor. The clear implication is that the cleric considered Fra Guido's actions to be unjust and was willing to oppose him at some personal risk. This effort was to no avail: Giuliano was imprisoned, tortured despite an "infirmity," and ultimately burned at the stake. Manfredo was excommunicated and then absolved after a penance and a fine of one hundred libre.[53]

A local parish priest was also punished for showing mercy to a Cathar: Don Giacomo Benintendi, rector of San Tommaso del Mercato, who gave the last rites to Rosafiore, the widow of the Cathar artisan Bonigrino (whose views were discussed in chapter 5). Bonigrino was first questioned in 1273, was condemned several times—ultimately as a relapsed heretic in September 1297—and died at the stake. Rosafiore was also condemned for heresy and required to wear the yellow cross. She was a fierce old woman who hated Fra Guido with an understandable passion, and when he personally came to her house to question her and her granddaughter Bonafiglia about their possible relapse into heresy, she drove him off with a torrent of threats and vituperation.[54] Soon afterward, when she was at the point of death, Don Giacomo, their parish priest, cared for her. He believed her statement that she had not returned to heresy, gave her penance and absolution and the sacrament, and after her death allowed her burial in the parish cemetery.[55] He was suspended from performance of the divine office, heavily fined, threatened with excommunication and the loss of his benefice, and required to exhume Rosafiore with his own hands and at his own expense.[56] His care of Rosafiore was apparently not intended as a challenge to the inquisitor, since his sentence ultimately was mitigated because of his "simplicity."[57] Rosafiore's choice to seek absolution and the sacrament from her parish priest is good evidence that she was not committed to Cathar dualism; Don Giacomo must, as he told Fra Guido, simply have believed her, and therefore done his pastoral duty.

The inquisitor and his assistants were not popular in the Bolognese countryside: when they passed through the villa of San Martino even before the trials, the locals detained and threatened them. And after the trials began in Bologna, some townsmen were openly furious. When the purser Bompietro was locked in the inquisition's prison, a mercer named Jacobo, who was his friend, went to the episcopal palace and asked to see the bishop. Told that the bishop was meeting in a council with the inquisitor, Jacobo said, "Is the inquisitor here: I would freely cut him with a knife, more freely even than I would eat. If I did not fear the commune of Bologna more than I fear God, I would freely cut him." When people remonstrated with him, he insisted that Bompietro was a good man and the inquisitor had accused him to get hold of his goods.[58] Questioned later by Fra Guido about his threats, Jacobo admitted that he had even said that he would kill the inquisitor if he could get him in the right spot. He had spoken from great agitation, he said, because he loved Bompietro, but had retracted the words before he even left the palace. Jacobo was fined one hundred imperial libre.

On 12 May 1299, Fra Guido condemned Giuliano, Bompietro, and the bones of Rosafiore to be handed over to the secular arm and burned for heresy. The sentence was first read in the Dominican church, and according to two witnesses a Suor Agnese protested loudly. She was a neighbor of Rosafiore and thought it was evil to exhume her bones and burn them. Rosafiore had been a good woman, one of the best in the contrata.[59] Agnese also detested what the inquisitor had said against their parish priest, Don Giacomo, and muttered a curse or threat against the inquisitor, suggesting perhaps that what he had done to the priest should be done to him.[60] Her reaction, like Jacobo's, was based on familiarity, on practice: she knew Rosafiore, who had been one of the best women in the neighborhood, and knew the priest as well.

After the inquisitor condemned the men for heresy, the bells were rung for an assembly and the men were handed over to the podestà in the piazza comunale to be judged. When people heard the sentences, the piazza buzzed with angry discussion. A notary argued that the inquisitor and friars deserved to be burned rather than Bompietro and Giuliano: it would be a good thing to go to the brother's house and burn it and the inquisitor and the brothers, as was done in Parma.[61] He was recalling a direct precedent for an assault on the friars. When a woman was burned for heresy in Parma in 1279, people sacked the Dominican convent, beat a number of the friars, and even killed one of them.[62]

Bompietro and Giuliano were marched out to a pyre, to be burned along with Rosafiore's bones. Bompietro asked the inquisitors for the sacrament at the last. He was denied it, as an excommunicated heretic, and he and Giuliano were killed. The town reacted with horror and anger to the spectacle of a man they knew and respected denied the sacrament and burned to death. Some people wept openly: a man called Vallariano told the inquisitor later that he shed tears "for compassion."[63] Others cursed the friars.[64] Some threw rocks and dirt, or even drew their knives, calling out to let the men go, or to burn the inquisitor instead. One woman cried out that they could summon the popular neighborhood militias, to go to the friar's convent: another threat of a direct attack.[65]

There is an extensive record of these Bolognese reactions; perhaps Fra Guido threatened excommunication if those who took part did not come in and confess to their words and actions during the riot.[66] About 337 people either confessed or were accused by others of specific actions in the tumult. Their comments offer an extraordinary look at popular attitudes, although they must be analyzed with care. People surely calculated what to confess and what to omit, although many people walked in and admitted to calling the inquisitor things like the devil or the Antichrist, which certainly seems candid. There is sometimes a marked difference between what a person reported he or she had said and what someone else accused them of saying. And, of course, the people who confessed were self-selecting: only a minority showed up because they were cited. As a result, the text is more revealing of Catholic beliefs than of the views of non-Catholic or irreligious people.

Who took part? Paolini has shown that the people involved were not confined to artisans or the city's poor, but were a social mix including both men and women and many nobles. Gonto, who was the son of a butcher, yelled comments that are characteristic: this execution was a sin and an evil deed. Bompietro had asked for the sacrament and should not die. He was a good man. If he had had money, this would not have happened. And Gonto called out that the inquisitor had wanted Bompietro's sister, and both she and Bompietro had refused.[67] Many people, like Gonto, knew and respected Bompietro, including the shoemaker named Michael, who said he was a "good man and he was a good neighbor."[68] The inquisitor's actions violated their moral judgment.

People were terribly troubled by seeing bones burned. Marchexana, daughter of Ubaldini, said of the bones, "What cheating trick is this?"[69] Her neighbor Diana, daughter of a master artisan, said, "What good is it to deride some bones?"[70] Others found the action derisive as well.[71] Many of the comments suggest a lack of belief or perhaps even comprehension of the Catholic view that the dead remain identified with their bodies and will rise again to be judged. A Suor Luchexia said, "What does it signify to burn bones from which the persons have died?"[72] Suor Agnexia, who lived with a noblewoman and was perhaps a tertiary, pointed out that nothing rose up when the bones were burned.[73] This statement is a bit obscure but perhaps meant that no soul or spirit visibly rose from the bones, suggesting that Rosafiore herself was not affected by the burning because she was not present in her bones. If so, the comment recalls the woman in the Fournier Register who watched a child die and saw no soul escape its lips. Another woman, astonishingly, said it was better to burn the living than the dead.[74] It was deeply troubling to see the dead dishonored.

One common theme was to urge that the friars were corrupt. Many attacked them for greed. It is a sin to give them alms, or to give them bread.[75] One of the most common statements was that they only wanted money. Some, like Gonto, said that if Bompietro and Giuliano had given the inquisitor money they would not have been killed. Others said that the men were being killed so the friars could get their property. The impact on Bompietro's family was troubling: one argued that it was wrong to take Bompietro's property from his heirs. The idea that the sentence was imposed because the inquisitor could not get his hands on Bompietro's sister was also common. Others, rather than attacking the friars for lust or greed, considered them outright evil. People called Fra Guido the devil, or the Antichrist. It is ironic that the friar's pursuit of dualist heresy got him labeled the embodiment of evil.

These comments were not an expression of simple anticlericalism, as local sympathy for the parish priest Don Giacomo suggests. Hostility was specifically directed at the inquisitors and the Dominican friars. The emphasis on their greed, as Paolini points out, reflected their actions: Fra Guido did, in fact, levy huge fines, and a case could be made that he targeted moneylenders, people who could pay. In 1308 Clement V even launched an inquiry into his accounting.[76]

Some comments were deeply Christian. There was outrage that Bompietro was denied the sacrament when he asked for it. One person said, "Those cursed friars should have received Bompietro, because Christ received all."[77] Others pointed out that his very request meant that he was not a heretic. And others unfavorably compared the friars' actions to those of Christ.[78] Many people condemned the execution on religious or moral grounds: it was an evil deed. There were a few who called the inquisitors the heretics and even expressed hope of a miracle.[79] The comments of Iacobina, the daughter of a notary, are revealing. She "said that the friars were more heretical than Bompietro, and that Christ would produce a miracle for him because it was not judgment day, and said that she was grieved over the priest of San Tommaso who was condemned."[80] Iacobina, by this one comment, was very much a Catholic Christian. She believed that Christ was merciful and that Bompietro would be saved, but that it would require a miracle because of his excommunicate death. She apparently respected the parish priest who had cared for Rosafiore and was troubled by his punishment. She repudiated the authority and judgement of the inquisitors, and she emphasized the relative nature of heresy.

Several people, like Iacobina, commented that the friars make heresy, or that the friars are heretics. On 17 May, four days after the executions, Fra Guido had the inquisition's notary read the sentences of Bompietro and Giuliano in the neighborhood church of San Martino dell' Aposa during the Mass, immediately after the Gospel. Messer Paolo Trintinelli denounced the sentences and the inquisitors, before the people. His comments were not a hasty emotional reaction to the awful spectacle of the executions, but a more considered response. Messer Paolo was a wealthy and prominent man with a long career in public office in Bologna, and his comments carried authority.[81]

Messer Paolo said that "the thing that had been done to Bompietro and Guiliano was an evil deed and that the inquisitor could have anything he wanted written, so that he himself would not give one bean for those writings." Another noble, Messer Pace of Saliceto, tried to stop him: "You are speaking evil and will be excommunicated because of the things you said." Paolo answered, "The inquisitor cannot excommunicate, nor do I believe that his excommunication has any validity." He went on to say that Bompietro had been a good man and unjustly condemned. A great sin had been done to him, and it was another great sin to take the inheritance of Bompietro's sons and destroy his household. Messer Paolo condemned the Carmelite brothers who lived in San Martino, who he said were *viles et miseri*, because Bompietro had given them wine for the mass and they did not defend or excuse him or aid him in any way.[82] Messer Paolo acted with some courage in stating the moral outrage of at least part of the Bolognese community directly to the inquisitor, Fra Guido. He was ultimately condemned for it and forced not only to pay a large fine but, in what must have been a bitter moment, to beg mercy from Fra Guido, on his knees in the bishop's palace in the presence of the town's leading officials.[83]

The conclusion that emerges from these powerful actions and comments is that the sophisticated folk of a late-medieval Italian town—at all social levels—were not easily convinced that the brutal repression of heresy was justified. At times, they questioned the close association of Catholic orthodoxy and legitimate authority. It is true that the mendicants were sometimes hated for other reasons: they were foreigners, rivals to the local clergy, forever threatening damnation and begging for money. But as this record suggests, people also reviled the inquisitors when they simply did not believe them: many Bolognese were not convinced by the friars' portrayal of heresy and thought their actions were evil and un-Christian. Messer Paolo Trintinelli judged that because Fra Guido's actions were evil, his sentences were illegitimate, not worth a bean. Repression did not, in this case, foster popular acceptance of the concept of heresy.

Coercion, then, had its limits. As historians of heresy have long argued, the Catholic Church in the thirteenth century combated Catharism not only through direct measures like the inquisitions, but through the clearer definition of Catholic orthodoxy. In Orvieto, officials developed a close ritual association of civic authority with Catholic orthodoxy and hierarchy. Representations of orthodox belief emphasized the sanctification of the human body, in the celebration of the Corpus Domini feast and in visual representations of creation and the human ancestry of Jesus.

EIGHT

Corpus Domini and the Creation of Adam and Eve

ORVIETO WAS a town with a strong Cathar presence, probably unbroken, from the 1190s until the 1260s. The Cathars who can be identified from the surviving register tended to be members of recently established houses, families that were quick to take advantage of the social and political transformations of the thirteenth century. Hardly the disaffected laborers or rural nobles of older historiographic traditions, they were instead merchants, moneylenders, civic treasurers, prosperous artisans. A startling number of them held high popular office in the 1240s and '50s, notably Domenico Toncelle, who as prior of the guilds and società acted for a time as the town's executive. Circles of Cathars in Florence and Bologna were similar, including minor urban elites and skilled artisans. They derived not from a fading social group but from the historical winners, thriving new houses responsible for many of the great political innovations of the duecento.

What drew these people to Cathar dualism? Catharism was a religious faith, and the motives of Cathar believers cannot be reduced to politics. Still, in the thirteenth century politics and religion were not easily separable. I have argued that Cathar beliefs were not odd dualist anomalies in a time of normative Catholic orthodoxy but expressed concerns shared by many European Christians. Italian Catharism is better understood as a cluster of beliefs within a broader spectrum of contemporary belief and skepticism. Judging from the meager statements that remain to us, Italian Cathars were driven by a concern with purity, an insistence that the sacred is in no way contaminated or compromised. God is not responsible for pain and suffering, for wolves, flies, the execution of criminals, or the soul of Judas Iscariot.

Why the special association with the early popolo? The popular movement of the 1240s and '50s sought to build a prosperous, independent commune with the strength to dominate its region. In Orvieto, as elsewhere, civic autonomy grew in opposition both to older forms of lordship, including ecclesiastical lords, and to the newly extended papal jurisdiction and monarchy. Orvieto, like other towns in the Patrimony of Saint Peter, was directly at odds with the papal curia over territory and jurisdiction. The curia was quick to use the interdict to pressure a town by depriving its folk of the sacraments. Surely the long jurisdictional struggles with the popes bred skepticism of claims about papal authority. For popular leaders like Domenico Toncelle, Catharism offered a faith that condemned the secular entanglements of pope and bishop as contamination and by implication, allowed a free, independent commune. Furthermore, the Catholic faith in the thirteenth century provided the ideological underpinnings for political and social hierarchy. The ritual practice of the Catholic Church taught and expressed hierarchy and authority, particularly in the veneration of the Host. The men who built the early popular institutions espoused not hierarchy but a new corporatism.

The austerity and renunciation of the Cathar perfects made them a powerful social model. As Durkheim argued:

> asceticism does not serve religious ends only . . . society itself is possible only at [the price of a certain disdain for suffering]. Though exalting the strength of man, it is frequently rude to individuals; it necessarily demands perpetual sacrifices from them; it is constantly doing violence to our natural appetites, just because it raises us above ourselves.[1]

The critical problem in thirteenth-century towns was the establishment of order, a vita civile. In a society torn by violent conflicts, there was a desperate need for restraint, for individuals to put aside self-interest and family interest and live in a peaceful corporate order. Cathar perfects were exemplars of self-restraint, people who renounced the gratification of their appetites and all but the most intangible self-interest. Cathar understandings of creation depicted humankind as angels victimized by the devil and Lucifer, without agency or responsibility for sin. Curiously, that emphasis allowed them to celebrate a human capacity for self-restraint, for perfection in life. Citizens and guildsmen similarly needed to put aside their immediate interests for the common good. Heroic abstinence was an appropriate ideal. Cathars, then, carefully defined civic and spiritual authority as entirely distinct. The perfects they venerated represented an ideal self-restraint, in no way contaminated by mundane affairs.

Perhaps this understanding of authority had resonance for their contemporaries. Certainly, Orvietans who knew that men like Domenico Toncelle came from Cathar houses were nevertheless happy to see them serve in high civic office. In the political climate of the 1240s, Provenzano Lupicini could do penance for Cathar heresy and serve as town consul the same year, just as Barone del Baroni served on a civic council in Florence. Orvietans were unconvinced by the concept of heresy, the association of Cathar beliefs with pollution and treason. The friars preached the idea of Cathar heresy as a threat to society and used labels associating local Cathars with dirtiness and dishonorable animals, but Orvietans at first paid little heed: even after 1268 a few convicted Cathars enjoyed long public careers.

The change was a gradual redefinition of authority, and this final chapter explores that process. I examine the ways in which the Orvietan commune, from the mid-1260s on, became identified with the papal curia and the celebration of the Corpus Domini feast. Ecclesiastical and civic authority became closely linked: men in high popular office were now more apt to be papal appointees than former Cathars. The town's ceremonies and processions in the late duecento and early trecento linked hierarchy and orthodoxy: in the Corpus Domini play, the town's popular executives, the Seven, accompanied by the clergy, carried the bloody altarcloths that constituted proof of transubstantiation to the pope. On the facade of the new cathedral, Lorenzo Maitani's workshop carved one of the masterpieces of early-fourteenth-century sculpture, reliefs that portrayed in detail the sanctity of physical creation.

Papal Curia and Corpus Domini

Orvieto's character in the late thirteenth century was shaped by the recurrent visits of the popes and their entourages, including Gregory X, the French Martin IV, the Colonna client and first Franciscan pope Nicholas IV, and then Benedetto Caetani, Boniface VIII.[2] This presence was overwhelming. Thirteenth century popes had as many as two hundred salaried officials and retainers. With papal merchants and copyists, the cardinals and their staffs, and miscellaneous followers, including plaintiffs seeking justice, in all perhaps five to six hundred people depended on the curia and traveled with the pope.[3] Two more palaces were added to the Orvietan cathedral complex to house the curia, the first built by Urban in the 1260s, the second at the end of the century. The curia drew many visitors, notably the Angevin court and garrison: Charles of Anjou was resident in 1268, returned during the stay of Gregory X in 1272–73, and returned again during the long residence of Martin IV in 1281–84.[4] Angevin political influence seems to have lasted only as long as Charles and his garrison were actually in town. The presence of the papal courts had a more lasting impact, giving the town a cosmopolitan quality. Scholars of the caliber of Albertus Magnus and Thomas Aquinas visited the town for extended periods in the 1260s; Louis IX was canonized there; the extraordinary tomb of the French cardinal Guillaume de Braye was carved by Arnolfo di Cambio and placed in the Dominican church.

The repeated presence of the papal court profoundly shaped Orvietan politics. The guilds had a strong interest in encouraging these visits, which enriched some local proprietors and tradesmen. Rents doubled when the curia was in town, and luxury trades flourished.[5] In the 1280s, a bipartisan popular regime arose, under the leadership of Neri della Greca. The council of the popolo gained power in fits and starts. By 1286 the council elected consuls, who then chose the podestà, and from 1292, Orvieto enjoyed guild-based rule, with guildsmen executives, the Seven, answerable to the council of the popolo. Similar guild-based regimes associated with the Guelf Party arose in many towns, notably Siena and Florence. Popular rule by now was staunchly identified with Catholic orthodoxy. Orvietan councils often elected popes to high civic office, including Martin IV, Nicholas IV, and Boniface VIII; the action must have been intended as flattery. Some popes actually did serve by proxy.[6] Officials with close ties to the papacy were appointed, like Bertoldo degli Orsini, who served as podestà in 1278 and again in 1287–88.[7]

The Seven's enthusiasm for visits from the curia is evident in the council minutes. When the funds for the second papal palace ran out in 1298, the council of the popolo voted to expend revenues from the gabelles or the collective property to complete the building.[8] In 1301 they somewhat ironically elected Boniface VIII capitano del popolo. When Boniface settled a dispute with the town and planned a visit, the Seven's preparations were frantic. Among plans for festive games, lodgings, and other arrangements, they appropriated funds to have the arms of the pope's family, the Gaetani, painted on the Palazzo del Popolo and statues of him placed over two of the main gates of the city. If the statues could not be finished in time, painted images would be slapped up to serve as temporary substitutes.[9] The statues are still in place over the city gates.

The effect was a closer interweaving of ecclesiastical and civic authority. Few hints survive of any popular hostility to this identification of the commune with the curia. In 1277 a group of twenty-nine lesser guildsmen met in a secret council and decided to refuse to house any more foreign guests. Clearly, some trades benefited from the court's presence more than others, notably provisioners of foodstuffs, tavernkeepers, and producers of luxury goods. Those who met to protest must have been weary of having visitors quartered on them, and perhaps they were hostile to the curia as well.[10] They were fined for an action characterized in the sentence as dishonoring the commune.

Orvieto was specially identified not only with the papal court but with late-medieval celebration of the Corpus Domini. This feast was implicitly, and perhaps explicitly, an answer to Cathar ideas, as a powerful affirmation of Catholic doctrine that was antithetical to dualism, and a powerful assertion of priestly authority as well.[11] The development of late-medieval Eucharistic piety and the Corpus Christi feast has been often recounted. As the Fourth Lateran Council defined membership in Christian society in terms of one communion a year, the Mass took on a new centrality as the focus for lay piety. Worship of the Host was fostered, paralleling older forms of veneration of saints and relics. As Jean-Claude Schmitt has shown, during this period performance of the Mass changed as the gestures of the officiant became increasingly theatrical, setting out the elements of Christian theology while reenacting the actions of Christ. The climax of the ceremony became the elevation of the Host. At the moment of consecration, "the point at which God came into presence," the priest, his back turned to the faithful, raised the Host so that it could be seen and venerated by all.[12] The gesture both emphasized the miracle of transubstantiation and reinforced the authority of the officiant and his distance from the laity.[13] Worshippers were expected to make gestures of reverence: to kneel, perhaps to bow slightly, to incline the head. Respect for the Host and for the priest who consecrated it thus became an important element of lay religious practice. The ritual taught hierarchy and authority as it celebrated the miracle of Christ's Body and Blood.

The significance of Orvieto in the establishment of the universal Corpus Christi feast has been debated. The feast originated in the intense Eucharistic piety of female Cistercians and the early beguines in Liège, especially Juliana of Cornillon, and was promoted by the Dominican theologian Hugh of Saint-Cher, among others.[14] This milieu influenced Jacques Pantaleon, who served as an archdeacon in the diocese of Liège at the time of the local feast's 1246 foundation and who in 1261 became Pope Urban IV. It was during a long residence in Orvieto that Urban instituted the universal feast, and he celebrated it twice before his death in October 1264. According to Orvietan tradition, his decision to institute the feast was sparked by the Eucharistic miracle at Bolsena; Fredegand Callaey, among others, has argued convincingly that Urban's long association with Eucharistic devotion in Liège was a more important influence.

Surely Urban's decision was shaped both by his experience in Liège and by his immediate military and political concerns in Orvieto. Urban in the summer of 1264 was virtually beseiged within the fortress town of Orvieto: confronted with the serious threat of imperial capture, he even urged efforts to call up a crusading army for his defense.[15] At the same time, Urban was again at odds with the Orvietan government and local nobles over the Martana island and Aquapendente, and considered himself pressed by enemies within the town's walls. When he left, he stated bitterly that the town's Ghibellines had driven him out. Urban must also have been aware that the town government had long been riddled with Cathars and considered their heresy to be treason. In these difficult circumstances, Urban drew on long-established strengths. Many of his appointments were old, northern friends and allies, as Miri Rubin points out. Urban also turned to a powerful expression of orthodox Catholic piety and clerical authority, Eucharistic devotion. The enthusiastic promoter of the feast, the Dominican Hugh of Saint-Cher, was in fact a member of his entourage until his death in March 1263.[16] Urban's bull instituting the feast, "Transiturus de hoc mundo," is dated 11 August 1264, the summer of Manfred's campaign to beseige the city and the pope within it.[17]

What of the miracle at Bolsena? The story is a tale of doubt of the Eucharist confounded. A Bohemian priest, named—in Orvietan tradition—Peter of Prague, was troubled by doubts over transubstantiation, the literal transformation of the bread and wine of the Mass into the flesh and blood of Christ. While passing through the little town of Bolsena, he celebrated Mass at the church of Santa Cristina. The altarcloths dripped blood, a vivid answer to his doubt and statement of the doctrine of transubstantiation. The priest rushed to Pope Urban in Orvieto and told him the story. The pope had the relics of the miracle carried with great ceremony to Orvieto and instituted the Corpus Christi feast.

The status and real influence of the miracle has been open to debate because the written documentation is very late: the earliest versions of the miracle story date from after 1323.[18] It is mentioned in the chronicle of Luca di Domenico Manenti, a chronicle compiled in the late fourteenth and early fifteenth centuries from earlier sources, many of them now lost. The text reads: "In that year [1264] in the Church of Santa Christina of Bolsena the miracle of the Corpus Domini appeared and was carried to Orvieto by the bishop of the city and with solemn ceremony placed in Santa Maria Prisca, where at present it can be seen."[19] The reference to Santa Maria Prisca suggests that this line was written after the 1297 demolition of the old cathedral. The text may well have been redacted between 1317 and 1338, the years immediately after Clement V reinstituted the universal feast and probably the period of the development of the regular Orvietan celebration. Some scholars on these grounds have questioned the actual date of the miracle and its connection with the Eucharistic feast.

Jaroslav Polc has recently put some of these doubts to rest with his identification of the Bohemian priest, described in a nineteenth-century source derived from Orvietan tradition as a priest of Prague called Peter. Polc points out that Urban's registers do refer to a Master Peter, canon of Prague and protonotary of the king of Bohemia, who passed through Bolsena on a visit to the curia in Orvieto in late April or May 1264 in order to seek dispensation to reside away from his benefice.[20] The pope's letter granting the dispensation is dated at Orvieto 4 June 1264, as is a letter to the king of Bohemia that was entrusted to Peter. The presence

of a Bohemian priest called Master Peter of Prague in Bolsena and then
Orvieto in the summer of 1264 certainly strengthens the case for the date
and influence of the miracle. The Corpus Domini feast in Orvieto on 19
June 1264, as Polc suggests, was probably a celebration of the translation
of the relics from Bolsena to Orvieto. Urban's bull "Transiturus" is dated
11 August. He also wrote on 8 September to Eve of St. Martin in Liège
and described the scale of the celebration, emphasizing his inclusion of
all the cardinals, archbishops, bishops, and other clerics then present at
the curia, so that they could then imitate the model feast he was establishing.[21]

Thomas Aquinas may have composed the Roman liturgy for the Corpus Christi feast. Aquinas came to Orvieto in the fall of 1261, as lector
of the Dominican priory, and lectured on the book of Job.[22] He became
friends with Urban and did write a number of works for the pope, including the commentary on all four Gospels that came to be termed the
"Catena aurea" and a short work "Against the Errors of the Greeks."[23]
The Roman Corpus Christi liturgy is considered remarkable for its theological precision and the use of Aristotelian terminology to state with
some exactness the idea of the Real Presence, which suggests Thomas's
hand.[24] Furthermore, in one sermon Thomas linked pastoral emphasis on
Eucharistic devotion with the condemnation of heretics. The sermon was
on a parable from Luke 14:16–24, "Homo quidam fecit cenam magnam
et vocavit multos." The story concerns a man who plans a feast: when a
number of people choose not to attend, he invites the poor and the
maimed instead. Probably, the sermon was preached after Thomas's stay
in Orvieto, either at Rome or Paris. Thomas gave the text a Eucharistic
meaning that, according to Louis-Jacques Bataillon, was a novel interpretation of the parable. The sermon paralleled the Corpus Christi office,
particularly in the choice of scriptural texts. Thomas also linked the parable, with his Eucharistic reading, with the condemnation of heretics. Heretics, along with Jews and pagans, are the *extraneos*, the outsiders who do
not come to the feast.[25] Thus Thomas linked in a sermon popular devotion to the Eucharist with the exclusion of heretics.

Orvieto became a center for Corpus Domini celebration and ultimately
saw the construction of a chapel in the Duomo frescoed with an ambitious program depicting Eucharistic miracles from popular exempla, again
emphasizing doubt confounded. Probably the tale of the miracle was read
aloud, and the extant account was a derivative of that version.[26] The

feastday came to include a major public procession and a theatrical performance, or *sacra rappresentazione*, of the miracle, performed by members of the confraternity of the Disciplinati of San Martino. The play probably dates from 1325–30.[27]

The extant version of the performance emphasizes the intersecting roles of Orvietan clerical and political authorities. The play begins with the Bohemian priest and his doubt. His confessor asks how he can continue to perform his office, and for the sin of doubt imposes on him the penance of a pilgrimage to Saint Peter in Rome. The priest stops to lodge at Bolsena, performs Mass, and experiences the miracle. Then the authorities step in. The miracle is reported by the bishop of Orvieto to the pope, and the pope responds by giving the bishop a privilege and sending him to Bolsena for the relics. It is the Seven who present the pope with the bishop's messenger carrying the bloody altarcloths. The pope institutes the Corpus Domini procession and asks Thomas Aquinas to write the office. At the end of the performance a voice from heaven compliments Thomas on his work.[28] In effect, Orvieto developed a major public celebration that brought together an emphasis on the Corpus Domini and the miraculous transubstantiation at the heart of the Mass with an orderly procession of authorities, including clerics and civic officials.[29] The ritual was a show of power: the miracle of transubstantiation confounded doubt and upheld a carefully articulated association of civic and ecclesiastical authority.

Civic Authority

The close link between civic authority and Catholic practice was displayed not only in religious processions but in public judicial proceedings. The late thirteenth-century civic courts policed marriage and sexual morality, holding inquisitions even into cases of adultery.[30] As early as 1269, civic authorities enforced laws punishing blasphemers who cursed God and the saints, insulted the Virgin Mary, or swore by the Corpus Domini. A Pucio de Montefalco, for example, was accused of blasphemy as a result of a judicial inquiry: he "had cursed God and his saints and the Roman Church."[31] Convictions were common, and the penalties were heavy and cruel. Men and women were fined twenty-five libre—as opposed to a modest twenty soldi for an insult—and threatened with a beating and the

loss of their tongues. This was especially severe: in Bologna the punishment was a fine or a beating, but not mutilation.[32] There is no direct
evidence of blasphemers who were actually mutilated at Orvieto, but it is
suggestive that the instrument used to mutilate the tongue, the *mordaccla,*
appears in popular insults and threats: a person thought to have a sharp
tongue would be told that he or she deserved the mordaccla.[33] This implies that the horrible instrument was familiar to people.

The Orvietan court offered an incentive for accusations of blasphemy
by making them lucrative: as for many other crimes, the fine was split
between the commune and the accuser. However, the profits of justice
cannot have been the overriding concern, as the targets of these accusations were often poor and often women. In 1269 a "little pauper woman
named Rosa," an emigrant from a nearby town, was sentenced to a fine
of twenty-five libre for blasphemy against the Virgin Mary. She was imprisoned and threatened with the loss of her tongue in ten days if she
was unable to pay. The case was heard by the exgravator, who lifted the
sentence and "replaced her in that state in which she had been before."[34]
In 1288, a female emigrant from Montepulciano accused of cursing God
was called only by the ugly name of Socza.[35] *Socza puttana,* or dirty whore,
was an actionable insult.[36] Her response, that as she recalled she had
blessed rather than cursed God, apparently annoyed the court. She was
sentenced to either a fine of twenty-five libre or a public whipping through
the town followed by the loss of her tongue. Like most offenders of her
status, she probably fled to escape the sentence.

Elites might be treated more leniently. A Monaldo, perhaps a Monaldeschi, was first convicted of cursing God and then absolved when several
witnesses stated that he had been drunk at the time.[37] Another blas-
phemer in 1295 must have been a marginal: he was nicknamed Neri
Pazzo, Crazy Neri. He was mercilessly fined one hundred libre for four
curses.[38] Blasphemy convictions publically identified social outcasts—people without homes or even patronymics, often disreputable women—with
sacrilegious comments.[39] It was a Socza, a dirty woman from another
town, who would curse God.

The commune, with the dedication of the new cathedral, had a special
association with Mary, and honored her not only by the punishment of
blasphemy but by the display of mercy. As Marilena Rossi has shown, the
city from 1295 on occasion offered up convicted prisoners on the altar:
they were "freed and removed from prison and offered on the altar of the

Blessed Mary."[40] In 1300, Bernardo Staiuli, imprisoned for brawling and unable to pay the fine, was chosen to be "exhibited, donated and offered to the new church of the glorious Virgin Mary, in order that she might conserve the Orvietan people and commune."[41] The text has an odd whiff of sacrifice; in practice, at least one of the freed prisoners was made to work for six months on the new cathedral.[42] The commune depended on the Virgin's favor. Civic authority and well-being were defined in terms of the honor and favor of Mary.

Orvietan lay piety in the late thirteenth century followed spiritual currents common in northern and central Italy. Confraternities proliferated in Orvieto from the 1250s, but there is little internal evidence about their nature before the 1320s.[43] In 1258 Bishop Jacomo had given a forty-day indulgence to all who joined an antiheretical confraternity.[44] The emphasis in most confraternities was probably on death and commemoration: the Franciscan confraternity of Santa Maria, granted a papal indulgence between 1254 and 1261 and disbanded before 1323, demonstrably kept a list of dead members for this purpose.[45] Death confraternities essentially provided their members with solemn funerals and then prayed for the release of their souls from Purgatory. Lay religious enthusiasm was encouraged in a form that emphasized the orthodox Catholic understanding of death, purgation, and resurrection.

Creation Retold

The late-thirteenth-century redefinition of authority was expressed in an insistence on the potential of the human body for sanctity. The connection between these ideas was most clearly stated in the Corpus Domini procession and feast, directly linking civic and ecclesiastical officials and the relics of transubstantiation. It was also expressed in the career of the Beata Vanna, with her poses of death and elaborately perfumed corpse. But the most powerful and, certainly, the most beautiful Orvietan statement of the presence of the sacred in the physical world can still be read in the frieze on the facade of the new cathedral in Orvieto. Four monumental reliefs fill the broad pilasters flanking the doors in the facade. The carvings narrate salvation history: Creation, the Tree of Jesse, the Life of Christ, and the Last Judgement. Overall, the reliefs express an intense physicality and natural beauty. In Romanesque reliefs—as in thirteenth-century mosaic—the figures often seem immaterial, like spiritual rather than earthly presences. Here, solid human bodies are located in a lyrically beautiful natural world.

The iconography of the reliefs emphasizes the capacity of the physical world for sanctity. The second panel depicts the Tree of Jesse: the human ancestry and prophecies of Jesus—an idea abhorrent to Cathars, who taught that Christ was pure spirit. The sophisticated iconography has long fascinated and, in fact, eluded art historians; Michael Taylor in 1972 published a detailed analysis developed with the aid of parallel images from the Balkans (which are conveniently labeled).[46] Taylor argues convincingly that the Jesse panel tracing the human ancestry of Jesus is explicitly anti-Cathar, close in its Old Testament content to the treatise of Moneta of Cremona. He speculates, less convincingly, that the lost original of the iconography was a now-destroyed frieze on the facade of the Dominican convent in Orvieto, completed in the 1260s.

A precise connection between the reliefs and anti-Cathar efforts is elusive. The date of the carving of the reliefs is uncertain, let alone the date of their design. The agreement to build the church was made on 22 June 1284, and the foundation stone was laid by Nicholas IV on 15 November 1290. The facade reliefs were carved in the decades after 1300, though the exact dates are disputed. John White read a text of 1310 to imply that the facade had not been begun when the Sienese architect Lorenzo Maitani took charge of the project. This reading means, he argues, that the reliefs were carved between 1310 and Maitani's death in 1330.[47] White convincingly demonstrates that all four reliefs were carved simultaneously. Portions of the upper sections remain incomplete. David Gillerman has recently argued, on the basis of a stylistic gulf between the designs of earlier and later nave capitals, that Lorenzo Maitani took over as early as 1300 and may have begun the facade reliefs before 1310.[48]

The origin and date of the design for the reliefs is also elusive. Two remarkable sketches for the facade survive, evidence perhaps of a design competition. White dates the sketches to the period of Maitani's arrival. However, the overall iconographic program could well date earlier. Both designs incorporate wide pilasters to hold the relief; the design that was left unbuilt in fact indicates reliefs—circles framed by vines.[49] This fact strongly suggests that the decision to include some sort of reliefs on the facade had already been made, so that the artists were asked to incorporate them in their designs. And, as Taylor argues, the sophistication of the second panel, in particular, suggests the advice of a theologian conversant with the anti-Cathar polemical literature. One possible source is the curia of Nicholas IV. Nicholas, a Colonna client and the first Franciscan pope, was very much interested in facilitating the construction of the church and even aided in the settlement of a local property dispute that had blocked the project. It was Nicholas who placed the first stone in 1290. An agreement of 1290 between the cathedral chapter and the papal chamberlain famously specifies that the church be built "in the image" of Santa Maria Maggiore, the great Roman basilica on which Nicholas had lavished his patronage.[50] The contemporary painted decoration of the left transept at Santa Maria Maggiore included a Genesis cycle, probably begun in 1295 and now largely destroyed.

The first panel of the Orvietan reliefs, like the second, spoke directly to concerns raised by Cathar teachings. The panel tells the story of Genesis. The lower level is remarkable in the development of a beautiful natural landscape of rocks, trees, and flowers. Within this natural frame, a gentle, bearded, youthful God creates first the plants, then the animals, then humankind. John Pope-Hennessey speaks of "lyrical fantasies with the pellucid texture of a fairy tale," and of "beguiling innocence."[51] The creation of Adam and Eve is drawn out into four episodes.[52] God calls a reclining Adam into being from the dust of the ground, then in the next scene animates him. In the third vignette, Adam again reclines, sleeping on the ground, as God leans over him to reach into a gaping opening in his side. Finally, in the fourth scene, God, touching the newly emergent Eve at the shoulder, pulls her forth. The sequence affirms the divine origins of the natural order and the loveliness of creation: luxurious and exquisite plants and heroic animals. The figures are remarkable for their beauty and their innocence.

The remainder of the panel depicts a dignified, almost courtly temptation, followed by an expulsion scene in which Adam and Eve cower under bushes in fear. Then they are shown spinning and delving in dignity, still in a beautiful natural landscape; the upper vignettes show Cain and Abel, and the invention of the arts, with the rather odd choices of Geometry and Tubalcain. The sacrifice scene is certainly a reference to the Mass and thus to the Corpus Domini. The emphasis is not only on sin and the Fall, but on an idea fully developed in the Andrea Pisano carvings in Florence a few decades later: the links between divine and human creativity.

This depiction seems to be unique to Orvieto. The idea of large reliefs on the facade perhaps derives from the Italian Romanesque. David Gillerman has explored one antecedent, the facade at Spoleto, where friezes depict the life of Peter. Another possible influence is the Duomo at Modena, where four reliefs tell stories from Genesis, from Creation to Noah's ark. The panels were carved by Wiligelmo, around 1100. The first panel moves from creation to sin: God appears in a mandorla, then in the second scene creates the upright figure of a fat, sagging Adam. The central scene shows Adam reclining as God grasps Eve by the wrist and pulls her from Adam's side. In the final scene, the stiff figures of Adam and Eve simultaneously express temptation, sin, and shame: Eve reaches for the forbidden fruit as she looks back at Adam, Adam lifts his hand to his mouth; both figures clutch fig leaves to their privates with stiff right arms. In the second panel God reproves them, the angel drives them from Eden, and they both toil, fully dressed and hoeing the ground. As Roberto Salvini has stated, they give the impression of humanity in a brute state, doomed by fate to fall into sin. Adam's heavy body suggests the weight of the flesh.[53]

The Genesis scenes carved by Andrea Pisano for the Florentine campanile offer a revealing contrast. The hexagonal reliefs, begun around 1336, include four Genesis scenes, including the creation of Adam, the creation of Eve, and their work.[54] Andrea was markedly influenced by the reliefs at Orvieto in his portrayal of trees and drapery.[55] He also shared with Maitani an emphasis on the beauty of the garden. But the creation of Eve shows an upright God looking down as he grasps Eve by the wrist and pulls her from Adam. In marked contrast to the Eve at Orvieto, God seems to be physically hauling the sinuous body of Eve—seen sideways—from Adam. Eve's pose in the Florentine relief lacks the grace and dignity of the Orvietan figure—there is instead real motion in the scene carved by Andrea: she is hauled out and born. Andrea went on to develop a cycle that stresses not temptation and sin but rather creativity, as Marvin Trachtenberg has argued. The Adam and Eve scenes lead to their work and the works of their descendants: the mechanical and liberal arts.[56]

At Orvieto, the bodies of Adam and Eve are displayed for the viewer in all their physical beauty. There is a careful attention to anatomy in the rounded forms of pectorals and thighs.[57] Male and female genitalia are indicated, in their beauty and innocence. There is no whiff of concupiscence and shame, let alone the tears of the angels forced into sexed bodies

FIGURE 8-1: God animates Adam and begins the birth of Eve, Genesis relief, cathedral of Santa Maria Della Stella.

FIGURE 8-2: The birth and injunction of Eve. (Photograph by Marcello Bertoni.)

FIGURE 8-3: Adam hoes and Eve spins. (Photograph by Marcello Bertoni.)

in the Cathar Creation recounted in the *Interrogatio Iohannis.* The scene depicts the divine creation of an original human sexual difference, a sexual difference without sin. The picture of Adam and Eve working in dignity after the fall also portrays gender as natural and appropriate, the different work of men and of women.

God is very much physically engaged in creation. This God is not the Creator seen in twelfth-century illustrations who stands back, waves his hand and issues commands. Nor is he the slow old man of the Modena reliefs, creating a human race he knows is doomed to fall. The Orvietan Creator is young, handsome, even tender. He holds Adam up by the head as the upright figure sags like a puppet. The scene derives from Prometheus imagery.[58] The most remarkable moment is God stretching out over Adam to pull Eve from his side, lightly grasping her by the shoulder, and with great tenderness, fixing her gaze to admonish her. Her naked body, like that of Adam in the previous scene, is fully presented to the viewer in its graceful, linear beauty. Nothing could contrast more powerfully with the Cathar picture of angels trapped in flesh by Lucifer and the devil. These scenes imagine the Creation as a moment of youth and great promise, an innocent and sinless male and female humanity.

Yet the image has a curious sexual ambivalence. The hole in Adam's side evokes not only Christ's wound but female genitals and human birth. Adam reclines passively; God acts as a midwife as he reaches over, opens up the wound in Adam's side, and draws forth Eve. The image recalls the medieval theme of the femininity of Jesus.[59] Adam is represented as male, while his activity, perhaps his sexuality, is female: he gives birth. This reproduction is of course without lust or copulation, birth without original sin. The artist—perhaps to underscore the naturalness of human sexual characteristics—portrayed innocent birth from Adam's side in a way that evokes female sexuality as well.

We find, then, in late thirteenth-century Orvieto a triumphant emphasis on forms of piety that interwove clerical and civic authority as they interwove matter and spirit. The extraordinary friezes on the facade of the new Duomo described God's presence in the created order with exquisite beauty; in the Corpus Domini procession, a long line of civic and church officials carried the relics that were visual proof of the sacrament itself. Civic judges expressed a similar identification of orthodoxy and authority when they punished blasphemers or offered up prisoners to the

Virgin. These were public expressions of the nature of authority. Were they consciously intended to answer dualism and the insistent Cathar separation of the spiritual from any contamination by secular interest? The answers are irrecoverable. My own guess is that Urban's recourse to Eucharistic piety in a town riddled with Cathars was not accidental. Taylor's evidence that the Tree of Jesse iconography was repeated in areas that were Cathar centers also suggests an explicit anti-Cathar purpose. Consciously or not, late thirteenth-century understandings of authority were shaped by the struggle over popular dualism.

Finally, how convinced were Orvietans by this understanding of orthodoxy and authority? This population was sophisticated, and the extended visits of the papal curia surely fostered not only the luxury trades but considerable cynicism. When the Seven settled a long fight with Boniface over property and then desperately raced to place statues of the pope over the gates before the old man arrived for a visit, surely their flattery was more than a little tongue-in-cheek. However, no popular movement articulated an opposing view; I know, for example, of no evidence of Orvietan enthusiasm for the radical Franciscans, whose personal austerity and attacks on the propertied church attracted so much sympathy elsewhere.

One case of popular mockery of the Mass and the commune does survive in the Orvietan judicial records. In 1295 a group of men, including apprentices and young nobles, were fined for a series of destructive actions on the evening before Good Friday. Going about with their hoods pulled up and clothing reversed in some fashion (*contrafactos in vestibus*) so they could not be recognized, they set traps and tripped people on their way to church. They stole holy water sprinklers along with holy water and even bread from church altars. They chose domini, lords, among their bands, adjourned to a tavern, and—incredibly—picked one of their number to be a *Christus contrafactus*, a mock Jesus. Presumably, they used the things they had swiped from the churches to parody the Mass, perhaps even the Last Supper, in the tavern. They also attacked symbols of the commune and civic authority, throwing rocks at the fountains and tearing down markers identifying the neighborhoods.[60]

Taken seriously, these actions were an attack on the central symbols of orthodoxy and authority. It is significant that the two were linked: forty years before, a Cathar from the early popular movement would not have connected civic and Catholic symbols. A Toncelle or Lupicini would have mocked the Mass but respected the neighborhood societies. By 1295 the two went together. It is also significant that the attacks were not taken seriously: the account in the sentences suggests not blasphemy or treason but pranks. The court treated the youths mildly; though admittedly the court may have been cautious because of the high status and political connections of some of them. The participants were required to produce guarantors and to pay large fines, but were not accused of blasphemy. One youth who was unable to pay was ultimately let off by the town council.[61] Their actions were harmless, mockeries that resemble carnival reversals but took place out of season. The attacks only strengthened the established order.

Catharism, then, probably simply faded, at least in Orvieto. Bits of Cathar teaching show up in later testimony to the inquisition from northern Italy, typically mixed with other faiths and ideas. It is also true that one central aspect of Cathar belief became a dominant intellectual current in the late fourteenth and fifteenth centuries. Cathars, as I have shown, found in a dualist reading of the Genesis story a strong statement of human capacity: the idea that humans are kidnapped angels, temporarily trapped in matter but free of original sin and capable of perfection in life. Renaissance humanists similarly looked to the Creation narrative for an understanding of human identity and capacity: the creation of humankind in the divine image.[62] An argument for a causal link would be too strong, documentation of influence implausible. Nevertheless, the shared impulse again suggests the centrality of Cathar ideas in late medieval Italian culture.

The statement of Andreas and Pietro

IN PRIMIS NOS Andreas et Petrus dicimus et protestamur hanc esse fidem Paterinorum, quam hactenus credebamus fuisse catholicam. In primis duo fuisse principia, scilicet boni et mali et ii deos fuisse ab eterno, scilicet lucis et tenebrarum. Deum lucis fecisse omnem lucem et partem spirituum, Deum vero tenebrarum scilicet diabolum fecisse omne malum et omnes tenebras et quosdam angelos, et dictus diabolus cum suis angelis ivit et decepit luciferum et angelos ipsius, qui cum eo ceciderunt, qui erant de populo dei lucis. Item diabolus et lucifer cum suis angelis ceciderunt de celo. Item quidam angelus bonus, scilicet dei lucis cum quibusdam sotiis suis venit ad tenebras istas, ut redimeret luciferum et sotios, qui ceciderunt de celo. Item diabolus, scilicet draco mangnus et lucifer [*concorditer opera huius mundi in vi diebus fecerunt,*] simul ceperunt illum angelum et sotios suos et abstulerunt ab eo coronam et splendorem quem habebat. Item permittente deo lucis diabolus et lucifer concorditer opera huius mundi fecerunt in vi diebus. Item lucifer penituit de deceptione, quae facta fuit Deo lucis, fuit in concordia cum dracone ut facerent hominem de terra. Draco volebat ut esset homo immortalis et lucifer mortalis et sic factus est mortalis et miserunt in corpore hominis, scilicet Adae, illum angelum qui venit redimere luciferum et angelos suos a quo abstulerunt coronam, de qua fecerunt luminaria que sunt in firmamento et fecerunt Adae sociam mulierem et specie istorum hominum postquam fuerunt in corpore obliti sunt omnium bonorum et retinuerunt factores corporum eorum deos et lucifer precepit ut non commederent de lingno scientie boni, scilicet quod non commiscerent se ad invicem et draco fecit eos prevaritare, scilicet commiscere ad invicem. Item cum draco videret quod homo esset mortalis penituit se quod hominem fecerat unde, Deo lucis permittente, inmisit diluvium super terram et lucifer, permittente Deo lucis, reservavit Noe et socios suos. Item draco fecit turrem di bebel hedificari, ubi fecit multa genera linguarum ut si contingerit quod aliquis veniret de regno celestiali predicaturus homines eum non intelligerent. Item lucifer loquebatur Abrae, Ysaac et Iacob ostendendo se deum lucis et huic dedit legem Moysi et isti salvi sunt. Item deus lucis loquebatur per prophetas annuntiando adventum filii dei et dicit Iohannem missum a deo lucis. Item dicit quod filius dei venit in beatam Virginem Mariam quae erat facta de superioribus elementis et ab ea carnem suscepit et non de istis elementis et descendit de celis cum cxliiii milia angelorum et post mortem descendit ad infernum et reduxit secum sanctos patres et prophetas et qui obedierant prophetis. Item in die Pentecostes misit Spiritum Sanctum et docuit apostolos omnes linguas a contrario illius, qui linguas confusit et credit per illum Spiritum sanctum habere salvationem, quam se dicit habere et nullum alium. Item credit nullum salvari sine manus impositione et nullam confessionem peccatorum dicit esse necessariam in persona illorum qui de novo veniunt ad fidem illorum. Item dicit per malum ministrum vel sacerdotem nichil bonum operari vel dari quod ad salvationem pertineat. Item dicit Romanam ecclesiam fidem catholicam non habere, nec aliquam salvationem esse in ea nec aliquem per eam salvari et omnes constitutiones Romanae Ecclesiae abominantur. Item matrimonium dampnant, carnes, caseum et ova commendendes dampnant et iuramentum penitus dicit esse prohibitum. Item de corpore Christi et baptismo nichil credit fieri in ecclesia Romana. Dixit tamen dictus Petrus, quod de multis capitulis, qui in hanc carta continentur nihil ab aliquo intellexit. Andreas vero hanc esse vitam Paterinorum penitus refermavit, quod supra invenitur fidei.

For an English translation, see chapter 5.

Source: Archivio di Stato di Firenze, Diplomatico, Santa Maria Novella, 26 giugno 1229. This copy emends the edition by G. B. Ristori, "I Patarini in Firenze nella prima metà del secolo XIII," *Rivista storico-critica delle scienze teologiche* I (1905), pp. 15–17, printed also in Ilarino da Milano, "Il dualismo cataro in Umbria al tempo di San Francesco," *Filosofia e cultura in umbria tra medioevo e rinascimento,* Atti del IV convegno di studi umbri, Gubbio, 22–26 maggio 1966 (Perugia, 1967), pp. 187 n–89 n.

A 1212 Marriage Case
from the Bishop's Court

IN NOMINE DOMINI AMEN. Currente anno millesimo ccxii mense no-
vembris die [   ].

Oderisio peteret Riciadonnam ingenuam et nobilem mulierem in uxorem, promittens de veritate dicenda, dixit se iurasse recepturum illam in
uxorem et invadiasse inmissione anuli et ipsam consensisse et iurasse
eodem modo quo ipse iuraverat, apud Balneum in domo Gerardini, super
sacco iuxta ingnem, presente Ildibrandino Canuti, Algina serviente Gerardini et Viviano Petri Lambertucii, et diceret quod nesceret utrum Vivia-
nus intellexisset. Riciadoma, promittens de veritate dicenda, similiter dixit
quod numquam in eum consensit nec primo consentiret nec primo liber
tactus fuisse, et quod numquam osculata fuit eum ut eum haberet in
virum, et quod ipse per vim manum eius posuit super librum sed ipsa
numquam iuravit, et quod duos anulos inmisit ei sed utrumque reiecit.
Super hiis non est producta Algina, sed Ildibrandinus Canuti, Paltonerius
et Angelus. Ildibrandinus concordat cum Oderisio de tempore gemalii, de
loco, de presentia Viviani, et dixit quod erat ibi amasia Girardini et erat
Riccadoma, sed non erat ibi Paltonerius. Vidit Oderisium et Riccadonnam

colloquentes sed non intellexit quod dicerent et non vidit aliquem eorum iurare. Vidit quod ipse loco inmisit ei anulum sed ipsa statim reiecit eum in sacco, et ipse tunc collegit anulum et reddidit Oderisi. Paltonarius, iuratus, dixit quod ipse invenit Oderisium tenentem sub pellibus Riccadonnam et iam iuraverat. Interrogatus si vidit eos iurare, dixit quod non. Et vidit quod ille osculabatur eam iuxta matrem. Preter ea ivit ad civitatem et ocurabit anulum et inmisit eidem Riccadonnam, dicendo "Per istum anulum quem micto in tuum digitum tu sis meam uxorem ego tuus maritus." Interrogatus quis erat ibi quando iuravit, respondit ipsa scit quare tu me interrogas vero dicam tibi non verum. Interrogatus quis esset ibi quando inmisit ei anulum, respondit quod quidam sutcifer Oderisi de Celle et Algina serviens Gerardini. Interrogatus de tempore, dixit quod non recordat multum temporis est, non est adhuc annus, ultra natale fuit. Interrogatus si de die vel de nocte inmisit ei anulum, dixit quod de die ante tertiam et de consensu Ricadonne inmisit ei anulum. Interrogatus qualiter sciat quod de illius consensu, respondit quia illa porrexit digitum et retinuit anulum, sed non audivit quid responderet tunc. Nec erat ibi Ildebrandinus Canuti. Hic testis confessus est se esse subdiaconum sed non habebat tonsuram neque habitum clericalem. Angelus, iuratus, dixit quod fuit in domo quondam Ranieri Tiniosi in qua vidit et audivit quando Oderisio inmisit anulum in digitum Riccadonne, dicendo "Per istum anulum quem tibi micto tu sis mea uxor et ego tuus maritus." Interrogatus quod illa Riccadonna dixit quod consensit et placuit ei. Et hic fuit prefatti Paltonerio et quodam scutifero Oderisi cuius nomen ingnoret. Interrogatus si ludendo hic fuit Oderisio. Respondit hoc vidit, et vidit eam osculantem et ante et praeterea sepe et sepius praeterea pluria. Interrogatus utrum ioco vel facto, dixit hoc vidit fieri. Post aperturam testium predictorum et in disputatione quia obviebatur Ildebrandinus Canuti quod dixit inmissio anuli facta fuit ludendo, dixit Oderisio duas fuisse invadiationes, unam presenti Ildebrandini Canuti, aliam presentibus predictis testibus. Visis igitur confessionibus partium et eorundem conditionibus, et testium qualitatibus et conditionibus et dispositionibus diligenter consideratis, Ego Johanes divina patientia Urbevetanus Episcopus de causa congnoscens, licet Riccadonnam veluisse testes producere ad repellum testium ante publicationem, nos consideravimus quia non exspediebat. Idcirco, hiis et aliis rationibus motus, pronumptio inter predictos non esset matrimonio. Idcirco Riccadonnam absolvo et itatque licentiam nubendi in domino tribuo.

Datum in palatio episcopali anno MCCXII indictione xv die veneris vii mensis dicembris, presentibus archydiaconi et canonicis, et Raniero de Ripisano, Ormanno, Falco de Casale, Struffaldo, Berardino Andree de Vila, Benedicto Miscinelli, Massa Petri de Oliuario, Iamforte et Ranaldo Peri.

In the name of the Lord Amen. In the year 1212 in the month of November on the day [   ].

Oderisio sought Riciadonna, a free and noble woman, as a wife, and swearing to speak the truth, stated that he swore to receive her as a wife and entered into the placing of the ring, and she consented and swore in the same way that he had sworn, near Bagno, in the house of Gerardino upon a sack by the hearth, in the presence of Ildibrandino Canuti, Algina the servant of Gerardino, and Viviano di Pietro Lambertuci, and said that he did not know whether Viviano had knowledge.

Riciadonna, swearing to speak the truth, similarly stated that she never consented to him nor would she have consented to him, at first, nor at first was the book touched, and that she never kissed him to indicate that she would have him as her man, and that he placed her hand upon the book by force, but she never swore, and that he put two rings on her, but she cast away both. In these matters Algina was not produced, but Ildibrandino Canuti, Paltonerio, and Angelo were produced.

Ildibrandino agreed with Oderisio on the time of the pairing, on the place, and on the presence of Viviano, and said that the concubine of Girardino was there and Riciadonna was there, but Paltonerio was not there. He saw Oderisio and Riciadonna speaking together, but he did not know what they had said, and he did not see either of them swear. He saw that he put a ring on her there but she immediately threw it on the sack, and then he picked up the ring and returned it to Oderisio.

Paltonario, having sworn, stated that he found Oderisio holding Riciadonna under the hides and so swore. Asked whether he saw them swear he said no, and said that he saw him kiss her by the mother. Further, he went to the city and obtained the ring and put it on Riciadonna, saying, "By this ring which I place on your finger, you are my wife and I am your husband." Asked who was there when he swore, he answered, "She knows why, when you question me, in fact I do not speak the truth." Asked who was there when he put the ring on her, he responded a certain squire of Oderisio of Celle and Algina the servant of Gerardino. Asked about the time, he answered that he did not remember much about the time, it was not yet the new year, but after Christmas. Asked if it was day or night when he put the ring on her, he said that it was in the day before terce and by the consent of Riciadonna that he put the ring on her. Asked how he knew of her consent, he responded that she extended her finger and kept the ring but he did not hear what she said then. Nor was Ildebrandino Canuti there. This witness confessed that he is a subdeacon but has neither tonsure nor clerical habit.

Angelo, having sworn, stated that it was in the house of the late Ranieri Tiniosi where he saw and heard when Oderisio put the ring on Riciadonna's finger, saying, "By this ring which I give to you, you are my wife and I am your husband." Asked, he stated that Riciadonna said that she consented and that it pleased her. And the aforementioned Paltonerio was there, and a certain squire of Oderisio's whose name he did not know. Asked whether Oderisio was joking in this, he responded that he saw this, and saw him kissing her before, and often, or rather more often, or rather many times. Asked whether it was a joke or a serious deed, he said that this is what he saw take place.

After the opening of the aforementioned witnesses, and in the disputation because of the impediment that Ildebrandino Canuti said that the placing of the ring was done in jest, Oderisio said that there were two placings, one in the presence of Ildebrandino Canuti, and the other in the presence of the aforementioned witnesses.

Having seen the statements of the parties and their conditions, and the qualities of the witnesses, and having diligently considered these conditions and dispositions, I John, by divine sufferance Orvietan bishop, knowledgeable in the case, while Riciadonna had wished to produce witnesses in order to rebut the witnesses before publication, consider that there is no need. Therefore, moved by these and other reasons, I pronounce that there is no marriage between those mentioned above. Therefore I absolve Ricciadonna and so bestow on her license to wed in the lord.

Dated in the episcopal palace in the year 1212, in the 15th Indiction, on Friday December 7, in the presence of the archdeacon and canons and Raniero de Ripisano, Ormanno, Falco de Casale, Strufaldo, Berardino Andree de Vila, Benedicto Miscinelli, Massa Petri de Olivario, Iamforte and Ranaldo Peri.

Source: Archivio Vescovile di Orvieto cod. B, 112v–113r. A summary appears in CD, no. 89, p. 64.

Notes

ONE Introduction

1. "[Q]uod mundus iste et omnia visibilia a dyabolo erant creata; animas humanas esse spiritus, qui ceciderunt de celo, qui salvari debent in cordibus patarenorum; humanorum eorum resurrectionem non esse futuram; presbiteros Romane Ecclesie nullam habere potestatem absolvendi contritos et confessos a peccatis; matrimonialiter viventes in statu fore dampnationis; baptismum aque materialis non proficere ad salutem." ASO, Liber inquisitionis, 28r; All archival references are to the Archivio di Stato di Orvieto unless noted otherwise, and all translations are by me unless noted otherwise. See Luigi Fumi, ed., *Codice diplomatico della città di Orvieto. Documenti e regesti dal secolo XII al XV* (Florence, 1884), no. 314, pp. 258–59 (hereafter CD or Fumi). On Orvietan Catharism, see Luigi Fumi, "I paterini in Orvieto," *Archivio storico italiano* 3:22 (1875), pp. 52–81; Wanda Cherubini, "Movimenti paterinici in Orvieto," *Bollettino istituto storico-artistico orvietano* 15 (1959), pp. 3–42. An excellent thesis on Orvietan heresy and confraternities (with an approach to heresy very different from mine) appeared after I completed the bulk of my archival research: Mary Henderson, "Medieval Orvieto: The Religious Life of the Laity, c. 1150–1350" (Ph.D. diss., University of Edinburgh, 1990). I have credited her study whenever I learned of archival citations

from her very careful research, most notably the fact that a woman convicted of Catharism in 1268 had been a witness to a miracle of the Franciscan Ambrose of Massa decades before.

2. The classic reference is Mary Douglas, *Natural Symbols* (New York, 1982). See, for example, Ernst Kantorowicz, *The King's Two Bodies: A Study in Medieval Political Theology* (Princeton, 1957) and Sergio Bertelli, *Il corpo del re: Sacralità del potere nell'Europa medievale e moderna* (Florence, 1990). For a recent discussion, see Sarah Stanbury, "The Body and the City in 'Pearl,'" *Representations* 48 (Fall 1994), pp. 30–47.

3. Marie-Christine Pouchelle, *The Body and Surgery in the Middle Ages*, trans. Rosemary Morris (Paris, 1983; Eng. trans. New Brunswick, N.J., 1990), ch. 7, p. 122. The work is a study of the surgical treatise of Henri de Mondeville.

4. A number of Italian scholars of heresy have stressed the necessity of local studies: see, for a recent discussion, Francesca Lomastro Tognato, *L'eresia a Vicenza nel Duecento,* Fonti e studi di storia veneta, no. 12 (Vicenza, 1988), p. ix.

5. See Cinzio Violante, "Premessa," in *La storia locale: Temi, fonti e metodi di ricerca* (Bologna, 1982).

6. On the curia see Agostino Paravicini Bagliani, *La cour des papes au XIIIe siècle* (Paris, 1995), and his "La mobiltà della Curia romana nel secolo XIII. Riflessi locali," in *Società e istituzioni dell'Italia comunale. L'esempio di Perugia (secoli XII–XIV)* (Perugia, 1988), pp. 155–278. On the scholars, see the discussion of Aquinas's stay in Orvieto in James A. Weisheipl, *Friar Thomas d'Aquino: His Life, Thought and Works* (Garden City, N.Y., 1974), pp. 147–63.

7. As Antoine Dondaine pointed out, the early Cathar communities probably were not even in communication with each other; "La hiérarchie cathare en Italie I," *Archivum fratrum praedicatorum* 19 (1949), p. 293. Gabriele Zanella, "Malessere ereticale in valle padana (1260–1308)," *Rivista di storia e letteratura religiosa* 14: 3 (1978), pp. 341–90, notes the disorganization of heretical groups, p. 347.

8. The sentences are partially edited in CD, nos. 414–79, pp. 258–95, and by Riccetti in *Chiese e conventi degli ordini mendicanti in Umbria nei secoli XIII–XIV. Inventario delle fonti archivistiche e catalogo delle informazione documentarie. Archivi di Orvieto,* ed. Marilena Caponeri Rossi and Lucio Ricetti, (Perugia, 1987), pp. 85–100.

9. Liber inquisitionis, 5r. The relative lightness of the sentence probably does reflect political influence.

10. See the summary of the debate by Lorenzo Paolini, *L'eresia catara alla fine del duecento,* in *L'eresia a Bologna fra XIII e XIV secolo,* Istituto storico italiano per il medio evo, Studi storici, fasc. 93–96 (Rome, 1975), vol. I, pp. 86–87. There is an enormous bibliography on Catharism; see Gabriele Zanella, "L'eresia catara fra XII e XIV secolo: in margine al disagio di una storiografia," *Bollettino dell'istituto storico italiano per il medio evo e Archivio Muratoriano* 88 (1979), pp. 239–58, especially pp. 240–46; reprinted in his *Hereticalia: Temi e discussioni,* Centro italiano di studi sull'altomedioevo di Spoleto, Collectanea 7 (Spoleto, 1995), pp. 127–44, for a

historiographical survey on Italy. Synthetic discussions of the social makeup of Italian Catharism include Cinzio Violante, "Hérésies urbaines et hérésies rurales en Italie du 11e au 13e siècle," in *Hérésies et sociétés dans l'Europe pré-industrielle, 11e–18e siècles,* ed. Jacques Le Goff (Paris, 1968), pp. 171–202. Classic studies include Raoul Manselli, *L'eresia del male* (Naples, 1961); Grado Merlo, "Eretici nel mondo comunale italiano," reprinted in his *Eretici ed eresie medievali* (Bologna, 1989), pp. 233–59, is a recent survey. There has been a recent round of sharp debate between Lorenzo Paolini and Renato Orioli, on one side, and Gabriele Zanella, on the other, over the nature of heresy and the motives of heretics. For a response from Zanella that provides extensive citations to both sides, see Zanella, "Boni homines, bona opera, bona verba," in his *Hereticalia,* pp. 209–24.

11. Manselli, *L'eresia del male,* p. 88.

12. See, for studies that explicitly accept this view, Lorenzo Paolini, "Domus e zona degli eretici: l'esempio di Bologna nel XIII secolo," *Rivista di storia della chiesa in Italia* 35 (1981), pp. 371–87; Zanella, "L'eresia catara," especially p. 251.

13. Luigi Fumi, ed., "Cronaca di Luca di Domenico Manenti," in *Ephemerides Urbevetanae,* vol. 15, part 5 of *Rerum Italicarum Scriptores,* ed. L. A. Muratori (Città di Castello, 1910), appendices.

14. Emile Durkheim, *The Elementary Forms of the Religious Life* (originally published 1913; trans. Joseph Ward Swain, New York, 1965), pp. 463–64.

15. See, for a recent survey based in the medical literature, Joan Cadden, *Meanings of Sex Difference in the Middle Ages* (Cambridge, 1993).

16. For the recent debate over interpretation of heresy, see Grado Merlo, *Contro gli eretici* (Bologna, 1996), esp. pp. 109–111, and André Vauchez, "Un Moyen Age sans hérésies?" in his "Les recherches françaises sur les hérésies médiévales au cours des trente dernières années (1962–1992)," *Bollettino della società di studi valdesi* 174 (1994), pp. 99–101. See, for example, Gordon Leff, *Heresy in the Later Middle Ages* (Manchester, England, 1967), introduction.

17. Robert I. Moore, *The Formation of a Persecuting Society* (Oxford, 1987). For a survey of historians' efforts to define heresy, see Gabrielle Zanella, "L'eresia catara," especially pp. 240–46.

18. See the essays collected in *Mistiche e devote nell'Italia tardomedievale,* ed. Daniel Bornstein and Roberto Rusconi (Naples, 1992), especially the articles by Clara Gennaro, Mario Sensi, and Anna Benvenuti Papi. English translations appear in *Women and Religion in Medieval and Renaissance Italy,* trans. Margery Schneider (Chicago, 1996).

19. For an account of the complex Florentine case, see the discussion and bibliography in Anna Benvenuti Papi, "Un vescovo, una città: Ardingo nella Firenze del primo Duecento," in her *Pastori di popolo: Storie e leggende di vescovi e di città nell'Italia medievale* (Florence, 1988), pp. 21–124.

20. For examples of toleration, see Giovacchino Volpe, *Movimenti religiosi e sette ereticali nella società medievale italiana (sec. XI–XIV)* (Florence, 1972), p. 145.

21. Lorenzo Paolini and Raniero Orioli, eds. *Acta Sancti Officii Bononie ab anno 1291 usque ad annum 1310*, Fonti per la storia d'Italia, vol. 106 (Rome, 1982), part I, no. 22, p. 49. For other versions of Paolo Trintinelli's reaction, see nos. 21–32, pp. 47–60.

22. See Paolini, *L'eresia catara*, p. 30. For an emphasis on popular intolerance see Raoul Manselli, "Aspetti e significato dell'intolleranza popolare nei secoli XI–XIII," in *Il secolo XII: religione popolare ed eresia* (Rome, 1983), especially pp. 35–41.

23. Lorenzo Paolini, "Italian Catharism and Written Culture," in *Heresy and Literacy, 1000–1530*, ed. Peter Biller and Anne Hudson (Cambridge, 1994), pp. 83–103.

24. Paolini and Orioli, *Acta Sancti Officii Bononie*, part I, pp. 13–16, and no. 21, p. 48.

25. See Zanella, "L'eresia catara," pp. 252–53; Gabriele Zanella, *Itinerari ereticali: patari e catari tra Rimini e Verona*, Istituto storico italiano per il medio evo, Studi storici, fasc. 153 (Rome, 1986); appendix I is an edition of the documents. It is reprinted in his *Hereticalia*, without the appendix but with corrections to the edition, pp. 225–29.

26. For the literature on Christianization, see the very useful survey and critique by John Van Engen, "The Christian Middle Ages as an Historiographical Problem," *American Historical Review* 91: 3 (1986), pp. 519–52, and the response by Jean-Claude Schmitt in his introduction to *Religione, folklore e società nell'Occidente medievale*, trans. Lucia Carle (Rome, 1988), pp. 1–27.

27. See Zanella, *L'eresia catara*, p. 241.

28. See Antoine Dondaine, *Un Traité néo-manichéen du XIIIe siècle: le 'Liber de duobus principiis'* (Rome, 1939). This text is published in English translation along with several Bogomil accounts in Walter L. Wakefield and Austin P. Evans, *Heresies of the High Middle Ages* (New York, 1969; 2nd ed. 1991), pp. 511–591.

29. "James Capelli on the Cathars," in Wakefield and Evans, *Heresies*, pp. 301–306. The quotation appears on p. 304. A flawed edition exists: Dino Bazzochi, *La Eresia catara: Saggio storico filosofico con in appendice "Disputationes nonnullae adversus haereticos'* (Bologna, 1919 and 1920). There is a useful review of the Italian anti-Cathar polemical literature in Anne Reltgen, "Dissidences et contradictions en Italie," Actes de la 2e Session d'Histoire Médiévale de Carcassonne, *Heresis* 13–14 (1989), pp. 89–113.

30. See the comment by Jean Duvernoy in Reltgen, "Dissidences et contradictions," p. 110: he considers the work to be a fourteenth- or fifteenth-century compilation. See Dino Bazzochi, *La eresia catara: Saggio storico filosofico con in appendice "Disputationes nonnullae adversus haereticos," codice inedito del secolo XIII della biblioteca Malatestiana di Cesena* (Bologna, 1919–20); Ilarino da Milano, "La 'Summa contra haereticos,'" *Collectane franciscana* 10 (1940), pp. 66–82. A partial English translation appears in Walter L. Wakefield and Austin P. Evans, *Heresies* no. 49, pp. 301–6.

31. Raineri Sacconi's account of the Cathars is edited in Dondaine, *Un Traité néo-manichéen*, pp. 64–78.

32. "Processus Canonizationis B. Ambrosii Massani," *Acta Sanctorum* 66 (10 November) in Vincenzo Natalini, ed. *San Pietro Parenzo. La Leggenda scritta dal Maestro Giovanni canonico di Orvieto* (Rome, 1936).

33. For Armanno Punzilupo, see Gabriele Zanella, *Itinerari ereticalia: Patari e catari tra Rimini e Bologna*, Istituto storico italiano per il medio evo, Studi storici 153 (Rome, 1986), appendix I.

34. The Orvietan inquisitorial sentences are Archivio di Stato di Orvieto, Liber Inquisitionis. For partial editions, see note 8 above. There is a new edition, which I have not been able to consult: Mariano d'Alatri, ed. *L'Inquisizione francescana nell'Italia centrale del Duecento: con in appendice il testo del 'Liber inquisitionis' di Orvieto trascritto da Egidio Bonanno.* Biblioteca seraphico-cappucina, 49. (Rome, 1996).

35. The Florentine sentences were edited by Felice Tocco, *Quel che non c'è nella Divina Commedia, o Dante e l'eresia* (Bologna, 1899). For the sentences from Bologna, see Paolini and Orioli, *Acta Sancti Officii Bononie*, part I.

TWO   THE MURDER OF PARENZO

1. Paul Fabre and Louis Duchesne, ed., *Liber Censuum* (Paris, 1910–1952). See Daniel Waley, *The Papal State in the Thirteenth Century* (London, 1961), chs. 1–2.

2. On the reforms and their effects in one Italian bishopric, see Maureen Miller, *The Formation of a Medieval Church: Ecclesiastical Change in Verona, 950–1150* (Ithaca, N.Y., 1993), ch. 6

3. For a recent study with extensive comparative discussion, see George Dameron, *Episcopal Power and Florentine Society, 1000–1320* (Cambrdge, Mass., 1991).

4. See Ilarino da Milano, "Il dualismo cataro in Umbria al tempo di San Francesco," *Filosofia e cultura in Umbria tra medioevo e rinascimento.* Atti del IV convegno di studi umbri, Gubbio, 22–26 maggio 1966 (Perugia, 1967), pp. 175–216.

5. See Louis Duchesne, ed., *Liber Pontificalis* (Paris, 1955), vol. 2, p. 390; Daniel Waley, *Medieval Orvieto* (Cambridge, 1952), pp. 2–3; Peter Partner, *The Lands of St. Peter* (London, 1972), pp. 193–94. They probably had already sworn an oath of fealty to Lucius III: see Partner, *Lands of St. Peter*, pp. 215–16n. On the Via Cassia and its connection with the Via Francigena, see Renato Stopani, *La Via Francigena: Una strada europea nell'Italia del Medioevo* (Florence, 1988), p. 17.

6. "Gesta Innocentii Papae III," in *Patrologia cursus completus, Series Latina*, ed. Jacques-Paul Migne (Paris, 1844–1891), vol. 214, pp. 27, 29.

7. See Elisabeth Carpentier, *Orvieto à la fin du XIIIe siècle: Ville et campagne dans le cadastre de 1292* (Paris, 1986), p. 32.

8. On Innocent and the Patrimony, see Achille Luchaire, *Innocent III, Rome et l'Italie* (Paris, 1904), ch. 3.

9. On the dispute over Aquapendente, see Waley, *Medieval Orvieto,* chaps. 1, 2.

10. For an extensive recent study of a central Italian bishopric during this period, see Robert Brentano, *A New World in a Small Place: Church and Religion in the Diocese of Rieti, 1188–1378* (Berkeley, 1994). A thorough understanding of the Orvietan bishopric will be available with the completion of the doctoral thesis of David Foote of the University of California, Davis, tentatively titled, " 'Thou didst set a boundary': The Bishopric of Medieval Orvieto."

11. "[L]apsu carnis." Pericle Perali, ed., *La Cronaca del vescovado orvietano (1029–1239), scritta dal vescovo Ranerio* (Orvieto, 1907) p. 6. Lucio Riccetti is preparing a modern edition of this remarkable text; see L. Riccetti, "La cronaca di Ranerio vescovo di Orvieto (1228–1248), una prima ricognizione," *Rivista di storia della chiesa in Italia* 43: 2 (1989), pp. 480–509.

12. The use of the office of procurator to exploit and usurp episcopal resources was a common pattern; in Florence, the job was taken over by laymen and held by a large noble family, the Visdomini. See George Dameron, "Conflitto rituale e ceto dirigente fiorentino alla fine del Duecento: l'ingresso solenne del vescovo Jacopo Rainucci nel 1286,"*Ricerche storiche* 20: 2–3 (May–December 1990), pp. 263–86.

13. "Quia qui deberent esse vacante sede custodes pariter et pastores destructores sunt potius atque lupi, usurpantes bona patris . . ." Perali, *La Cronaca del vescovado,* p. 7. See CD, no. 47, p. 32.

14. For reconstructions of the Monaldeschi genealogy, see Waley, *Medieval Orvieto,* appendix 3, and Carpentier, *Orvieto,* pp. 261–64. The Monaldeschi were probably episcopal tenants who for a time usurped their lands. In July 1157 Bishop Guiscardus, an Orvietan, was able to regain possession of *Caiu,* described as a *terra Sancte Marie* that lay along the Paglia, from the first documented Monaldeschi, Petrus Cittadini, together with Bertramo and Petrus Amidei and their *nepote* Malefuge: see CD, nos. 37 and 38, p. 25. As Waley pointed out, Petrus Cittadini also held property at Parrano; see CD, no. 46, p. 32. Waley's suggestion that he "farmed a small patch of land by the Paglia," is misleading; see Waley, *Medieval Orvieto,* p. xxv. Two references indicate that the property was more important. In November 1181 the prior of S. Costanzo relinquished the "homines de Caio" in favor of the bishop; see Archivio vescovile di Orvieto (AVO), cod. B, 107r; CD, no. 49, pp. 33–34. The land was evidently farmed by serfs or tenants. Second, the *Cronaca* of Ranerio mentions the recovery of Caiu as the sole accomplishment of Bishop Guiscardus: "Huic successit Guiscardus Natione Urbevetanus, qui recollegit Caium, cui successit Milo natione"; Perali, *Cronaca del vescovado,* p. 7. This reference suggests a significant piece of property. Monaldeschi appear as titled noble landlords with retainers and a serf in the early miracles of Pietro Parenzo; see the discussion in chapter 3.

15. Rustico appears in a text of 1172 ratifying the possession of the castrum of Parrano by Count Ranierius: AVO, cod. B, 103; CD, no. 45, pp. 31–32.

16. "[M]agister pontis et populus." AVO, cod. B, 103; CD, no. 40, pp. 27–28.

17. See AVO, cod. B, 70r, 103r, 101r, 102v, and 108r.

18. AVO, cod. B, 107r; CD, no. 49, pp. 33–34.

19. Perali, *La Cronaca del vescovado*, part 9.

20. AVO, cod. B, 80r.

21. "Nam in tantam maior devenerat ecclesia vilitatem, ut omni tempore, preterquam in festo Assumptionis beate Virginis, in Nativitate Domini et solempnitate Paschali, ab hominum reverentia et frequentia videretur penitus aliena et vix in ea trium lampadum lumina resplenderent." Vincenzo Natalini, ed., *San Pietro Parenzo. La Leggenda scritta del Maestro Giovanni canonico di Orvieto* (Rome, 1936), section 7, p. 166.

22. "Cumque una illarum, Milita nomine, tamquam altera Martha, videretur esse sollicita pro tecto maioris ecclesie reparando." Ibid., section 2, p. 154.

23. See John Hine Mundy, *Liberty and Political Power in Toulouse 1050–1230* (New York, 1954), p. 82 and pp. 293–94, n. 34.

24. For Magister John, see Perali, *La Cronaca del vescovado*, part 6. For an analysis of the *Leggenda*, its motivation, and its relation to Innocent's bull "Vergentis in senium," see Ovidio Capitani, "Patari in Umbria: Lo 'Status Quaestionis' nella recente storiografia," *Bollettino istituto storico-artistico orvietano* 39 (1983), pp. 37–54.

25. This point was made by Vincenzo Natalini in his edition of *Leggenda*, p. 54.

26. See Francesco Lomastro Tognato, *L'Eresia a Vicenza nel Duecento*, Fonti e studi di storia veneta, no. 12 (Vicenza, 1988), p. 12.

27. See Jean Guiraud, *L'Inquisition au XIII siècle en France, en Espagne et en Italie*, *Histoire de l'Inquisition au Moyen Age*, vol. 2 (Paris, 1938), pp. 421–23.

28. "[Q]uidam Florentinus . . . doctrinam manicheorum pesssimam in Urbeveteri seminavit, asserens: nihil esse Christi corporis et sanguinis sacramentum; baptismum, quem catholica tradit Ecclesia, nihil proficere ad salutem; orationes et heleemosinas ad absolutionis beneficium non proficere defunctorum; beatum Silvestrum et omnes suos successores eterne pene cruciatibus alligatos; omnia visibilia esse a diabolo facta et eius subdita potestati; quemlibet bonum beato Petro, apostolorum principi meritis et premiis adequari, quemlibet malum cum Iuda proditore penam similem sustinere." Natalini, *Leggenda*, section 1, pp. 153–54.

29. "[P]ars maxima matronarum nostre civitatis et quidam earum amici eas ceperunt sicut sanctissimas feminas venerari"; "sub religionis pretextu multos et viros et mulieres attraxerunt in laberintum heresis memorate." Ibid., section 2, p. 154.

30. See Ilarino da Milano, "Il dualismo cataro," p. 193n; Arno Borst, *Die Katharer* (Stuttgart, 1953); French trans. *Les Cathares* (Paris, 1974), pp. 111–12.

31. On Peter Lombard, the Master of the *Sentences*, see Richard W. Southern. *Scholastic Humanism and the Unification of Europe*, vol. 1 (Oxford, 1995), pp. 213–14, 270.

32. There was a famous Cathar stronghold established in southern France, at the castle of Montségur. However, the parallel is weak, since Montségur was a late effort by refugee Cathars, after the Albigensian Crusade and the extraordinary efforts of the inquisition in the region. Nothing on this scale had taken place in Italy by 1198. Montségur comprised a castle and village, not an entire town.

33. Master John calls Parenzo a "rectorem qui summi pontificis gratiam urbevetanis acquireret, pacis et gratie romanorum beneficium impetraret." Natalini, *Leggenda*, section 3, p. 156.

34. See Pierre Toubert, *Les structures du Latium médiéval* (Rome, 1973), p. 1049; see 1327 n for a Parenzo who served as a judge in 1155.

35. See Vincenzo Natalini in his edition of *Leggenda*, ch. 5; Waley, *Papal State*, p. 131.

36. For a recent general biography of Innocent, with an extensive bibliography, see Jane Sayers, *Innocent III: Leader of Europe 1198–1216* (London, 1994).

37. On this problem see Ovidio Capitani, "Patari in Umbria." Diana Webb, "The Pope and the Cities: Anticlericalism and Heresy in Innocent III's Cities," in *The Church and Sovereignty c. 590–1918*, ed. Diana Wood (Oxford, 1991), pp. 135–52 is a useful survey but lacks a clear definition of heresy. For a general analysis of the development of the Church's response to heresy from the Third Lateran Council to the 1230s, see the essays of Grado Merlo in his *Contro gli eretici* (Bologna, 1996).

38. For the legal reasoning behind the decretal, see Walter Ullmann, "The Significance of Innocent III's Decretal 'Vergentis,'" *Études d'histoire du droit canonique dédiées à Gabriel Le Bras* (Paris, 1965), vol. I, pp. 729–41.

39. See Brenda Bolton, "Tradition and Temerity: Papal Attitudes to Deviants, 1159–1216," *Schism, Heresy and Religious Protest*, ed. Derek Baker (Studies in Church History, vol. 9) (Cambridge, 1972), pp. 79–91.

40. On temporal rectors, see Waley, *Papal State*, pp. 96–104. For a brief and lucid overview of the role of papal rectors in the later period and the ineffective working of thirteenth-century papal government, see Philip Jones, *The Malatesta of Rimini and the Papal State* (Cambridge, 1974), ch. 1. The quote is from p. 6.

41. See Grado Merlo, *Tensioni religiose all'inizio del duecento*, in *Tra eremo e città* (Assisi, 1991), pp. 33–92; Letizia Pellegrini, "*Negotium Imperfectum:* Il processo per la canonizzazione di Ambrogio da Massa (O. M., Orvieto 1240)," *Società e storia* 64 (1994), pp. 253–78, especially 264; Lucio Riccetti, *La città costruita: Lavori pubblici e immagine in Orvieto medievale* (Florence, 1992), p. 101.

42. For evidence from thirteenth-century Viterbo, including statutes, that does suggest that violent carnival games led to homicides, see Quirino Galli, "Presente e passato nel Carnevale della Tuscia meridionale. Le fonti medioevali," *Il Carnevale: dalla tradizione Arcaica alla traduzione colta del Rinascimento*, Centro studi sul teatro medievale e rinascimentale, atti del XIII convegno, Rome, 31 maggio–4 giugno 1989 (Viterbo, 1990), pp. 515–37.

43. Capitani argues that the only reference in the *Leggenda* to heresy as a *crimen lesae maiestatis* (as it is understood in "Vergentis") is after Parenzo's Easter visit to Rome, suggesting that Parenzo learned of the bull during his Easter visit. If so, Master John knew when Parenzo learned of the bull but referred to it only in this very indirect fashion, an interpretation that seems strained. See Capitani, "Patari in Umbria: Lo 'Status Quaestionis' nella recente storiografia," pp. 37–54.

44. "[A]lios pena mulctavit pecunie, que, amissa, veris lacrimis ab avaris possessoribus deploratur." Natalini, *Leggenda*, section 6, p. 159.

45. A number of quitclaims dating from 1217 show men termed the *creditores Parentii* repaid sums of money, and Fumi considered that these might have been fines associated with the repression of heresy. However, Pietro Parenzo's brother served as rector from 1200–1203. There was also a Roman podestà called Dominus Parenza in 1209, and there is another reference to a Parentius before 1217. The 1217 references might well be to exactions by any of these men. Furthermore, the texts refer to the fines as paid to Toncella as treasurer. This reference is intriguing, since he died a consoled Cathar. However, he is first documented as treasurer beginning 6 September 1215.

Perhaps the creditores Parentii were men who were first fined by Pietro's brother, and then had their convictions overturned by a later podestà. See CD, no. 72, p. 51 (27 September 1201); Giuseppe Pardi, "Serie di supremi Magistrati" *Bollettino della società umbra di storia patria* I (1895), pp. 25–86; 4 (1898), pp. 1–46; 10 (1904), pp. 169–97; 11 (1905), pp. 263–380, lists the podestà. The repayments to the creditores Parentii are Titolario, cod. A, fasc. I, 1v–3v. Some were printed in CD, no. 110, p. 79.

46. The term used, *iuratoriam cautionem*, derived from Roman law and meant an oath used to strengthen an obligation.

47. "Curia flebat, quia, licet ius esset in civitate, non erat tamen qui redderet, nec etiam postularet, sed leges et plebiscita, morte sua coacta patroni, silentium tenuerunt." Natalini, *Leggenda*, section 11, pp. 165–66.

48. For example, when a woman recounted a vision of Parenzo to an Orvietan physician, Master Anselm, he thought for a time about why Parenzo was killed and then said to her to go to that holy martyr who was killed because of justice *(propter iustitiam)* and can perhaps heal you. Ibid., section 15, p. 173

49. Enrico Guidoni has suggested that a move of civic functions away from the cathedral complex in many towns in this period was part of a *prova di forza* between bishop and commune: see his *La città dal Medioevo al Rinascimento* (Rome, 1981), pp. 75–76. Riccetti is dubious; see *La città costruita*, pp. 98–99. Michael Goodich reads the debate over moving the corpse as a response to the size of the crowd of mourners rather than the symbolic importance of the two churches: see his *Violence and Miracle in the Fourteenth Century* (Chicago, 1995), p. 16.

50. Natalini, *Leggenda*, section 11, p. 166.

51. AVO, cod. B, 108v, dated 20 February 1200.

52. Natalini, *Leggenda*, section 18, pp. 175–6.

53. For the attribution of the murder to the Prefetti, see "Cronaca di Luca di Domenico Manenti," in Luigi Fumi, ed., *Ephemerides Urbevetanae, Rerum Italicarum Scriptores*, ed. Ludovico A. Muratori, vol. 15, part 5 (Città di Castello, 1910), p. 279.

54. See, for example, the sentence of Stradigottus Ricci de Toste: "cuius domus dudum a progenitoribus suis dampnati erroris tamquam virulenta progenies et genimina viperarum nephariam contrahens disciplinam de hereticorum conversatione"; Liber inquisitionis, 3v. For another example, see Provenzano Lupicini's sentence, 13v.

55. Ibid., 9v. Mary Henderson derives *avultronis* from *avulsor*, or *shearer*, "Medieval Orvieto: The Religious Life of the Laity, c. 1150–1350," (Ph. D. diss., University of Edinburgh, 1990), p. 85. Perhaps this word was the source of the name, but his sentence mentions explicitly usury, and it is doubtful that he was a shearer as well.

56. The tower is mentioned in the 1268 excommunication of Cristoforo: Liber inquisitionis, 1v. In 1280–81 Toste and former Toste property was sold to the commune to become the Piazza del Popolo; see Istrumentari 878; CD, no. 524, pp. 324–25. "Bartahalomeus Ranucci Magistri" and "Ranuccius Tosti" agreed to the treaty. The text is printed in the appendix to Fumi, "Cronaca di Luca di Domenico Manenti," pp. 281–84n.

57. AVO, cod. B, 67r–66v (the document was placed in the volume upside down); CD, no. 87, pp. 62–63, lists Tostus Raneri Magistri. A Toste also witnessed a 1220 compromise: Istrumentari 871 (de Bustolis) 105r–v. The name appears to be "Tatii" Tosti.

58. Archivio di Stato di Siena (hereafter ASS) Riformagioni Diplomatico, 5 gennaio 1221. The Caleffo vecchio copy of this document erroneously reads "Ranuccius Torte"; the original is clearly "Toste." Presumably the name was unfamiliar to the copyist. See the edited version, Giovanni Cecchini, ed., *Il Caleffo vecchio del comune di Siena* (Siena, 1931), vol. I, no. 198, p. 295. A 1220 quitclaim over a shipwreck was made to a "Jaquinto de Tosto," acting for his *nepos* Alberto Johanis Stefani Normandi: Titolario, cod. A, 20v; Fumi, CD, no. 128, p. 88. Probably Toste was simply his patronymic.

59. The pact had been made in the house of Stradigotto, in the presence of "Ranuccio fratre Tosti, Stradigotto et Aldebrandino Riccio, et Ranierio Bartholomei Rainuctii Magistri;" it was now performed "ad pedem quercus Monaldi seu Ranieri Stefani apud Petrorium presentibus domino Jacobo judice de Florentia, Ranuccio Tosti, et Ildribandino Riccio." Titolario, cod. A, 88r; CD, no. 192, p. 121.

60. ASS, Diplomatico, 25 giugno 1235; CD, no. 218, pp. 147–48.

61. AVO, cod. B, 100v includes an 1177 transfer of part of a farm in Parrano by Lupicinus filius Neronis Raneri; one border is the "land of the sons of Johannes Lupicini." The fifteenth-century chroniclers Luca and Cipriano Manenti mention Lupicini service as consuls in the twelfth century; see Fumi, "Cronaca di Luca di Domenico Manenti," *Ephemerides Urbevetanae*, Rerum Italicarum Scriptores vol. I, p. 275. On the Lupicini see despite some errors Bernardino Lattanzi, "La Famiglia Lupicini di Orvieto," *Bollettino istituto storico-artistico orivetano* 21 (1965), pp. 74–83. Lucio Riccetti "Note in margine ad un testamento orivetano del trecento: Il testamento di Ugolino di Lupicino," [extract from *Bollettino istituto storico-artistico orivetano* 38 (1982)], pp. 13–15, corrects Lattanzi's assumption that Ugolino Lupicini, a wealthy and prominent Orvietan at the end of the thirteenth century, was the son of Provenzano Lupicini, identifying him instead as Ugolino di Lupicino di Pietro di Gianni (Iannes), based on Liber donationum, 25r; thus Lupicini was both his patronymic and his surname. For his Lupicini connection, see the 1182 reference to his grandfather's house as "domo Petri filii Iohannis Lupicini: AVO, cod. B, 108r-v, cited by Riccetti, "Note in margine," p. 14 n. The Iohannes Lupicini who appears in the 1202 list of Orvietans agreeing to a pact with Siena cited in note 56 was probably his great-grandfather.

62. See Giovanni Cecchini ed., *Il Caleffo vecchio del comune di Siena* (Siena, 1931), vol. I, no. 59, p. 76.

63. For Provenzano's service as consul, see CD no. 256, p. 170 (AVO, cod. B, 133); as treasurer in 1239, see, for example, Istrumentari 871 (De Bustolis), 54r; Titolario, cod. A, 71v, CD, no. 248, p. 162. He was a witness as early as 1220: Titolario, cod. A, 9v; CD, no. 127, p. 88; Fumi erroneously transcribed: "Provenzano," "Lupicini" di Bertramo "Bernarducci." In fact, the names are separated by periods and read: "Provenzani Lupicini. Bertramis Bernarducci." He was also a witness in 1222 and 23: Titolario, cod. A, 34v and 38r; CD, no. 157, p. 102, no. 159, p. 103.

64. Titolario, cod. A, 68v; CD, no. 246, p. 164. The Cathar Pietro di Ranierio Adilascie also appears.

65. Istrumentari 868 (Galluzo), 2v; CD, no. 293, p. 190. For his service as rector, see Giudiziario, Busta I, fasc. 1, 1r.

66. He was "Ninus Amidei Provenzani de Lupicinis." See CD, no. 548, p. 338.

67. He is named as Toncella Aronis in the original text, ASS Riformagioni, Diplomatico, 5 gennaio 1221. (The Caleffo vecchio copy erroneously reads Toncella Aronnis; see Cecchini, *Caleffo vecchio*, vol. I, no. 198, p. 299.) An Arone took the oath in 1202: *Caleffo vecchio*, vol. I, no. 59, p. 78.

68. See Istrumentari 871 (de Bustolis), 133r; CD, no. 100, p. 69. In 1217 a group of men termed the "creditores Parentii" were repaid sums they had given to "messer Toncella the former treasurer"; see Titolario, cod. A, 1v, 2r, 47r. CD, no. 110, p. 79 contains a short example.

69. Domenico owned a half share of the tower and in 1253 donated it to his daughter; see Liber donationem, 14v. By 1291 the tower was used by the commune as a prison: see Giudiziario, Busta II, fasc. 3, 17r for an escape.

70. For the deaths of Arone or Artone and his father, Toncella, see the heresy conviction of Domenico's wife, Syginetta, Liber inquisitionis, 9v.

71. Domenico Toncelle is listed as a witness as early as 1217: Titolario, cod. A, 1v.

72. A text of 8 January 1235 refers to Domenico's service as treasurer: Titolario cod. A, 85v; CD, no. 211, p. 143.

73. ASO, Riformagioni, vol. 69 (1295) contains many mentions of "dominus Petrus domini Mathei Toncelle legum doctori." For example, one of his students carried off a married woman: Guidiziario, Registro I, 601v.

74. Natalini, *Leggenda* section 21, p. 179.

75. AVO, cod. B, 138r; CD, no. 209, p. 141–42.

76. Perali, *La Cronaca del vescovado*, part 5.

77. The account of the visit was recorded in two brief notices written in the margins of a codex containing portions of the Old and New Testament, probably by someone attached to the canons of San Costanzo. It is now owned by the Morgan Library, identified there as M 465. The text is described and edited in Michele Maccarone, "La notizia della visita di Innocenzo III ad Orvieto nel cod. M 465 della Morgan Library di New York," in *Studi sul Innocenzo III* (Padua, 1972), Italia sacra, vol. 17, pp. 3–9.

78. See Anna Benvenuti Papi, "Un vescovo, una città: Ardingo nella Firenze del primo Duecento," in *Pastori di popolo: Storie e leggende di vescovi e di città nell'Italia medievale* (Florence, 1988), pp. 21–124; see also the discussion in André Vauchez, *Les Laics au Moyen Age: Pratiques et expériences religieuses* (Paris, 1987), ch. 11. On crusades against heresy, see Grado Merlo, " 'Militare per Christo' contro gli eretici," in *Contro gli eretici*, ch. 1.

79. Michele Maccarone, "Orvieto e la predicazione della Crociata," in *Studi sul Innocenzo III*, pp. 30–48.

80. "Numerus cruce signatorum de civitate ipsiusque districtus fuit plus quam duo milia virorum et mulierum tamen paucarum." Maccarone, "Orvieto e la predicazione," p. 137.

THREE   ORVIETAN SOCIETY AND THE EARLY POPOLO

1. In March 1223 a civic judge confiscated a house on the grounds that the owners, Guarniero de Cannano and his wife, Benvegnate, had confessed that they had received heretics in the building. The house was located in the rione of Santa Maria, and the perfects received there were Jacobus, called Peter of Spoleto, and Olivierio. The owners were each fined fifty libre. Guarnerio was dead within two

months; the cause of his death is unknown. The house was rented at a cheap ten soldi per year to nobles who had recently submitted to the commune and were required to live in town. The condemnation is Istrumentari 865 (Titolario, cod. A), 37v, dated 30 March 1223; the rental is 38r, dated 25 April; CD, no. 162, p. 106. For the submission of the nobles Ugolino, Veriterio, and Oderisio de Castroiovis, Istrumentari 865 (Titolario, cod. A), 40r, 2 January 1223: CD, no. 165, p. 101.

2. The currency used was the libra of Cortona, employed by papal tax officials, termed decimators, in the period. See Elisabeth Carpentier, *Orvieto à la fin du XIII siècle: Ville et campagne dans le cadastre de 1292* (Paris, 1986) p. 87. In Orvieto in 1291, forty-five soldi of Cortona were worth a Florentine florin: see Peter Spufford, *Handbook of Medieval Exchange* (London, 1986), p. 57.

3. For example, Enrico Fiumi found that 27.5 percent of households in Prato in 1325 rented rather than owned their residences: Fiumi, *Demografia, movimento urbanistico e classi sociali in Prato dall'età comunale ai tempi moderni* (Florence, 1968), p. 70.

4. A total of 2,827 hearths are included in the tax register and another 186 were recorded on a few pages that are now missing. With the 10 percent of households Carpentier believes were left out of the survey because of poverty, the total number of hearths would be 3,347. A multiplier of three would put the population at 13,388; four yields 16,735. The clergy probably numbered six or seven hundred. Carpentier, *Orvieto*, p. 237.

5. There were 3,473 hearths in the countryside. The Orvietan catasto explicitly surveys the contado, which meant the diocese of the bishop of Orvieto and the *districtus*, the town's zone of influence. Ibid., pp. 56–59.

6. Ibid., p. 251.

7. Carpentier argues that assessments were inflated for families considered heretical and Ghibelline: the Miccinelli, della Terza, and Toste; Ibid., p. 281 n. 274.

8. Ibid., p. 290. Carpentier argues that study of ecclesiastical property, omitted from the catasto, reveals a similar pattern.

9. Ibid., p. 225.

10. Average surface area of 24,961 hectares valued at an average of 3,991 libre; Ibid., p. 226.

11. The five comital households held 4.37 percent of the parcels of land, representing 8.94 percent of the overall acreage but 3.87 percent of the overall appraised value.

12. Ibid., p. 226.

13. The average surface area was 828 hectares, the average value 336 libre.

14. Carpentier provides a list of the guilds, the number of guild members identified in the catasto, and their total landed property; Ibid., pp. 228–29.

15. See Paolo Cammarosano, "Aspetti delle strutture familiari nelle città dell'Italia comunale (secoli XII–XIV)," *Studi medievali* 16 (1975), pp. 417–36.

16. On Siena, see Edward English, "Five Magnate Families of Siena, 1240–1350" (Ph.D. diss., University of Toronto, 1981). For the Florentines, see Carol Lansing, *The Florentine Magnates: Lineage and Faction in a Medieval Commune* (Princeton, 1992).

17. See Sandro Carocci, *Baroni di Roma: Dominazioni signorili e lignaggi aristocratici nel duecento e nel primo trecento* (Rome, 1993) (Collection de l'École française de Rome, no. 181), ch. 5.

18. "Feminam enim prolem a nostra successione penitus escludimus." quoted in Carocci, *Baroni di Roma* pp. 160–61. He cites Agostino Paravicini Bagliani, *I testamenti dei cardinali del Duecento* (Rome, 1980), p. 198.

19. On dowry custom and law, see Manlio Bellomo, *Ricerche sui rapporti patrimoniali tra coniugi: Contributo all storia della famiglia medievale* (Milan, 1961); Julius Kirshner, "Wives' claims against insolvent husbands in late medieval Italy," *Women of the Medieval World*, ed. Julius Kirshner and Suzanne Wemple (Oxford, 1985); Thomas Kuehn, "Some Ambiguities of Female Inheritance Ideology in the Renaissance," *Continuity and Change* 2 (1987), pp. 11–36.

20. See Christiane Klapisch-Zuber, "The 'Cruel Mother': Maternity, Widowhood and Dowry in Florence in the Fourteenth and Fifteenth Centuries," in her *Women, Family and Ritual in Renaissance Italy*, trans. Lydia Cochrane (Chicago, 1985), pp. 117–31.

21. A statute concerning inheritance and the transmission of property to children is included in the 1325 Carta del Popolo; its original date is unknown. It provides that fathers divide the paternal goods equally among all of their sons and not favor the sons of second wives; mothers similarly were to treat sons equally. And male and female children were to succeed to their mother's and grandmother's property in equal amounts. Carta del Popolo, rubric 50, CD, pp. 774–75. Two statutes concerned a marital family's claim to dowries and maternal property: if a wife died without legitimate children, the husband was to receive a third share of her dowry, rubric 115, CD, p. 802; children could not alienate goods derived from their mother, rubric 124, CD, pp. 812–13.

22. The text is Insinuazioni delle donazioni. See Lucio Riccetti, "Orvieto: i testamenti del 'Liber donationum' (1221–1281)," in *Nolens intestatus decedere: Il testamento come fonte della storia religiosa e sociale*, Archivi dell'Umbria: Inventari e ricerche, vol. 7 (Umbria, 1985), pp. 95–103.

23. The thirteenth century law is lost. The first extant statute requiring copies is in the 1334 Colletta edited by Giuseppe Pardi, "Gli Statuti della Colletta del comune di Orvieto (sec. XIV)," *Bollettino Deputazione di storia patria per l'Umbria* 9 (1905), pp. 324–25.

24. Liber donationum, 5r.

25. Ibid., 51v.

26. Ibid., 39v.

27. Ibid., 40r.

28. Ibid., 42v.

29. Ibid., 15r.

30. Ibid., 19v.

31. See, for example, the 1258 will of Johane di Ruberto Saraceni of Aquapendente, who made a widow who was no obvious relation his heir: Liber donationum, 6v. Andricotto di Andree Balzani after gifts to two men made his sister's sons his heirs: Liber donationum, 8r.

32. On emancipation of women, see Thomas Kuehn, *Emancipation in Late Medieval Florence* (New Brunswick, N.J., 1982), pp. 116–20. See Edward English, "Emancipation, Succession and Honor: Family Strategies in Medieval Siena," in *Medieval Manuscript Studies in Honor of Leonard E. Boyle*, ed. Jacqueline Brown and William Stoneman (Notre Dame, forthcoming 1997).

33. It is not obvious that Toncelle should be considered his surname rather than his patronymic; the distinction was probably unimportant to Domenico. The name was used by subsequent generations as a surname: Pietro di Matteo Toncelle, and so forth.

34. Liber donationum, 14v.

35. See Giudiziario, Busta II, fasc. 4, 17v.

36. Liber donationum 46v.

37. See Lansing, *Florentine Magnates*, p. 91.

38. Liber Donationum, 165r–167r.

39. Giudiziario, Busta I, fasc. 8.

40. Ibid., fasc. 5.

41. Ibid., fasc. 3.

42. Titolario, cod. B, 55r (CD, no. 497, pp. 303–4. Fumi's citation to Istrumentari 871 [de Bustolis] was discovered by Marilena Rossi to be an error).

43. "[A]d unam familiam ad unum panem ad unum vinum." Liber donationum, 79v. On this kind of arrangement and its diffusion in fifteenth-century Tuscany, see Christiane Klapisch-Zuber and Michel Demonet, "'A uno pane e uno vino': The Rural Tuscan Family at the Beginning of the Fifteenth Century," in Christiane Klapisch-Zuber, *Women, Family and Ritual*, pp. 36–67.

44. For late medieval Italy, the classic study using letters to reconstruct elite political patronage is Dale Kent, *The Rise of the Medici: Faction in Florence, 1426–1434* (Oxford, 1978). There are two very useful collections on patronage: F. W. Kent and P. Simons, eds. *Patronage, Art and Society in Renaissance Italy* (Oxford, 1987), and the essays collected in *Ricerche storiche* 15: 1 (1985). On twelfth-century rural clientage and the formation of rural communes, see Chris Wickham, *Comunità e clientele nella Toscana del XII secolo: Le origini del comune rurale nella Piana di Lucca* (Rome, 1995).

45. Andrew Wallace-Hadrill, ed., *Patronage in Ancient Society* (London and New York, 1989); see, in particular, Peter Garnsey and Greg Woolf, "Patronage of the Rural Poor in the Roman World," pp. 153–70.

46. "Fredum qui stat prope domum domini Muntanari," Giudiziario, Busta II, fasc. 8, 75r.

47. Vicenzo Natalini, ed., *San Pietro Parenzo. La Leggenda scritta del Maestro Giovanni canonico di Orvieto* (Rome, 1936), section 23, p. 181.

48. Ibid., section 22, pp. 180–81.

49. "Sancte Ambrosi, tibi voveo filium meum ut michi tuis meritis gloriosis reddere digneris; quod si feceris, ad tuum servitium omni tempore permanebo et imaginem ceream ad tuum sepulchrum portabo." "Processus Canonizationis B. Ambrosii Massani," in *Acta Sanctorum* 66 (10 November), 578C.

50. "[D]evovit, ut Deus meritis gloriosius viri Dei dignaretur suum filium reddere sibi sanum, dicens quod si faceret, quod ad suum servitium permaneret toto tempore vite sue, et donec vixerit de suo dabit eius amore." Ibid., 579C–D.

51. Ibid., 578B.

52. See Jeremy Boissevain, "When the Saints Go Marching Out: Reflections on the Decline of Patronage in Malta," in *Patrons and Clients in Mediterranean Societies,* ed. Ernest Gellner and John Waterbury (London, 1977) pp. 81–96.

53. See Peter Brown, *The Cult of the Saints: Its Rise and Function in Latin Christianity* (Chicago, 1981); for a recent look at saintly patrons in medieval Italy with a detailed bibliography by region, see Paolo Golinelli, *Città e culto dei santi nel medioevo italiano* (Bologna, 1991).

54. Garnsey and Greg Woolf, "Patronage of the Rural Poor," p. 159.

55. Carpentier, *Orvieto,* pp. 250–51.

56. Carpentier details the patrimonies of the wealthiest Orvietans; *Orvieto,* pp. 198–204.

57. "Non laboravit tempore congruo": Giudiziario, Busta II, fasc. 4, 17v.

58. See, for example, the many cases in two largely duplicate registers from 1291: Giudiziario, Busta II, fascs. 3, 4.

59. Emphasis on the whole system is urged by Garnsey and Woolf; "Patronage of the Rural Poor," p. 154.

60. Terry Johnson and Christopher Dandeker, "Patronage: relations and system," *Patronage in Ancient Society,* ed. Andrew Wallace-Hadrill (London, 1989), p. 223.

61. For a recent critique of the view that a corporate ideology can be ascribed to wage laborers in the textile industry in fourteenth-century Florence, see Alessandro Stella, *La révolte des Ciompi* (Paris, 1993).

62. See, for example, John Grundmann's account of Perugia, where there was civil war between knights and foot soldiers: *The Popolo at Perugia, 1139–1309,* (Ph.D. diss., Washington University, 1974), ch. 2; this thesis was published with

few emendations, in the series *Fonti per la storia dell'Umbria,* vol. 20 (Perugia, 1992). For a careful look at the institutions of the Florentine Primo Popolo, see Daniela De Rosa, *Alle origini della repubblica fiorentina: Dai consoli al 'Primo popolo'* (Florence, 1995), chs. 6, 7.

63. His mother was probably the "domina Camera uxor olim Rainucci de Arari" who was convicted, among other things, of meeting heretics in the home of her son, called Rainucetti; Liber inquisitionis, 26r. I suspect that the notary used the two names, Ranerio and Rainuccio, interchangeably in Latin and Italian. Istrumentari 865 (Titolario, cod. A), at 87v, includes a receipt for the return of four mules by "Bonifatio et Ranerio fratribus filiis olim Ranutii de Harari." It may be that there were three brothers, Bonifatio, Ranerio, and Rainucetto; more probably, the latter was a nickname.

64. The texts are two receipts from the tailor: "Jacobum sartor de Miscina Apuglensis fuit confessus se habuisse et recepisse et restitutus fuisse a domino Petro Berardini Iuliani et Phylippo Paganuzzi et Rainerio Ranerii de Arari rectoribus populi urbevetani nomine comunis Urbevetani unum equum de pilo rubeo quem sibi Petrus Velle et eius sozii cives Urbevetani dicebant quod abstulerent occasione scolte." Istrumentari 865 (Titolario, cod. A), 82r; CD, nos. 260–61, p. 172.

65. For the first reference to the Carta del Popolo, see the 1244 survey of the *beni comunali* edited by Sandro Carocci, "Le Comunalie di Orvieto fra la fine del XII e la metà del XV secolo," *Mélanges de l'École française de Rome* 99: 2 (1987), pp. 701–28. The first extant copy is the much-revised version of 1325.

66. Istrumentari 865 (Titolario, cod. A), 92r; CD, no. 264, pp. 173–74.

67. Titolario, cod. B, 1v; CD, no. 284, p. 185.

68. Istrumentari 865 (Titolario, cod. A), 95v–96r; CD, no. 276, pp. 180–81. Daniel Waley, *Medieval Orvieto* (Cambridge, 1952), ch. 6.

69. See Jean-Claude Maire Vigueur, *Comuni e signorie in Umbria, Marche e Lazio* (Torino, 1987). Istrumentari 874. See the discussion in Carpentier, *Orvieto,* p. 214.

70. Istrumentari 865 (Titolario, cod. A), 83v; CD, no. 272, p. 176. See Lucio Riccetti, *La città costruita: Lavori pubblici e immagine in Orvieto medievale* (Florence, 1992), pp. 107–116.

71. Istrumentari 865 (Titolario, cod. A), 73v; CD, no. 243, p. 162. I have called them rural nobles because of references to their lands *(terre)* and to clients: the prohibition extended not only to the men themselves but to any person who had submitted to them ("aliquam a vobis submissam personam").

72. See the fine survey of the documentation: Marilena Caponeri Rossi, and Lucio Riccetti, eds., *Chiese e conventi degli ordini mendicanti in Umbria nei secoli XIII–XIV. Inventario delle fonti archivistiche e catalogo delle informazione documentarie. Archivi di Orvieto* (Perugia, 1987), especially see Riccetti, "Primi insediamenti degli ordini

mendicanti a Orvieto," pp. xxi–xxii, on the initial establishment of the Dominicans.

73. "Post hec coram dicto Inquisitore denu o reddierunt et idem Barthus extitit confessus quod credidit bonam esse vitam patarenorum et vidit eos quibus locutus est in pluribus locis et dixit quod primo denegravit propter timorem Inquisitoris prefati." Liber inquisitionis, 18r.

74. Daniel Waley, *Medieval Orvieto* (Cambridge, 1952), p. 32. See Luigi Fumi, "Chronica Potestatis 3" and "Cronaca di Luca di Domenico Manente," in *Ephemerides Urbevetanae*, vol. 15, pt. 5 of *Rerum Italicarum Scriptores* (Città di Castello, 1910), pp. 150, 297; from the condemnation of Cristoforo de Tosti (Liber inquisitionis, 1v; CD, no. 415, pp. 262–63): "non nullis hereticorum credentibus, qui ausu temerario loci sancti Dominici ordinis Predicatorum inmunitatem fregerunt, et in fratres Predicatores manus iniecentes predictum Inquisitorem usque ad effusionem sanguinis gradierunt [sic]." From the sentences of Bartholomeus and Rainerius Rainutii Tosti and his brother it is clear that Rainerius attacked the inquisitior: "cupientes pro viribus impedire immunitatem Sancti Dominici fratrum predicatorum temere violarunt et in fratrum Rogerium inquisitorem prefatum idem Rainerius manus violentas iniecit eundem usque ad effusionem sanguinis gladiando." Liber inquisitionis, 18r.

75. "Proinde cum dictus Provenzanus et plures alii stimulum et aculum temporalis et actioris pene timerent nuditis pedibus et vestibus usque ad camisiam spoliati corrigiis ad collum appensis coram omnium populi multitudinem prefati inquisitoris misericordiam fuerunt in humilitate cordis consecuti." Ibid., 13v.

76. See, for example, Istrumentari 871 (de Bustolis), 40v–41r; CD no. 249, p. 165. The dispute is Archivio vescovile di Orvieto (AVO), cod. B, 124v, dated 15 June 1241. It took place in the field: "actum in campo." The bishop claimed that the produce was held by the "heremi de Laureto."

77. Liber inquisitionis, 7v.

78. The surviving account is the inquisitor's sentence of January 1249, condemning Biviero in a fine of two thousand libre and the destruction of his tower and houses. Several thirteenth-century copies of the original text survive: Istrumentari 865 (Titolario, cod. A), 94r, Istrumentari 871 (de Bustolis), 30r; a flawed edition was published in CD, no. 279, pp. 182–83. Mary Henderson, "Medieval Orvieto: The Religious Life of the Laity, c.1150–350" (Ph.D. diss., Univ. of Edinburgh, 1990), pp. 240–41, also prints the text. I have relied on the Titolario cod. A version: "Nam Cristoforus, Ildribandinus, Julianus et Bivienus iamdicti volentes penam effugere temporalem qui se perpetue eximanitate tanti facineis [the de Bustolis text reads: "facinoris"] obligarunt Boniohannem notarium qui fideliter et legaliter inquisitionis eorum acta scripserat universa proditorie ad domum quondam Juliani de Tuderto ducentes et eidem mortem minantes falsificare quedam instrumentam contra eos inita compulerunt sicut per iuramentum dicti Boniohanis notarius et famam publicam attestatur."

79. "Et cum nobilis vir dominus Jacobus Petri Octaviani Urbevetanis potestas vir catholicus et fidelis ecclesie brachium ad mandatum meum et prout juramento tenetur ex forma constituti sententiam a me contra contra [sic] Julianum et Ildribandinum prefatos latam vellet executioni mandare se pro viribus obponentes et congregando armatos in domibus suis muniendo turres ad sedditionem et guerram homines concitando, ut possit circumvenire vindictam executionem ipsam conati sunt multipliciter impedire." Istrumentari 865 (Titolario cod. A) 94r.

80. This crucial line is garbled in every version. The Titolario, cod. A version is probably the oldest (de Bustolis was copied in 1286; see 1r). It reads: "Et spetialiter dictus Bivienius triginta annis fuerit credens hereticorum et post hec omnia in platea comitatis Urbisveteris tribunal contionandi concedens surreserit in publica concione loquaci pro cacitate potestati in hiis que contra hereticos locutus fuerat contradicens." Istrumentari 865 (Titolario cod. A) 94r.

FOUR   THE CATHARS

1. John Mundy, *The Repression of Catharism at Toulouse* (Toronto, 1985).

2. His sentence, Liber inquisitionis, 11v, mentions his receiving in his house seven perfects, one of them Jacobus de Urbeveteri.

3. Ibid., 26r.

4. The text reads "mandato suo filio." He is named as Rainuccetti and was probably the Ranerio who served in popular office.

5. His 1244 service as consul is Istrumentari 865 (Titolario, cod. A). 82r; CD, no. 260, p. 172. The mule exchange is in Istrumentari 865 (Titolario, cod. A), 87v; CD, no. 252, p. 167; the text explains that Bonifatio had received them as his "paragio." The kinsmen's guarantee of Pietro Munaldi is Istrumentari 871 (de Bustolis), 137r.

6. Istrumentari 865 (Titolario, cod. A), 84r; CD, no. 267, p. 175. Fumi has "Martinello," but the name in fact is given as "Martino."

7. Ibid., 83v; CD, no. 271, p. 176. Fumi's version is somewhat garbled.

8. CD nos. 377, 378, pp. 233–34 for his service as anziano; the heresy conviction is Liber inquisitionis, 19v.

9. Liber inquisitionis, 9v.

10. Petrus Coriza's sentence is ibid., 19v.

11. For a claim against his heirs, see Liber donationum, 98v.

12. Liber inquisitionis, 10r.

13. Ibid., 8r; Amata's sentence is 19v.

14. Ibid., 25v. The conviction states that they learned heresy from their progenitors.

15. His condemnation is ibid., 20r. The sentence reads "absente dicto Martino," but it is clear from the text that he was dead. The family persisted, despite

the condemnations, and continued to live in Santa Pace: the modest catasto returns of descendants of Martino Guidutii appear in Catasto, 6v (total value: twenty-five libre, ten soldi) and 16r (total value 1,287 libre 6 soldi).

16. They are: Martinus Martini Guidutii, consul of merchants in 1247: Istrumentari 865 (Titolario, cod. A), 83v; CD, no. 271, p. 176; Raynerius Stradigotti Ricci de Tostis, anziano in 1262: Istrumentari 871 (de Bustolis), 177v; CD, no. 378, p. 234; Bevenutus Pepi, anziano in 1256, named in the conviction of his widow, Domina Benamata: CD, no. 331, pp. 208–9 (I have not verified the original, which Fumi cites as Archivio Comunale di Perugia, Sommissioni c. XXII); Rainutius de Arari, rector populi in 1244, named in the conviction of his mother, Camera (mentioned earlier); Amideo Lupicini, guild prior in 1255 and rector populi 1266: CD, no. 406, p. 252; Giudiziario, Busta I, fasc. I, 1r; Provenzano Lupicini, consul in 1241: Archivio vescovile di Orvieto; CD, no. 256, p. 170; and anziano in 1256: CD, no. 331, pp. 208–9 (I have not verified the original, Archivio Communale di Perugia Sommissioni: XXII); Petrus Raineri Adilascie, sindic for the commune in 1256 and anziano in 1262: Istrumentari 871 (de Bustolis], 39v–40v (CD, no. 333, p. 210), 177v (CD, no. 378, p. 234); Domenico Toncelle, "prior of the guilds and societies" in 1255, 1256 and 1259, and capitano del popolo in 1257: for 1255, see Diplomatico, R1, final text,; and Istrumentari 871 (de Bustolis), for 1256, see Istrumentari 871, 41r–v, (CD, no. 332, p. 209), for 1259, see Istrumentari 871, 172v–173v (CD, no. 359, p. 224) (he is named in the conviction of his widow, Domina Syginetta); Messer Munaldo Ranieri Stefani served as treasurer in 1245: Istrumentari 865 (Titolario, cod. A) 89v; CD, 262, p. 172; his son was convicted but treated gently, perhaps because of his high status; it could be that the father was also involved but left unmentioned for the same reason.

17. Ranutio Toste appeared as a witness: Liber donationum, 13v.

18. See Diplomatico, R1, a roll of copies, dated 1296, of a number of texts concerning Aquapendente.

19. See the series of texts in Istrumentari 871 (de Bustolis), 172v–176r; CD, no. 359, p. 224. Toncelle is mentioned as prior through 2 April 1259; Cittadino Bertrami was prior on 7 April.

20. The chronicles mention his death and date it to 1256 and 1257. They are published by Luigi Fumi as "Annales Urbevetani," in *Ephemerides Urbevetanae*, vol. 15, pt. 5 of *Rerum Italicarum Scriptores*, ed. Ludovico A. Muratori (Città di Castello, 1910). "Cronica Antiqua A" places it in 1257, "Annales Urbevetani," p. 128; "Cronica Potestatum 3" puts it in 1256 and names Arto Petri Gani, "Annales Urbevetani," p. 152–53; "Chronica Potestatum 4" states "dominus Dominicus Toncelle capitaneus populi, in platea fuit percussus et non fuit scitum a quo," "Annales Urbevetani," p. 154. Luca Manenti dates it in 1256 and names Bartholomeo de Pietro Tani: Luigi Fumi, ed., "Cronaca di Luca di Domenico

Manenti,"in *Ephemerides Urbevetanae,* vol. 15, pt. 5 of *Rerum Italicarum Scriptores,* ed. L. A. Muratori (Città di Castello, 1910), p. 304.

21. Benvenuto is described as having received perfects "eighteen or sixteen years ago" in the 1268 condemnation of his wife, Benamata: Liber inquisitionis, 26r. He is listed as an anziano in the 1256 pact with Perugia: CD, no. 331, pp. 208–9. I have not seen the original, cited by Fumi as Archivio Comunale di Perugia, Sommissioni. c. XXII.

22. Istrumentari 871 (de Bustolis), 176r–v and 177r–v; CD, nos. 377 and 378, pp. 233–34.

23. The 1202 oath is *Il Caleffo vecchio del commune di Siena,* ed. Giovanni Cecchini (Siena, 1931), vol. I, no. 59, pp. 74–78. For Nanzilotto Ranieri Miscinelli, see Istrumentari 865 (Titolario cod. A), 37 v; CD, no. 154, p. 101. For the 1212 marriage dispute, see appendix B.

24. Miscinello Ricci Miscinelli's heresy sentence is Liber inquisitionis, 11v. The sale of land to Manfred Lancia is Istrumentari 869 (Titolario cod. B), 7 v; CD, no. 291, p. 188. There is a damaged copy of the will of Maffutio di Guilelmo Miscinelli in Liber Donationum, 40v, which describes two branches of the family, one of them the Ricci Miscinelli. The only legible date is "tempore domini Innocenti pape," surely Innocent IV, dating the will between 1243 and 1254. Cecchini, *Caleffo vecchio,* vol. 2, no. 598, pp. 824–25.

25. Liber donationum, 149r, a donation dated 1287, includes a house in Santa Pace "iuxta plateam populi et iuxta rem filiorum Boniohannes Ricci Miscinelli."

26. The 1280–81 purchase is Istrumentari 878; see the discussion in Riccetti, *La città costruita: Lavori pubblici e immagine in Orvieto medievale* (Florence, 1992). p. 114 n.

27. Liber inquisitionis, 11v.

28. Ibid., 21v.

29. Ibid., 29r.

30. His sentence mentions repayment of usury: ibid., 16r.

31. The tower is mentioned in the 1268 excommunication of Cristoforo: ibid., 1v. In 1280–81 Toste and former Toste property was sold to the commune to become the Piazza del Popolo; see Istrumentari 878; CD, no. 524, pp. 324–25.

32. Liber donationum, 39v; they also donated rural property in 1250: 3r.

33. Liber inquisitionis, 18r.

34. A 1270 property transfer was witnessed by a "Petrus Ranieri Tosti notarius:" Istrumentari 869 (Titolario, cod. B), 57v. Fumi cited the wrong codex: CD, no. 497, p. 303–4.

35. Cristoforo's sentence is Liber inquisitionis, 1r; Ranucetto appears at 14r and Tafura at 33r.

36. Stradigotto Ricci is ibid., 3r; his son Raynerio, 2r, and Andriotto, 20r; Bartolomeo Rainuti, his brother Raineri, 18r, and his son Rayneri and grandson Barthutio, 5v.

37. Ibid., 5v.

38. Liber donationum, 39v.

39. Liber inquisitionis, 24r.

40. Ibid., 18r

41. Ibid., 10r; 31r is Vianese's conviction. His fine was in the smaller currency of Cortona.

42. I learned of this Claruvisi inventory from Mary Henderson, "Medieval Orvieto: The Religious Life of the Laity, c. 1150–1350" (Ph.D. diss., University of Edinburgh, 1990), p. 86. See Giudiziario, Busta I, fasc. 12, 3v–7v.

43. Liber inquisitionis, 12r.

44. Catasto 400, 40v–41r.

45. Istrumentari 826 mentions Ingilberto as a witness in December 1263. A series of parchments reveal that his house, which belonged to his sons Pietro and Johanuccio, contained property that was confiscated before the house was destroyed. Two men petitioned, claiming the property had been stolen from them: Diplomatico, nos. 773 (13 November 1269), 59 (21 November 1269), 12 (23 Nov. 1269). The nature of the property is unspecified.

46. His curious name derived ultimately from a public office: prefect or rector of a city or province. It appears in a list of officials in the "Gesta Innocentii," *Patrologia cursus completus, Series Latina* ed. Jacque-Paul Migne (Paris, 1844–1891), vol. 214, p. liii n.

47. Liber inquisitionis, 4r and 27v.

48. He was present in Orvieto to witness a donation on 8 December 1250 (Liber donationum, 3r) and a will in 1253 (Liber donationum, 9v).

49. Ibid., 68r.

50. "[D]ixit se nullo tempore credentem hereticorum erroribus extitisse. Dixit tamen quod ad suggestionem et preces Stradigottii pellipparii in domo qua inhabitabat receptavit Leonardellum et sotium patarenos audivit inibi predicationes ipsorum de hereticorum erroribus et reverentiam fecit eis doctus a Stradigotto prefato." Liber inquisitionis, 24r.

51. "[D]ixit quod nullo tempore fuit credens hereticorum erroribus nec reverentiam fecit aliqui patareno expressit tamen quod conduxit Nicolam de Casalveri et sotium ac alios plures hereticos ad plura loca ad petitionem Stradigotti pelliparii audivit monitiones Jacobi florentinis patarenis de vita patarenorum apud Castellonclum ex parte Stradigotti prefati hereticis unum piscem sapillitum portavit." Ibid., 24r. Nicola de Casalveri also met with the shoemaker Benefactus, 27v, and Rainerio Stephani, probably a smith, 34v.

52. "[P]rohanum corpus Josep dampnati heretici deposuit de furtis et devotissime sepellivit." Ibid., 15v.

53. A 1288 judicial sentence calls him Frederic "de Serancia": Giudiziario, Registro I, 83r.

54. Liber donationum, 88v; in Marilena Caponeri Rossi and Lucio Riccetti, eds. *Chiese e conventi degli ordini mendicanti in Umbria nei secoli XIII–XIV. Inventario delle fonti archivistiche e catalogo delle informazione documentarii. Archivi di Orvieto* (Perugia, 1987), the summary contains a minor error.

55. The witness is named as Blanco Ugolini and is not called a furrier. However, the name Blanco was not common, and my guess is that this witness was the Blanco pellipario condemned for heresy.

56. Giudiziario, Busta I, fasc. Ibis.

57. Liber donationum, 125v.

58. "[P]ropter varias et prudentes interrogationes . . . "Liber inquistionis, 6r. The transfer by the woman who bought his house of her rights in the property is Liber donationum, 90r.

59. Lorenzo Paolini, *L'eresia catara alla fine del duecento,* in *L'eresia a Bologna fra XIII e XIV secolo,* Istituto storico italiano per il medio evo, Studi storici, 93–96 (Rome, 1975), vol. I, p. 2.

60. Fourteen were termed *domini,* and ten were in aspects of the textile industry, including mercers, weavers, and drapers. Lorenzo Paolini, *L'eresia catara,* p. 163.

61. Lorenzo Paolini and Raniero Orioli, eds., *Acta Sancti Officii Bononie ab anno 1291 usque ad annum 1310,* Fonti per la storia d'Italia, vol. 106 (Rome, 1982), vol. I, no. I, pp. 2, 4.

62. "Item anno et die predictis B. de Podio Cauo testis juratus dixit quod in domo P. Columba heretici pillicerii fuit per biennium conductus ab eodem heretico causa discendi officii de pelliparia, et vidit ibi cum heretico P. de Sancto Juliano, socium dicti P. Columbi hereticum, et P. Garini et Arnaldum de Terren et Poncium Garini et Ramundum de Corduba et B. Esquirol et P. de Sancto Martino et P. de Feilhoneto discipulos dicti heretici, et W. de Lantario et Pictavinus (sic) Aruieu, et P. Garini maior (sic), patrem predicti P. Garini, et plures alios ementes et vendentes in domo dictorum hereticorum quorum nomina ignorat." The source is the mid-thirteenth century register of Bernard de Caux: Bibliotheque de Toulouse MS 609. Austin P. Evans, "Social Aspects of Medieval Heresy." *Persecution and Liberty: Essays in Honor of George Lincoln Burr* New York, 1931) pp. III n–II2 n.

63. See Robert I. Moore, "St. Bernard's Mission to the Languedoc in 1145," *Bulletin of the Institute of Historical Research* 47:115 (May 1974), pp. I–10, for a survey of the literature. References associating weavers with heresy were discussed by Herbert Grundmann, *Religious Movements in the Middle Ages,* trans. Steven Rowan (originally published 1935; rev. ed. 1955; English trans. Notre Dame, Ind., 1996), pp. 69–70, 151, 231–33.

64. See the discussion of the transmission of heresy in Jacques Le Goff, ed., *Hérésies et sociétés dans l'Europe pré-industrielle, 11e–18e siècles* (Paris, 1968), in particular the comments of Le Goff, Manselli, and Grundmann, pp. 278–80.

65. They are distinct from the tanners of cordovan leather—used, among other things, for expensive shoes, and tanned by a very different process. On tanning, see John W. Waterer, "Leather," in *A History of Technology*, ed. Charles Singer et al. (Oxford, 1957), pp. 147–87. For English tanners and a clear account of the technical processes used by tanners and cordwainers, see Heather Swanson, *Medieval Artisans* (Oxford, 1989), ch. 5.

66. On the late medieval fur trade, see the very extensive study by Robert Delort, *Le commerce des fourrures en occident à la fin du moyen âge (vers 1300–vers 1450)* (Rome, 1978); for the distinction between furriers who tanned and those who tailored the furs, see p. 711.

67. In 1277 the Orvietan Messer Raynaldo domini Petri Gani was found by the officers of the court to be carrying a knife concealed under a fur garment ("cultellum malitosum asconse sub pelle") in the city; he refused to give up the knife and was fined four libre of Cortona and forty soldi, because he was a knight and not allowed to carry arms. The penalty was doubled because he had the knife concealed, and again because he would not give it up, and then reduced because he ultimately did give it up. Giudiziario, Busta I, fasc. 6, 37r.

68. David Herlihy, *Pisa in the Early Renaissance* (New Haven, 1958), p. 148. He argues that the new availability of lambskin in fact made the style possible. Delort discusses the change; *Le commerce des fourrures*, p. 2, ch. 1, especially p. 324.

69. For a discussion of this process, see Delort, *Le commerce des fourrures*, pp. 713–28.

70. One frustratingly brief reference survives from thirteenth-century Orvieto, but it does not mention the location. In 1295 a man was convicted of theft from "the ditch where hides are scraped" where the furs of a particular artisan were soaking in water. The man stole four sheep and goat hides. The text is Giudiziario, Busta II, fasc. 9, 68r.

71. Franco D'Angelo, "Concia e conciatori nella Palermo del Duecento," *Schede medievali* 6–7 (1984), pp. 111–26.

72. See Delort, *La commerce des fourrures*, p. 716 n. For an extensive study of a fifteenth century leather shop in Perugia, see Romano Pierotti, "Aspetti del mercato e della produzione a Perugia fra la fine del secolo XIV e la prima metà del XV: la bottega di cuoiame di Niccolo di Martino di Pietro," *Bollettino della Deputazione di storia Patria per l'Umbria*, 72: I (1975), pp. 79–185; 73: I (1976), pp. 2–131.

73. Catasto 399, 515r.

74. The furriers appear in ibid., 399, 122v, 135v, 140r, 150v, 158v, 171r, 221v, 275v, 479r, 515r, 518r, 562v. There is one reference in the catasto to an urban pilliczaria, a leather shop, 158v. Not surprisingly, none of these men were identifiably descendants of the households linked to heresy. See Elisabeth Carpentier, *Orvieto à la fin du XIIIe siècle: Ville et campagne dans le cadastre de 1292* (Paris, 1986), pp. 228–31, for a general look at the trades in the catasto.

75. To my knowledge the first reference to a furrier's guild in Orvieto is a 1269 mention of the consul of the pelliciai. They were among the guilds included in the Carta del Popolo, which was first mentioned in 1247, although the first extant version dates from 1325. See Daniel Waley, *Medieval Orvieto* (Cambridge, 1952), p. 85.

76. Paolini and Orioli, *Acta Sancti Officii Bononie*, no. 1, pp. 2, 4.

77. Lorenzo Paolini, "Domus e zona degli eretici: l'esempio di Bologna nel XIII secolo," *Rivista di storia della chiesa in Italia*, 35 (1981), pp. 371–87.

78. See, for example, Cinzio Violante, "Hérésies urbaines et hérésies rurales en Italie du XIIIe siècle," in Jacques Le Goff, *Hérésies et sociétés*, pp. 171–197.

79. The major source for Florentine heresy is a series of parchments that survived in the collection of the Dominican convent of Santa Maria Novella and then were passed to the Florentine state archives. Most were edited by Felice Tocco, *Quel che non c'è nella Divina Commedia, o Dante e l'eresia* (Bologna, 1899) (hereafter Tocco). Tocco's edition is not always reliable, and I have cited the originals. One 1245 summary of the evidence against the Baroni brothers was not included by Tocco: Archivio di Stato di Firenze Diplomatico Santa Maria Novella (hereafter ASF SMN) 1245. . . . Later evidence does exist, though it is sparse: see Raoul Manselli, "Per la storia dell'eresia catara nella Firenze del tempo di Dante," *Bullettino dell'Istituto storico italiano per il medio evo e archivio muratoriano* 62 (1950), pp. 123–38, and Dinora Corsi, "Per la storia dell'inquisizione a Firenze nella seconda metà del secolo XIII," *Bollettino della società di studi Valdesi* 132 (December 1972). On the secondary literature, see Dinora Corsi, "Firenze 1300–1350; 'Non conformismo' religioso e organizzazione inquisitoriale," *Annali dell'Istituto di Storia*, Università di Firenze, Facoltà di Magistero I (1979), pp. 29–66. See John N. Stephens, "Heresy in Medieval and Renaissance Florence," *Past and Present* 54 (1972), pp. 25–60; Marvin B. Becker, "Heresy in Medieval and Renaissance Florence: A Comment," *Past and Present* 62 (1974), pp. 153–61. Georg Semkov, "Die Katharer von Florenz und Umgebung in der ersten halfte des 13. Jahrhunderts," *Heresis* 7 (1986), pp. 61–75, examines the Florentine cathars by social class, using the published evidence.

80. See, for example, Gherardo di Raineri Ciuriani, ASF SMN 6 giugno 1245; Tocco, no. 14, pp. 50–52.

81. "[D]ixit quod ipsa dejeraverat propter timorem viri et destructionem sue domus": ASF SMN 6 giugno 1245.

82. On the Macci banking, see Robert Davidsohn, *Storia di Firenze*, vol. 1, p. 1192 and vol. 6, p. 256. For their house, see Pietro Santini, ed., *Documenti dell'antica costituzione del comune di Firenze*, Documenti di storia italiana, vol. 10 (Florence, 1895), pt. 3, doc. 27, pp. 400–401.

83. ASF SMN 30 gennaio 1244; Tocco no. 3, pp. 37–38.

84. One of the Cavalcanti served as consul of the Calimala in 1192; see

Santini, *Documenti*, pt. 3, pp. 365–67; on the Cavalcanti merchants, see Davidsohn, *Storia*, vol. 6, p. 256. See Massimo Tarassi, "Il regime guelfo," in *Ghibellini, Guelfi e popolo grasso: I detentori del potere politico a Firenze nella seconda metà del Dugento* ed. Sergio Raveggi et al. (Florence, 1978), p. 112 n.

85. For the tower, see Santini, *Documenti*, appendix 2, pp. 537–39.

86. Davidsohn, *Storia*, vol. 2, p. 417; Santini, *Documenti*, pt. 1, pp. 190–92. The excerpt from his testimony to the inquisitors is ASF SMN 12 ottobre 1245; Tocco, no. 8, pp. 41–43. The name is actually written as Cavalcaconti.

87. ASF SMN 6 giugno 1245; Tocco no. 14, pp. 50–52.

88. Dante, *Paradiso* 14, 108. See the discussion in Tarassi, "Il regime Guelfo," p. 127 n. Biatrice is mentioned in ASF SMN 26 aprile 1245; Tocco, no. 13, pp. 48–50.

89. Santini, *Documenti*, appendix 2, no. 7, pp. 526–27.

90. See Davidsohn, *Storia*, vol. 2, p. 416. He cites Archivio di Stato di Siena, Riformagioni, for the date of 25 June 1235. On the Pulci see Daniela Medici, "I primi dieci anni del Priorato," in Raveggi et al., *Ghibellini, Guelfi e popolo grasso*, pp. 187 n.

91. ASF SMN 27 novembre 1244; Tocco, no. 1, pp. 34–35.

92. "Qui dixit suo iuramento quod iam sunt duodecim anni, quod ipse habuit notitiam hereticorum, qui veniebant in domo fratris sui ad cognatam eius dominam Tedoram et occasione ipsius domine Tedore, et dixit quod vita eorum placebat sibi, et eos bonos homines tenebat, et audivit predicationem eorum, et mittebat eis, cum essent in domo propria, pisces, panem et vinum et res conmestibiles": ASF SMN 26 aprile 1245; Tocco no. 13, pp. 48–50.

93. Santini, *Documenti*, appendix 2, doc. 3, pp. 519–20.

94. On the Nerli, see Carol Lansing, *The Florentine Magnates: Lineage and Faction in a Medieval Commune* (Princeton, 1992), pp. 72–75 and 81–83.

95. The witness is named as Guidone Bagoncini; Santini, *Documenti*, pt. 2, pp. 259–60.

96. Ibid., pt. 1, pp. 48–51.

97. Ibid., pt. 2, p. 277.

98. Ibid., pt. 3, p. 475.

99. The location is detailed in their first sentence: "domum supradictam muratam et altam, que iuxta domum filiorum Marchi et iuxta vicum qui protendit ab Arno usque ad Burgum sanctorum Apostolorum": ASF SMN 11 agosto 1245; Tocco, no. 15, pp. 52–54.

100. "Rosa mulier iurata dixit quod anno preterito ipsa vidit in domo Pacis de Barone sex hereticos horantes et mensam paratam coram eis": ASF SMN 12 ottobre 1245; Tocco, no. 7, pp. 40–41.

101. "Albese predicta, que rediit, dixit suo iuramento quod ante consolationem suam ipsa stetit in domo alta Pacis del barone murata et in alia que est ex

parte Porte Sancte Marie per quattuor menses ad recipendam doctrinam hereticorum a Meliorata, que combuste fuit Prati, et Floretta predicta que rediit": ASF SMN 12 ottobre 1245; Tocco, no. 8, pp. 41–43.

102. Catalogued under ASF SMN 12 ottobre 1245 are two lists of evidence against the Baroni. They are printed in reverse order by Tocco, nos. 7 and 8, pp. 40–43. A third list, whose contents duplicate much in the other two but are more detailed, was not printed by Tocco: ASF SMN 1245 . . . It was probably working notes, since it contains no notarial signature but an X by each rubric and a summary of which witnesses agreed on the presence of a major perfect: for example, "Notum quod Albese, Contelda, Uguicione, Amata, Clarus concordant de Torsello episcopo hereticorum. Item domina Peregrina, et Albese, et Scocta, concordant de Meliorata que combuste fuit."

103. See Davidsohn, *Storia,* vol. 2, pp. 410–13.

104. See Sergio Raveggi, "Il regime Ghibellino," in Raveggi et al. *Ghibellini, Guelfi e popolo grasso: I detentori del potere politico a Firenze nella seconda metà del Dugento* (Florence, 1978), especially the list on pp. 70–72.

105. Davidsohn, *Storia,* vol. 2, p. 417; Santini, *Documenti,* part 2, pp. 462, 475.

106. Davidsohn, *Storia,* vol. 2, p. 417; Santini, *Documenti,* part 2, p. 190.

107. Santini, *Documenti,* vol. 2, doc. no. 56, p. 277.

108. See Raveggi, "Il regime Ghibellino," p. 209–10 n.

109. See Massimo Tarassi, "Il regime Guelfo," p. 130 n.

110. Santini, *Documenti,* part 2, p. 486 (ASF SMN 13 marzo 1245).

111. See Tocco, no. 17, p. 55.

112. See the documents of 13 and 24 agosto 1245 in Santini, *Documenti,* part 2, p. 487.

113. See Davidsohn *Storia,* vol. 2, p. 427 n.; *La cronica domestica di Donato Velluti* ed. Isidoro del Lungo and Guglielmo Volpi (Florence, 1914), p. 72.

114. John Martin explores the diffusion of heresy in the hierarchical society of sixteenth-century Venice in *Venice's Hidden Enemies: Italian Heretics in a Renaissance City* (Berkeley, 1993), ch. 6.

115. Bronislaw Geremek, "Activité économique et exclusion sociale: les métiers maudits," *Gerarchie economiche e gerarchie sociale, secc. XII–XVIII,* Istituto internazionale di storia economica 'Francesco Datini', dodicesima settimana di studio, Prato, 22 aprile 1980, p. 27, cited by D'Angelo, "Concia e conciatori," p. 118.

116. The Florentine chronicler Giovanni Villani spoke of this change as a loss of purity, a new oversophistication. Back in the good old days of the Primo Popolo, "I cittadini di Firenze viveano sobrii, e di grosse vivande, e con piccole spese, e di molti costumi e leggiadrie grossi e rudi; e di grossi drappi vestieno loro e le loro donne, e molti portavano le pelli scoperte sanza panno." Giovanni Villani, *Cronica* (Florence, 1823), book 6, ch. 69.

117. On the idea that animality was the source of sin, see Marie-Christine Pouchelle, "Représentations du corps dans la *Légende dorée*," *Ethnologie française* 6: 3–4 (1976), pp. 293–308, especially p. 300.

FIVE   BELIEF AND DOUBT

1. "Interrogatus dictus Bompetrus quam fidem et quam credenciam et quorum hereticorum fidem habebat respondit quod non bene dicernebat inter credencias et septas hereticorum, set credebat quod heretici essent meliores homines de mundo et quod in eis et in fide eorum esset vera salvatio, et quod in fide Romane Ecclesie esset dampnacio." Lorenzo Paolini and Raniero Orioli, eds., *Acta Sancti Officii Bononie ab anno 1291 usque ad annum 1310*, no. 12, p. 32.

2. Lorenzo Paolini has recently argued for a divergence between Cathar popular belief and the theologies developed by circles of learned perfects in "Italian Catharism and Written Culture," in *Heresy and Literacy, 1000–1350*, ed. Peter Biller and Anne Hudson (Cambridge, 1994), pp. 83–103.

3. Raoul Manselli, "Evangelisme et mythe dans la foi cathare," *Heresis* 5 (1985), pp. 5–17.

4. Grado Merlo, in his important study of heresy in the Piedmont in the fourteenth century, found considerable religious syncretism—a mix of beliefs drawn from Cathar and Waldensian teaching, and other sources as well—and argued convincingly that this pattern was due to the various preachers and currents of belief available in the Piedmont in this late period. See Grado G. Merlo, *Eretici e inquisitori nella società piemontese del Trecento* (Turin, 1977), ch. 2.

5. "Cum dominus Papa Gregorius nonus esset apud ecclesiam sancte Marie sororum. . . . Perusino in publica predicatione coram maxima hominum multitudine et mulierum, presentibus multis de cardinalis, Archiepiscopis, Episcopis et Cappellanis Romane Ecclesie, Andreas et Petrus patareni, qui reprehesentati fuerunt Romane Ecclesie per C. abbatem monasterii sancti Miniatis Florentie abiuraverunt omnem haeresim et specialiter Paterinorum et professi sunt fidem catholicam, quam Papa G. nonus tenet."

6. The text is ASF, SMN 26 giugno 1229. It was edited, with a number of errors, by G. R. Ristori, "I Patarini in Firenze nella prima metà del secolo XIII," *Rivista storico-critica delle scienze teologiche* I (1905), pp. 15–17, and there is a copy in Ilarino da Milano, "Il dualismo cataro in Umbria al tempo di san Francesco," *Filosofia e cultura in umbria tra medioevo e rinascimento*, Atti del IV convegno di studi umbri, Gubbio, 22–26 maggio 1966 (Perugia, 1967), pp. 187 n–89 n.

7. "Item, dixit idem Petrus quod omnes illi qui ululabant in ecclesia cantando voce non intelligibili decipiebant populum simplicem; et quod ipse habebat Passionem in domo sua in romano sicut fuerat in re." "Dépositions contre Pierre

Garcias," in Célestin Douais, ed., *Documents pour servir à l'histoire de l'inquisition dans le Languedoc* (Paris, 1900), vol. 2, p. 97.

8. "Item, audivit dictum Petrum Garcia dicentem quod illud pomum vetitum primis parentibus fuit nichil aliud nisi delectatio carnalis cohitus, et illud pomum porrexit Adam mulieri." Ibid., pp. 93–94.

9. "Dixit etiam idem Petrus quod illud quod Ecclesia Romana conjungebat, virum scilicet et mulierem, ut se et uxorem suam Aymam, [est meretricium]: nullum est matrimonium nisi inter animam et Deum. . . . Dixit etiam idem Petrus quod non jacuerat carnaliter cum uxore sua duo anni erunt in Pentecoste; et cum diceret Petro frater Guillelmus Garcia quod hoc erat quia ejusdem fidei erat cum ipso, dixit quod non set erat bestia sicut ipse frater Guillelmus." Ibid., p. 99.

10. "Item audivit Petrum dicentem quod matrimonium erat meretricium et quod nemo poterat salvari cum uxore sua, nec ipse cum uxore propria." Ibid., p. 93.

11. "Item, audivit dictum Petrum Garcia[m] dicentem, cum dictus frater Guillelmus Garcias requireret ab eo si caro resurgeret ostendens ei manum suam, dixit quod caro non resurgeret nisi sicut postis, percussiens postem cum manu." Ibid., p. 93.

12. "Item, dixit idem Petrum quod purgatorium non erat, et quo eleemosine facte a vivis non prosunt mortuo, et quod nullus salvatur nisi perfecte fecerit penitentiam ante mortem, et quod spiritus qui in uno corpore non poterat facere penitentiam, si deberet salvari, transibat in alium corpus ad complendum penitentiam." Ibid., p. 100.

13. "Dixit etiam idem Petrus quod si teneret illum Deum qui de mille hominibus ab eo factis unum salvaret et omnes alios damnaret, ipsum dirumperet et dilaceret unguibus et dentibus tanquam perfidum et reputabat ipsum esse falsum et perfidum, et spueret in faciem ejus, addens: de gutta cadat ipse." Ibid., p. 100.

14. There are detailed discussions of Bonigrino by Lorenzo Paolini, in *L'eresia catara alla fine del duecento*, in *L'eresia a Bologna fra XIII e XIV secolo*, Istituto storico italiano per il medio evo, Studi storici, 93–96 (Rome, 1975) pp. 96–107, and his "Bonigrino da Verona e sua moglie Rosafiore," in *Medioevo ereticale*, ed. Ovidio Capitani (Bologna, 1977), pp. 213–27.

15. Paolini and Orioli, *Acta Sancti Officii Bononie*, nos. 3–10, pp. 11–25.

16. Gerhard Rottenwoher considers that there is a Bagnolan influence, which is not surprising: see "Foi et théologie des cathares Bagnolistes," *Heresis* 7 (December 1986), p. 29.

17. Paolini argues that this position was consistent with the mitigated dualism taught by the Bagnolans; see *L'eresia catara*, p. 102 n.

18. Bagnolan Cathars taught that there was one God: one and not two principles. But Lucifer, the *minor creator*, was responsible for the creation of our bodies

and all transitory, visible things. See the "Disputatio inter catholicum et paterinum haereticum," cited by Paolini: *L'eresia catara*, 102 n. "Deum omnia creasse concedo, intellige bona, sed mala et vana et transitoria et visibilia ipse non fecit, sed minor creator scilicet lucifer . . . corpore nostra et omnia visibilia a minore creatore id est a diabolo facta sunt." Ilarino da Milano, "Fr. Gregorio O. P., vescovo di Fano, e la 'Disputatio inter catholicium et paterinum haereticum,'" *Aevum* 14 (1940), p. 130.

19. Paolini points out in *L'eresia catara*, p. 106, that this was consistent with the belief of Albanesi Cathars that the devil created evil spirits and used them to animate some humans.

20. For example, the inquisitors asked whether the good God and the God of light made the flood come in the time of Noah, and Bonigrino answered that these kinds of things do not proceed from the good God. The question: "si Deus verus et Deus lucis fecerat venire diluvium tempore Noe"; the answer: "quod a bono Deo talia et similia supradicta non procedebant." Paolini and Orioli, *Acta Sancti Officii Bononie*, no. 5, p. 15.

21. The condemnation of judicial execution was a Cathar teaching mentioned by Raineri Sacconi: see "Summa fratris raynerii de ordine fratrum praedicatorum, De Catharis et Pauperibus de Lugduno," in Antoine Dondaine, *Un Traité néo-manichéen du XIIIe siècle* (Rome, 1939), p. 65; trans. by Walter L. Wakefield and Austin P. Evans, *Heresies of the High Middle Ages* (New York, 1969; 2d ed. 1991) no. 51.

22. See the discussion in Gabriele Zanella, "L'eresia catara fra XIII e XIV secolo: in margine al disagio di una storiografia," *Bollettino dell'istituto storico italiano per il medio evo Archivio Muratoriano* 88 (1979), pp. 253–55.

23. "Sicut sunt lxxii lingue, ita sunt lxxii fides."

24. See Paolini, *L'eresia catara*, p. 104.

25. See Giovanni Boccaccio, *Decameron, Tutte le opere di Giovanni Boccaccio*, ed. Vittore Branca, vol. 4 (Milan, 1976), day I, story 3.

26. For his statement of belief, see Paolini and Orioli, *Acta Sancti Officii Bononie*, part I, no. 12, pp. 31–33. For a few examples of community comments (among a great many), see *Acta Sancti Officii Bononie*, part I, no. 152, p. 165; no. 168, p. 170. On Bompietro, see Paolini, *L'eresia catara*, pp. 110–26.

27. On Armanno's heterodoxy, Grado Merlo commented that his actions were interpreted in "a doctrinal and canonistic sense" by the inquisition. Grado G. Merlo, *Eretici e eresie medievali* (Bologna 1989), p. 109, and see the discussion in Lorenzo Paolini, *Eretici del Medioevo: L'albero selvatico* (Bologna, 1989), pp. 146–50.

28. It was copied by Peregrino Prisciano and conserved in the Archivio di Stato in Modena. There is a recent edition by Gabriele Zanella in *Itinerari ereticali: Patari e catari tra Rimini e Verona*, Istituto storico italiano per il medio evo, Studi storici, 153 (Rome, 1986), appendix I. See also the corrections to the edition printed by Gabriele Zanella, *Hereticalia* (Spoleto, 1995), pp. 225–29.

29. "Domina Bengepare, que fuit credens hereticorum, in .mcclxxiiii, die .x. intrante novembri, iurata dicit quod Punzilupus de Ferraria fuit credens hereticorum secte de Baniolo. Et dicit quod audivit catharos facere multas truffas et dicere verba derisoria de illis de ecclesia romana dicentes 'quomodo dicent postea illi de ecclesia romana quod nos simus mali homines cum ipsi fecerint unum de nostris sanctum'; et quod publica fama erat inter eos quod Punzilupus predictus erat de suis et credens eorum." Zanella, *Itinerari ereticali,* appendix I, p. 49.

30. See ibid., pp. 52–54.

31. "Dominus Iacobinus judex in .mcclxx. die quinto intrante iulio, iuratus dicit quod credit Punzilupum fuisse credentem hereticorum. Interrogatus quare, respondit quia non ibat ad ecclesiam nisi raro, et quia non habebat consilium ab aliquo sapiente ecclesiastico, et quia multa mala dicebat de clericis." Ibid., p. 50.

32. Ibid., pp. 86–89.

33. The notary Manfredino testified that he had often heard Armanno "dicendo quod erant mali homines et non faciebant opera Dei, nec erat in eis nec in fide romane ecclesie salus, sed erant deceptiones animarum, et quod erant lupi rapaces, qui persequabantur bonos homines et ecclesiam Dei, intelligendo de ecclesia hereticorum." Ibid., p. 54.

34. This came from Manfredino as well: "tempus combustus fuit quidam hereticus nomine Martinus de Capitello, et dum ducere⟨tur⟩ ad comburendum audivit Punzilupum dicentem pluribus audientibus: 'Videte qualia opera sunt ista, comburere istum vetulum bonum hominem; terra non deberet substinere illos qui faciunt talia opera.'" Ibid., p. 64.

35. "Item dicit quod Punzilupus frequenter ortatus fuit ipsum testem quod staret firmus in fide hereticorum, quia ut dictum est in ipsis solis erat salus." Ibid., p. 55.

36. Manfredino quoted him: "It has not been long since I saw the priest of St. Julian's who poured so much wine in the chalice that he became drunk." ("Et dicebat: 'Non est diu quod ego vidi sacerdotem sancti Juliani qui posuit tantum de vino in calice quod ipse sacerdos fuit inde inebriatus.'") Ibid., p. 56.

37. Domina Duragia stated, "[Q]uod idem Punzilupus consuevit in die Pasqe accipere unum magnum panem et unum butatium vini et dabat pluribus comedere et bibere. Et cum consumptum esset dicebat: 'Quid dicunt isti prevedones lupi rapaces corpus Christi non potest consummi: ecce nos consumpsimus unum tam magnum panem et butatium vini.'" Ibid., p. 56.

38. Armanno confessed that he once said, "'Quomodo sunt stulti isti sacerdotes qui credunt claudere Deum in piscide,' loquendo de corpore Christi quod sacerdotes sacrificant in altari; tamen dixit quod hoc dicebat pro ludo." Ibid., p. 56.

39. "[M]agister Castelanus calegarius, qui fuit credens hereticorum, in .mcclxxxviii. die .vi. intrante maio, iuratus dicit quod quando Punzilupus erat

mortuus cum adhuc corpus eius esset in ecclesia episcopali nondum traditum sepulture ipse testis una cum quondam Oldeberto et Bonomo iverunt ad videndum eum, et cum dictus testis diceret de corpore Punzilupi quod esset peius quam una bestia ipse Oldebertus respondit: 'Cave, compater, quid dicas, quia ipse fuit consolatus cum comatre tua', intelligendo de uxore ipsius Oldeberti." Ibid., p. 59; this excerpt is the third from Castellano's deposition in the dossier; the first excerpt includes the same anecdote but omits the address as compater; see pp. 50–51 and 53–54.

40. See Tocco, no. 8, pp. 41–42.

41. Liber inquisitionis, 16r: "ipsi erant boni et sancti homines et apostoli dei et quod solum in eis erat salvationem et quod omnes qui erant in fide Romane ecclesie non salvabantur nec solum qui faciunt vitam et tenent vitam patarenorum."

42. For a general discussion, see Susan Reynolds, "Social Mentalities and the Case of Medieval Skepticism," *Transactions of the Royal Historical Society*, 6th series, I (1991), pp. 21–41.

43. Alexander Murray, "Piety and Impiety in Thirteenth-Century Italy," in *Popular Belief and Practice*, ed. S. J. Cuming and Derek Baker (Cambridge, 1972), Studies in Church History, vol. 8, pp. 83–106.

44. "Or mi di, quanti cia di questi infedeli? Chi crede oggi i beni invisibili, i beni di paradiso, chissine cura? Non si ne curan le genti. Non studiano le genti in altro oggi se non in montare in ricchezze temporali. Non sanno che sè. . . . Ma oggi ne pieno tutto il mondo di questo peccato." "[O]gi, sicuri delleminaccie e delle pene di ninferno, nullo non credono." Giordano da Pisa, *Prediche*, MS Florence Biblioteca Nazionale xxxv, 222, 158v, 159v; the translation is in part from Murray, "Piety and Impiety," p. 101.

45. "Vedeano i buoni esse premuti e sostenere molte pene. Sike dixero che e questo non potrebe essere ke iddio fosse. Kome potrebbe sostenere tanti mali, e tante kose pessime? E ancora ogi si fa questa questione per li matti tutto die." Credo, 47r; Murray's translation, "Piety and Impiety," p. 102.

46. See Paolini and Orioli, *Acta Sancti Officii Bononie*, nos. 44, 46, 49–52, pp. 73, 76–77, 81–84; Paolini, *L'eresia catara*, pp. 147–49. Testimony survives from three monks of the house, a *confrater* from Cremona, the abbot, and a local canon. The monk Guidolino di Yvano, for example, testified that for the many years he had been in the monastery, "nunquam audivit nec vidit quod dictus dompnus Iacobus acciperet penitenciam vel communicaret, nec diceret missam, quamvis sit sacerdos . . . audivit ipse testis ab ipso dompno Iacobo quod ipse dompnus Iacobus comedit cum personis laicis in prandio et in cena splendide." Paolini and Orioli, *Acta Sancti Officii Bononie*, no. 46, pp. 76–77.

47. "Item dicit quod non vadit ad officium divinum, nec ad missas, nec ad oras alias, nec etiam dicit divinum officium per se nec cum aliis, cum tamen sit sacerdos, nec dicit missam." Ibid., no. 44, p. 74.

48. One of the witnesses stated that he had been banned for a homicide.

49. "Item audivit eum dicentem quod, si haberet potestatem, libenter inter-ficeret dominum papam Bonifacium et cardinales, quia ipse dominus papa Boni-facius fecerat interfici meliorem hominem qui esset in mundo, scilicet papam Celestinum, qui erat verus papa, et iste papa Bonifacius non erat papa de iure, licet esset de facto." Ibid., no. 44, p. 73.

50. "Item dicit quod audivit dictum dompnum Iacobum dicentem, postquam Bompetrus et Iulianus fuerunt condempnati et combusti, quod inquisitor et fra-tres fecerunt malum opus et magnum peccatum quia fecerant comburri bonos homines, quia dicti Bompetrus et Iulianus fuerunt boni homines et meliores quam essent inquisitor et fratres." Ibid., no. 44, p. 74.

51. "[D]ixit quod abbas non corrigit eum quia non audet, et si reprehendere-tur ab aliquo, qui dicat ei: 'Don Iacobe, non timetis vos pecatum, non habetis vos animam?'; ipse despicit et dicit quod persica habet animam." Ibid., no. 50, p. 82.

52. This differs with Paolini, who suggests it meant that only fish have souls; see p. 147.

53. "Item dicit quod audivit dictum dompnum Iacobum dicentem quod non erat alius infernus, nec alius paradixus, nisi mundus iste." Paolini and Orioli, *Acta Sancti Officii Bononie,* no. 44, p. 73.

54. "Item audivit ipse testis dictum dompnum Iacobum dicentem quod ille qui bene habet in hoc mundo bene habet in alio." Ibid., no. 46, p. 77.

55. "Item dicit quod audivit eum dicentem quod fecit miracula fiticia et falsa cum aqua vite circha velum beate Marie virginis, in civitate Barlette, et per istum modum seducebat personas et lucrabatur multam pecuniam." Ibid., no. 50, p. 82.

56. On the idea of popular rationalism see the discussion in Merlo, *Eretici e in-quisitori,* pp. 54–56. As he points out, Wakefield's attribution of currents of skepti-cism to marginal parts of the city and remote countryside is very much open to question. See Walter L. Wakefield, "Some Unorthodox Popular Ideas of the Thir-teenth Century," *Mediaevalia et Humanistica,* new series, 4 (1973), pp. 25–35.

57. Giudiziario, Busta II, fasc. 8, 95r. "Quod dictus Petrucius facere se in-firmum taliter quod appareret mori. Et eidem fecerunt dare penetentiam et Cor-pus Christi predicta occasione."

58. The tale of Ser Cepparello, a wicked man who made a false confession and came to be venerated as a saint, is told by Giovanni Boccaccio, *Decameron,* vol. 4, day I, story I.

59. For general accounts, see Jean-Claude Schmitt, *Medioevo superstitioso,* trans. Maria Garin (Rome-Bari, 1992); Richard Kieckhefer, *Magic in the Middle Ages* (Cambridge, 1989).

60. Palmeria went to Viterbo to a church consecrated that day by Gregory IX. When she tried to drink water a boy drew from a well, a woman (in her husband's account a prostitute) pushed before her and said, "Drink and a thou-

sand demons will enter your body." She miscarried and then suffered demonic possession. "Processus Canonizationis B. Ambrosii Massani" *Acta Sanctorum* 66 (10 November), col. 594 E–595C.

61. See Giudiziario Busta II, fasc. 8, 6r.

62. In the contemporary miracle at Offida, in southern Italy: a woman concerned that her husband was straying attempted to give him a potion containing ashes acquired by burning a consecrated Host. The Host, instead of burning, became bleeding flesh; she concealed it in the stables, where the animals venerated it. See Giuseppe Sergiacomi, *Il miracolo eucaristico di Offida* (Ascoli Piceno,1957).

63. Archivio di Stato di Bologna, Comune, Curia del Podestà, Accusationes 5a, Register I, 55v–56r.

64. Jean Duvernoy, ed., *Le Registre d'Inquisition de Jacques Fournier, èvêque de Pamiers (1318–1325)* (Toulouse, 1965), vol. I, pp. 151–59. (fols. 23b–24d). This edition contains some errors. See Emmanuel Le Roy Ladurie, *Montaillou; The Promised Land of Error*, trans. Barbara Bray (New York, 1978); Leonard Boyle, "Montaillou Revisited: Mentalité and Methodology," in *Pathways to Medieval Peasants*, ed. J. A. Raftis (Toronto, 1981), pp. 119–40; Wakefield, "Some Unorthodox Popular Ideas," pp. 25–35.

65. Duvernoy, *Registre d'Inquisition*, vol. I, pp. 263–67 (fols. 47d–49a).

66. Ibid., pp. 160–68. (fols. 24d–26d) This discussion parallels the debate by scholastic theologians

67. For a discussion of change in the actions of the priest celebrating Mass, see Jean-Claude Schmitt, *La raison des gestes* (Paris, 1990), pp. 330–55 .

68. For a general discussion, see Miri Rubin, *Corpus Christi: The Eucharist in Late Medieval Culture* (Cambridge, 1991).

69. "Nonne ego possum dicere ipsam lasagnam esse corpus Christi, ut presbiteri dicunt quando levant suas calesetas quando celebrant?" Francesca Lomastro Tognato, *L'eresia a Vicenza nel Duecento*, Fonti e studi di storia veneta, no. 12 (Vicenza, 1988), doc. 14, pp. 132–33. For a discussion of medieval lasagna, see Bruno Laurioux, "Des Lasagnes romaines aux vermicelles arabes: quelques réflexions sur les pâtes alimentaires au Moyen Age," in *Campagnes médiévales: Études offerts à Robert Fossier*, ed. Elisabeth Mornet (Paris, 1995), pp. 199–215.

70. "Quando vidistis hominem morientem redire ad nos, qui de victa alia portaverit nobis nova." Paolini and Orioli, *Acta Sancti Officii Bononie*, pt. 2, ed. Orioli, no. 573, pp. 323–26; no. 578, pp. 335–37.

71. Duvernoy, *Registre d'Inquisition*, vol. 2, pp. 118–27.(fols. 141d–143d).

72. "Non solvamus (carnalagia), set dabimus centum libras duobus hominibus qui interficiant dictum dominum episcopum!" Ibid., vol. 2, pp. 122 (fols. 142c, d).

73. Ibid., vol. I, pp. 533–36 (fols 113a–13d).

74. This phrase is from Sherry Reames, *The* Legenda aurea: *A Reexamination of Its Paradoxical History* (Madison, Wis., 1985).

75. See Ibid., ch. 6.

76. See Reames, *Legenda aurea*, p. 111.

77. "Saint Peter Martyr (April 29)," in *Jacobi a Voragine Legenda Aurea*, ed. Th. Graesse (3d ed. 1890; reprinted Osnabrück, 1965), ch. 61, no. 10, pp. 285–86; The translation is from Jacobus de Voragine, *The Golden Legend: Readings on the Saints*, trans. by William Granger Ryan (Princeton, 1993) vol. I, pp. 261–62. The tale of St. Mark's relics is p. 245.

78. "Saint Gregory (March 12)," in Graesse, *Jacobi a Voragine Legenda Aurea*, ch. 46, no. 11, pp. 197–98; Ryan, *Golden Legend*, pp. 179–80. On eucharistic miracles, see Rubin, *Corpus Christi*, ch. 2.

79. A witness testified that Cursio said "quod quicquid sacerdotes et eorum prelati et fratres predicatores et minores faciebant et opperabantur, fiebat ad detractionem et extorsionem peccuniarum hominium simplicum de mundo, qui dicuntur christiani et ad tenendum eos sub pedibus suis." Paolini and Orioli, *Acta Sancti Officii Bononie*, no. 89, p. 128; On Cursio, see Paolini, *L'eresia catara*, pp. 142–45. Paolini argues that the witnesses were other Florentine usurers out to destroy a business rival, implying that their evidence is not trustworthy. This theory seems to me possible but conjecture.

80. "[E]t audivit etiam a dicto Cursio asertive dicere pluribus vicibus et diversis temporibus, quod sacramentum quod publice dicitur corpus Christi, quod fit sub ostia, erat quedam subornatio sive delusio, et quod non erat credendum quod in manibus talium peccatorum posset corpus Christi consecrari." Paolini and Orioli, *Acta Sancti Officii Bononie*, no. 89, p. 128.

81. "Ob hoc etiam prevaricatores, qui dicebant illam speluncam latronum, redeuntes ad cor, ecclesie limina, ut videbatur, devotis mentibus visitabant." Vincenzo Natalini, ed., *San Pietro Parenzo. La Leggenda scritta dal Maestro Giovanni canonico di Orvieto* (Rome, 1936), section 21, p. 178–79.

82. "Hoc die, quo rector noster manibus occubuit impiorum, quedam mulier de castro Sermognani, Balneoregiensis diocesis, audita sinistra fama de morte martiris interfecti, qui amicum eius ereticum debita punierat, ultione, cepit non modicum exultare, flexisque genibus et elevatis manibus, cepit proferre contra martirem blasphemiam dicens: Benedictus Deus, quia mortuus est ille pessimus homo, qui multos iniuste homines affligebat. Expleto blasphemie sermone, statim oris in posteriori parte sustinuit tortionem, ut in eo, in quo deliquerat, puniretur." Ibid., section 17, pp. 174–75.

83. "Dum quidam castellanus de Lerona omnium horum esset incredulus et diceret martirem peccatorem fuisse nec aliquem cecum per se posse illuminari, continuo est cecitate percussus; nec ante oculorum lumen recepit, quam publice peccatum suum episcopo confiteretur, sed, uti ad martiris sepulcrum accessit et coram omnibus delictum suum fuit confessus episcopo, sine dilatione sanitatem suscepit. Item dum quidam nobilis de civitate Balneoregensi omnino ista non crederet, sed potius in derisum et contemptum martiris diceret: se quendam asi-

num cecum habere, illum se velle ad martiris sepulcrum adducere, ut in eo asino experiretur et martiris probaret potentiam, utrum posset cecum illuminare, et hic oculorum lumen amisit et tanto in oculis exurebatur incendio ac dolore, ut nullatenus in aliquo posset consistere, quiescere, nec aliquam quietem habere. Veniens autem ad sepulcrum quarto kalendas octobris et peccatum episcopo confitens, iurans etiam sic in veritate esse, ut diximus, statim oculorum incendium ac dolorem amisit, sed lumen non receperat in kalendis octobris, quando hec scriptura est condita." Ibid., section 30, pp. 188–89.

SIX SEXED BODIES, MARRIED BODIES, DEAD BODIES

1. See Arno Borst, *Die Katharer* (Stuttgart, 1953); French trans. *Les Cathares* (Paris, 1974), pp. 8, 101–2.

2. The critical edition is Edina Bozóky, ed., *Le livre secret des cathares: Interrogatio Iohnnis, Apocryphe d'origine bogomile* (Paris, 1980). The edition in Richard Reitzenstein, *Die Vorgeschicte der christlichen Taufe* (2nd. ed. Stuttgart, 1967), pp. 297–311, was translated by Walter L. Wakefield and Austin P. Evans, *Heresies of the High Middle Ages* (New York, 1969; reprint 1991), no. 56 B. The text, according to the Carcassonne version, was brought to Italy by the Concorezzan bishop Nazarius. See Borst, *Les Cathares*, p. 89; Anselm of Alexandria mentioned it c. 1260–70 in his "Tractatus de haereticis," edited by Antoine Dondaine in his "La Hièrarchie cathare en Italie, II," *Archivum Fratrum Praedicatorum* 19 (1949), p. 319; Wakefield and Evans, *Heresies*, p. 362.

3. "Et cogitavit facere hominem in servitio sibi et tulit limum de terra et fecit hominem similem sibi. Et praecepit angelo secundi celi introire in corpus luti et tulit de eo et fecit alium corpus in forma mulieris praecepitque angelo primi celi introire in illum. Angeli ploraverunt multum videntes super se formam mortalem esse in diversis formis." Bozóky, "Interrogatio Iohannis," p. 58; Wakefield and Evans, *Heresies*, p. 460.

4. "Praecipiebatque eis carnalia opera facere in corporibus luti, et illi nesciebant facere peccatum. Initiator autem peccati cum sua seductione ita fecit: plantavit paradisum et misit homines intus et praecepit eis, ne comederent ex eo. Diabolus intravit in paradisum et plantavit arundinem in medio paradisi et de sputo suo fecit serpentem et praecepit ei in arundine manere, et sic diabolus ascondebat sapientiam sue fraudis ut non viderent deceptionem suam. Et introibat ad eos dicens: De omni fructu comedite qui est in paradiso, de fructu iniquitatis ne comedatis. Postea malignus diabolus intrans in serpentem malum et decepit angelum qui erat in forma mulieris et effundit super caput eius concupiscentiam peccati; et fuit concupiscentia Evae sicut fornax ardens. Statimque diabolus exiens de arundine in forma serpentis fecit concupiscentiam suam cum Eva cum cauda serpentis. Ideo non vocantur filii dei sed *filii diaboli* et filii serpentis voluntates patris facientes diabolicas usque ad seculi finem. Postea dia-

bolus effundit suam concupiscentiam super caput angeli qui erat in Adam, et ambo inventi sunt in concupiscentia luxurie simul generando filios diaboli et serpentis usque ad consummationem seculi." Bozóky, ed., "Interrogatio Iohannis," pp. 58–62; Wakefield and Evans, *Heresies*, p. 460.

5. The text is a fascinating historical backdrop to contemporary debates about the relationship between gender, sexual difference and biology; one recent controversial text is Judith Butler, *Bodies That Matter: On the Discursive Limits of "Sex"* (New York and London, 1993).

6. See Caroline Bynum, *The Resurrection of the Body In Western Christianity, 200–1376* (New York, 1995).

7. See J. Van Oort, "Augustine on Sexual Concupiscence and Original Sin," in *Studia Patristica*, 22 (Leuven, 1989), pp. 382–86.

8. When the Concorezzans divided over the issue of materiality, the followers of Desiderius repudiated the *Interrogatio Iohannis*, believing that Christ and Mary were truly incarnate. Antoine Dondaine, ed., "La hiérarchie cathare en Italie, II, Le 'Tractatus de hereticis' d'Anselme d'Alexandrie, O.P.," *Archivum Fratrum Praedicatorum* 20 (1950), pp. 310–24; Wakefield and Evans, *Heresies*, doc. 54, pp. 361–73.

9. Christine Thouzellier, ed., *Un traité cathare inédit du début du XIIIe siècle d'après le 'Liber contra manicheos' de Durand de Huesca* (Louvain, 1961), pp. 65–66; 90–112.

10. This text is printed in appendix A.

11. "Disputatio inter catholicum et patarinum hereticum," in *Thesaurus novus anecdotorum*, ed. Edmund Martène and Ursin Durand (Paris, 1917) vol. 5, cols. 1710–14. Excerpts are translated in Wakefield and Evans, *Heresies*, no. 47, p. 295.

12. "Nos matrimonium non condemnamus, sed adulterium. Matrimonium est inter Christum et Ecclesiam . . . sed illud turpe negotium, quod homo facit cum muliere, quando ei carnaliter commiscetur, illud adulterium est quod nos prohibemus et Dominus prohibet."

13. See Dyan Elliott, *Spiritual Marriage: Sexual Abstinence in Medieval Wedlock* (Princeton, 1993), ch. 4.

14. See Penny S. Gold, "The Marriage of Mary and Joseph in the Twelfth-Century Ideology of Marriage," in *Sexual Practices and the Medieval Church*, ed. Vern Bullough and James Brundage (Buffalo and New York, 1982), pp. 102–17.

15. "[C]redunt corpus maris et foeminae a diabolo fuisse factum, et membrorum pudendorum distinctionem, unde omnem carnalem concubitum damnabilem dicunt." Thomas A. Ricchini, ed., *Monetae Cremonensis adversus Catharos et Valdenses libri quinque*, vol. I, *Descriptio fidei haereticorum* (Rome, 1743) book 2, pp. 1, 2; Wakefield and Evans, *Heresies*, no. 50, p. 315.

16. Ricchini, *Monetae*, p. 111; the translation is emended from Wakefield and Evans, *Heresies*, no. 50, p. 321.

17. See Odon Lottin, "Les théories sur le péché originel de Saint Anselme à Saint Thomas D'Aquin," in his *Psychologie et morale aux XIIe et XIIIe siècles* (Louvain, 1954), vol. 4, and Pierre Payer, *The Bridling of Desire: Views of Sex in the Later Middle Ages* (Toronto, 1993), ch. 2. See Marie-Christine Pouchelle, *The Body and Surgery in the Middle Ages*, trans. Rosemary Morris (Paris, 1983; Eng. trans. New Brunswick, N.J., 1990), ch.7.

18. For the view that Augustine was influenced by the Manichee understanding of matter as random motion, see Johannes van Oort, "Augustine and Mani on concupiscentia sexualis," in *Augustiana Traiectiana*, ed. Jan den Boeft and Johannes van Oort (Paris, 1987), pp. 137–52.

19. On this view in Augustine's *De Genesi contra Manichaeos*, see Payer, *The Bridling of Desire*, p. 43. See the discussion in Paul Agaesse and Armand de Solignac, *La Genèse au sens littéral en douze livres, Oeuvres de Saint Augustin*, Bibliothèque augustinienne, vol. 49 (Paris, 1972), notes, pp. 555–59. On concupiscence, see John Rist, *Augustine: Ancient Thought Baptised* (Cambridge, 1995), pp. 321–27.

20. See Payer, *The Bridling of Desire*, p. 43.

21. Thomas Tentler, *Sin and Confession on the Eve of the Reformation* (Princeton, 1977), pp. 166–68. See J. Roman, "Summa d'Huguccio sur le *Décret* de Gratien d'après le Manuscrit 3891 de la Bibliothèque Nationale. Causa 27, Questio 2 (Théories sur la formation du mariage)," *Revue historique de droit français et étranger*, ser. 2, 27 (1903): 745–805.

22. On the *Brevis summula*, see Célestin Douais, *La somme des autorités à l'usage des prédicateurs méridionaux au XIIIe siècle* (Paris, 1896); Charles Molinier, "Un Texte de Muratori concernant les sectes cathares: Sa provenance réelle et sa valeur," *Annales du Midi* vol. 22, (1910), 212–16. Wakefield and Evans *Heresies*, translated sections, no. 53, p. 351–61.

23. Wakefield and Evans, *Heresies*, p. 748 note 3.

24. "Albigenses dicunt quod Lucifer fuit filius mali dei et ascendit in coelum et invenit uxorem illius superni regis sine viro suo id est Deo et ibi tantum fecit quod jacuit cum ea, et ipsa primo defendente se dixit ei Lucifer, quod si filium procrearet, faceret eum Deum in regno suo et faceret eum adorari tanquam Deum, et sic acquievit ei, et inducunt illud Apoc.: Factum est regnum hujus mundi etc. et sic dicunt Christum natum et ipsum sic duxisse carnem de coelo, et illud est magnum secretum ipsorum. Volunt etiam dicere quod non fuit verus homo, sed angelus incarnatus et quod non fuit filius Beatae Mariae et sic non sumsit carnem ex ea et quod non comedit neque bibit corporaliter." Ign. von Döllinger, *Beiträge zur Sektengeschichte des Mittelalters* (Munich, 1890; reprint New York, 1960), pt. 2, pp. 612–13; see Dondaine, "La Hiérarchie cathare, I," p. 299 n. 38. The first part of this translation is from Wakefield and Evans, *Heresies*, p. 353; see p. 750 n. 23.

25. Archivio di Stato di Bologna, Curia del Podestà, Libri inquisitionum et testium, Busta III, 221r.

26. Jean Duvernoy, ed., *Le Registre d'Inquisition de Jacques Fournier, évêque de Pamiers (1318–1325)* (Toulouse, 1965), vol. 2, pp. 489–90, 94. The idea that a woman's spiritual advancement entailed that she become male appears in Gnostic teachings; see Elliott, *Spiritual Marriage*, pp. 25–27; the Gnostics also told the more conventional version of diabolic seduction, p. 492.

27. "Audivit etiam a dicto heretico quod quando aliquis cognoscebat carnaliter mulierem, fetor illius peccati ascendebat usque ad capam celi, et dictus fetor se extendebat per totum mundum." Duvernoy, *Registre d'Inquisition*, vol. 2, p. 500 (fol. 220b).

28. See Caroline Bynum, *Holy Feast and Holy Fast: The Religious Significance of Food to Medieval Women* (Berkeley, 1987).

29. Andreas's statement is ASF SMN 26 gennaio 1244; Tocco, no. 2, pp. 35–37.

30. "Item dixit quod commedere carnes est peccatum mortale" was crossed out and the following line inserted: "Item dixit quod Christus prohibuit commedere carnes [deletion: carnales]." "Carnales" was crossed out in favor of "carnes."

31. "Item dixit interrogatus quod non credit virum cum uxore sua in matrimonio [insertion: carnali] salvari possit."

32. See Pierre Bourdieu, *Outline of a Theory of Practice*, trans. Richard Nice (Cambridge, 1977); see Catherine Bell, *Ritual Theory, Ritual Practice* (Oxford, 1992).

33. "[P]er testes legittime probaverunt quod dictus dominus Marchus habuit uxorem, tempore domini Eccelini de Romano, et cum ea stetit in matrimonio donec vixerit, secundum mos ecclesie Romane et ex ea multos filios et filias habuit." Francesca Lomastro Tognato, *L'Eresia a Vicenza nel Duecento*, Fonti e studi di storia veneta, no. 12 (Vicenza, 1988), doc. 10, pp. 118–21.

34. Francesca Lomastro Tognato, *L'eresia a Vicenza*, p. 39n. "The Chronicle of William Pelhisson," trans. Walter L. Wakefield, in his *Heresy, Crusade and Inquisition in Southern France, 1100–1250* (Berkeley, 1974), p. 213. For the text, see C. Douais, *Les sources de l'histoire de l'inquisition dans le Midi de la France au XIIIe et XIVe siècles* (Paris, 1881), pp. 81–118.

35. For a general discussion of gender in heretical communities, see Shannon McSheffrey, *Gender and Heresy: Women and Men in Lollard Comunities* (Philadelphia, 1995), introduction. For an emphasis on the importance of understanding gender in terms of class rather than assuming that women in the thirteenth century were a unified category, see the recent work of Sharon Farmer, including "Matter Out of Place: *Elite Perceptions of Single Women in Thirteenth-Century Paris*," in *Single Women in the European Past*, ed. Judith Bennett, forthcoming.

36. Her post-mortem heresy conviction is Liber inquisitionis, 30v. She is condemned as a credens, who heard the preaching of the heretics, reverenced them, received them in her house, and gave them "auxilium et favorem;" she died

in error. Bonadimane was a widow at the time: her husband, described as the *suocero*, father-in-law, of Pietro Ferralloca, was dead when she testified in 1240. I learned of her testimony on behalf of Ambrose from Mary Henderson, "Medieval Orvieto: The Religious Life of the Laity, c. 1150–1350" (Ph.D. diss., University of Edinburgh, 1990).

37. Liber donationum, 17 verso; see Marilena Caponeri Rossi and Lucio Riccetti, eds., *Chiese e conventi degli ordini mendicanti in Umbria nei secoli: XIII–XIV, Inventario delle fonti archivistiche e catalogo delle informazione documentarie* (Perugia, 1987), p. xix.

38. The clearest example is the group comprising Benvegnate, Donnedellaltre, and Greca; Liber inquisitionis, 16r.

39. For lists of perfects, see Henderson, "Medieval Orvieto," pp. 220–22.

40. See Liber inquisitionis 19v, 8r, 10r, 31r, 26r. She is also mentioned in the sentences of the young trumpet player, Pietro di Guido Becci, 16r, and in that of Lord Jacopo Arnuldi, 19v.

41. Ibid., 24r.

42. "Probatur per dicta Biatricis filie olim Rugieri Sitii, Albensis que fuit de Senis et Contelde, que consolate fuerunt et ad fidem redierunt, contra dictum Renaldum, quod ipse receperunt consolationem in domo ipsius Ranaldi a Torsello episcopo et quod steterunt in ipsa domo. Item probatur contra ipsum per dominas nobiles et alias mulieres fide dingnas, quod viderunt in ipsa domo Torsellum et alios consolatos plures facere manuum impositionem. Item probatur contra ipsum per alias mulieres, que redierunt ad fidem et que fuerunt credentes, et per famulam quamdam ipsius domus quod viderunt plures hereticos in ipsa domo." ASF SMN 26 Aprile 1245, emended from Tocco, no. 13, pp. 48–50.

43. Her name is mentioned in her sons' condemnation, ASF SMN 11 agosto 1245; Tocco, no. 15, pp. 52–54.

44. "Item dixit quod antequam exiret de domo vendita Boldroni, vidit dominam Tedoram cum quadam Sanese qui claudebat oculos ad modum hominis dormientis et ventum eius exaltabat in altum et incipiebat loqui et predicabat et dixit quod ipsa dicebat quod Torsellus et Marcus et alii erant et stabant ad pedes maiestatis habentes vestes ex lapidibus preciosis ornatas." ASF SMN 1245; emended from Tocco, no. 11, p. 46.

45. Richard Abels and Ellen Harrison, "The Participation of Women in Languedocian Catharism," *Medieval Studies*, 41 (1979), pp. 215–51.

46. It was, of course, Herbert Grundmann who first pointed these similarities out in 1935: *Religious Movements in the Middle Ages*, trans. Steven Rowan (Notre Dame, Ind., 1996), especially ch. 4.

47. Vito of Cortona, "Vita de B. Aemiliana seu Umiliana," in *Acta Sanctorum* 27 (19 May), pp. 385–402. See Carol Lansing, *The Florentine Magnates: Lineage and Faction in a Medieval Commune* (Princeton, 1992), ch. 6. Anna Benvenuti Papi,

"Umiliana dei Cerchi. Nascita di un culto nella Firenze del Duecento," *Studi Francescani* 77 (1980), pp. 87–117.

48. "Et factum est, volente Deo, quod illo tempore mortua fuit mater mea quae erat mihi magnum impedimentum. Et postea mortuus est vir meus et omnes filii in brevi tempore. Et quia incoeperam viam predictam et rogaveram Deum quod morerentur, magnam consolationem inde habui, scilicet de morte eorum." *Il libro della Beata Angela da Foligno*, ed. Ludger Thier and Abele Calufetti (Rome, 1985), p. 138. On saintly laywomen and marriage, see Elliott, *Spiritual Marriage* ch. 5.

49. See Clara Gennaro, "Chiara d'Assisi, Agnese e le prime consorelle: dalle 'Pauperes Dominae' di S. Damiano alle Clarisse," in *Mistiche e devote nell'Italia tardo-domedievale*, ed. Daniel Bornstein and Roberto Rusconi (Naples, 1992), pp. 37–56.

50. Mario Sensi, "Incarcerate e recluse in Umbria nei secoli XIII e XIV: un bizzocaggio centro-italiano," in *Mistiche e devote, nell 'Italia tardomeidevale*, ed. Daniel Boornstein and Roberto Ruscani (Naples, 1992), pp. 57–84.

51. Anna Benvenuti Papi, "Frati mendicanti e pinzochere in Toscana: dalla marginalità sociale a modello di santità," in Bornstein and Rusconi, *Mistiche e devote*, pp. 85–106.

52. See Gabriel Le Bras, "La doctrine du mariage chez les théologiens et les canonistes depuis l'an mille," in *Dictionnaire de théologie catholique*, ed. A. Vacant et al. (1930–50), vol. 9, cols. 2196–2217. For a recent general history, see Christopher Brooke, *The Medieval Idea of Marriage* (Oxford, 1989).

53. On Bandinelli's view, Seamus P. Heaney, *The Development of the Sacramentality of Marriage from Anselm of Laon to Thomas Aquinas* (Washington, D.C., 1963), pp. 12–13. There is a large literature on the reformation of marriage, including the classic studies of Adhemar Esmein, *Le Mariage en droit canonique*, (Paris, 1891; reprint, New York, 1968), 2 vols.

54. See J. Roman, "Summa d'Huguccio," and the discussion in Elliott, *Spiritual Marriage*, p. 136; James Brundage, *Law, Sex and Christian Society in Medieval Europe* (Chicago, 1987).

55. See Charles Donahue, "The Policy of Alexander III's Consent Theory of Marriage," in *Proceedings of the Fourth International Congress of Canon Law*, ed. Stephan Kuttner, Monumenta Iuris Canonici, series C: Subsidia, vol. 5 (Vatican City, 1976), pp. 251–81. For an analysis of Gratian's formulation against the social background of contemporary cases involving forced marriage, see John T. Noonan, "Power to Choose," *Viator* 4 (1973), pp. 419–34.

56. See John T. Noonan, *Contraception* (Cambridge, Mass., 1965), ch. 6; Elliott, *Spiritual Marriage*, p. 134.

57. "Item communis opinio Catharorum est omnium quod matrimonium carnale fuit semper mortale peccatum, et quod non punietur quis gravius in futuro propter adulterium vel incestum, quam propter legitimum coniugium, nec etiam

inter eos propter hoc aliquis gravius puniretur." "Summa fratris Raynerii," ed. Antoine Dondaine, *Un Traité neo-manichéen du XIIIe siècle* (Rome, 1939), p. 64; Wakefield and Evans, *Heresies,* no. 51, p. 330.

58. "Ego autem frater Ranerius, olim heresiarcha, nunc Dei gratia sacerdos in ordine Praedicatorum licet indignus." Summa fratris Raynerii, p. 66.

59. "Non enim gravius punietur Iudas proditor quam infans diei unius, sed omnes erunt aequales tam in gloria quam in poena." Ibid.

60. James Capelli, "On the Cathars," *Heresies,* trans. Wakefield and Evans, p. 305. This text was edited by Dino Bazzochi, *La Eresia catara: Saggio storico filosofico con in appendice "Disputatione nonnullae adversus haereticos," codice inedito del secolo XIII della biblioteca Malatestiana di Cesena* (Bologna, 1919, 1920). Wakefield and Evans, *Heresies,* considered Bazzochi's edition flawed and collated it with the Cesena manuscript in translating the text: doc. 49, p. 301–6.

61. I differ with the view that Cathars were primarily motivated by the perfects' noninterference, or that Catharism was an easy religion in practice. See, for example, Malcolm Lambert, "The Motives of the Cathars: Some Reflections," in *Religious Motivation: Biographical and Sociological Problems for the Church Historian,* ed. Derek Baker, *Studies in Church History,* vol. 15 (Oxford, 1978), pp. 49–60.

62. Georges Duby, *The Knight, the Lady and the Priest: the Making of Modern Marriage in Medieval France,* trans. Barbara Bray (New York, 1983).

63. The letter appears in the Registers of Innocent III, *Patrologia cursus completus, Series Latina,* ed. Jacques-Paul Migne (Paris, 1844–1902), vol. 215, no. 28 (99), cols. 549–50.

64. The text is Archivio vescovile di Orvieto, cod. B, 87v, printed by Riccetti, "La cronaca di Ranerio vescovo di Orvieto 1228–1248, una prima recognizione," p. 497. Two lines were dropped from Riccetti's text; the last four lines should read:

Petrus Ildebrandini Rustici. Absolutus. Ranerius
Tabaldus Leonardi. Absolutus. Ranerius
presbiter Ranerius de Turre. Absolutus. Ranerius
Filie Tedore senensis. Absolute. Ranerius.

65. On the problem of proof of marriage, see the discussion in Esmein, *Le Mariage,* pt. 2, ch. 3 (vol. I, pp. 189–202). For comparable early cases from England, see Norma Adams and Charles Donahue, eds., *Select Cases from the Ecclesiastical Courts of the Province of Canterbury, c. 1200–1301,* Selden Society (London, 1981).

66. See Noonan, "Power to Choose."

67. The Cathar Ingilbertus mercator was identified in 1263 as Ingilberto Tignosi, and Tignosi was used by his sons as a surname: Johanucci Ingilberti Tiniosi.

68. See the discussion in Ilarino da Milano, "Il dualismo cataro in Umbria al tempo di San Francesco," *Filosofia e cultura in Umbria tra medioevo e rinascimento*, Atti del IV convegno di studi umbri (Perugia, 1967), pp. 194–96.

69. Benedicto was probably the Buonoditus Miscinelli in the 1226 Caleffo Vecchio list of Orvietans; Oderisio may have been the Riccus or Ricco Miscinelli. See *Il Caleffo vecchio del comune di Siena*, ed. Giovanni Cecchini (Siena, 1931), no. 233, pp. 331–36.

70. See Caroline Bynum, *Fragmentation and Redemption: Essays on Gender and the Human Body in Medieval Religion* (New York, 1991), p. 387 n. 125.

71. See Walter Wakefield, "Burial of Heretics in the Middle Ages," *Heresis* 5 (December 1985), pp. 29–32.

72. See Peter Brown, *The Cult of the Saints* (Chicago, 1981).

73. Lorenzo Paolini and Raniero Orioli, eds., *Acta Sancti Officii Bononie ab anno 1291 usque ad annum 1310*, Fonti per la storia d'Italia, vol. 106 (Rome, 1982), part I, no. 183, p. 176.

74. See Laura Andreani, "Un frammento di statuto del comune di Orvieto (1313–15). Note a margine," *Bollettino istituto storico artistico orvietano* 42 (1986–87), pp. 123–72. See also Lucio Riccetti, "Premessa," in *Il Duomo d'Orvieto*, ed. Lucio Riccetti (Rome, 1988), pp. viii–ix, for a text of 1392 describing the removal of corpses at night to make space for new ones.

75. "[A]lii, vitam suam male in suo finientes errore, feditam extra Ecclesie cimiterium aciperent sepulturam." Vincenzo Natalini, ed., *San Pietro Parenzo. La Leggenda Scritta dal Maestro Giovanni canonico di Orvieto* (Rome, 1936), section 2, p. 155.

76. "Alius autem, qui domino suo vulnus mortale intulerat, ad castrum quoddam confugiens, inflatus in proximo miseram animam exalavit. Cuius corpus, dum traditum esset ecclesiastice sepulture, ita inflando excrevit, ut vix posset in tumulo retineri, aerem pre nimio fetore inficiens; unde infirmitatis et mortalitatis pestis invaserat castellanos, irruente in illis partibus grandinis tempestate. Sed castellani, feditissimum effodientes cadaver, ipsum extra castrum in loco fedito tumularunt. Et sic, cessante causa, cessavit pariter quod urgebat." Ibid., section 12, p. 167.

77. "Nam cum rector noster . . . esset plagis maximis vulneratus et cadaver esset carnosum, in tumulo cultre coopertum velamine, nullum emittebat fetorem, sed odor ex eo quasi aromaticus emanabat. Unde stupebant omnes et multipliciter mirabantur, quod cum maximus esset calor nullum emittebat fetorem, sed calorem vivaciorem, quam dum viveret, continebat; nec palluit corpus, nec membra obriguerunt, vitali spiritu destituta." Ibid., section 13, p. 169.

78. "Nam presbiteri et milites digitos eius frequentissime contingebant et ita eos inveniebant plicabiles, quasi corpus vitalis spiritus et anima vegetarent." Ibid., section 13, p. 169.

79. "Quidam maligni spiritus, volentes hominum frequentiam a tumulo cohi-

bere, in quadam fenestra proxima carnem fetentem et marcidam proiecerunt, quod postmodum ab eo non extitit impunitum." Ibid., section 17, p. 175.

80. "Quidam etiam, rectoris nostri tunicam rapiens de sepulcro, lavit sanguinem ex eadem, prohiciendo ipsam in loco putredini deputato." Ibid., section 12, p. 167.

81. See, for example, Jean-Pierre Vernant, "La belle mort et le cadavre outragé," *La mort, les morts dans les sociétés anciennes,* ed. Gherardo Gnoli and Jean-Pierre Vernant (Cambridge, 1982), pp. 45–76.

82. "The Passion of Our Lord," Jacobus de Voragine, *The Golden Legend: Readings on the Saints,* trans. William Granger Ryan (Princeton, 1993) vol. I, p. 213. Jacobo added, "Thus far we have quoted the aforementioned aprocryphal history: let the reader judge whether the story is worth telling."

83. See the testimony of his fellow friars, especially Fra Morico, who himself became the center of a local cult: "Processus Canonizationis B. Ambrosii Massani," *Acta Sanctorum* 66 (10 November), 572E–75 B. On the cult, see Vauchez, *La sainteté,* pp. 584–87; A. I. Galletti, "I francescani e il culto dei santi nell'Italia centrale," *Atti del VII convegno,* Società internazionali studi Francescani (Assisi, 1981), pp. 313–63; Rossi and Riccetti, *Chiese e conventi,* pp. xxiii–iv. For a careful recent look at the context in which the cult appeared, including discussion of the papal decision not to canonize Ambrose as well as a complete bibliography, see Letizia Pellegrini, "Negotium Imperfectum: Il processo per la canonizzazione di Ambrogio da Massa (O.F.M., Orvieto 1240)," *Società e storia* 64 (1994), pp. 253–78.

84. The evidence was collected between 12 June 1240 and 16 February 1241.

85. The Franciscans first established themselves in Orvieto in the church of San Pietro in Vetere, probably in 1227. It is also possible that the *domus* was in fact the modest early church.

86. Testimony of Luca Tancredi Brance, his wife, domina Tedora, and his son Bartho, "Processus Canonizationis B. Ambrosii," in *Acta Sanctorum* 66 (10 November) 598B–E.

87. Ibid., 592E–F.

88. Testimony of "Domina Balseverina, filia Tedore Senensis," "Guidalocta, filia Tedore Senensis, mulier religiosa," and "Domina Balvina, soror predicte Guidolocte, mulier religiosa." Ibid., 594C–E.

89. Testimony of Domina Giugla, uxor domini Franki Zanponis, Ibid., 590D.

90. Testimony of Fredericus Pepi Prudentii, nepos domini episcopi Urbevetani, and of Domina Verdenovella, uxor Frederici, Ibid., 604D–E.

91. Testimony of "Ianni Ranuctii Zentii civis Urbevetanus, Domina Bona, uxor Zentii Ianni Ranuctii" and "Domina Adilascia, uxor Ianni," Ibid., 588C–F.

92. I. H. Sbaralea, *Bullarium Franciscanum,* vol. I (Rome 1759), p. 274.

93. "Annales Urbevetani," in Luigi Fumi, ed., *Ephemerides Urbevetanae*, vol. 15, pt. 5 of *Rerum Italicarum Scriptores*, ed. L. A. Muratori (Città di Castello, 1910) p. 150.

94. Marie-Christine Pouchelle, "Représentations du corps dans la *Légende dorée*," *Ethnologie francaise* 6: 3–4 (1976), pp. 293–308.

95. Orioli, *Acta Sancti Officii Bononie*, pt. 2, no. 572, pp. 320–22.

96. His sentence is Liber inquisitionis, 32v.

97. Liber Inquisitionis, 4r and 27v.

98. Her post-mortem heresy conviction is Liber inquisitionis, 30v. She is condemned as a credens, who heard the preaching of the heretics, reverenced them, received them in her house, and gave them "auxilium et favorem;" she died in error. Bonadimane was a widow at the time: her husband, described as the suocero of Pietro Ferralloca, was dead when she testified in 1240. I learned of her testimony on behalf of Ambrose from Henderson, "Medieval Orvieto."

99. The child was a nephew or grandson and—presumably, given his patronymics—related to her through the female line.

100. See Caroline Bynum, *Holy Feast and Holy Fast* (Berkeley, 1987).

101. P. Vincenzo Marredu, ed., *Leggenda della Beata Giovanna detta Vanna d'Orvieto del Terz' Ordine di San Domenico scritta dal Ven. P. Giacomo Scalza Orvietano de Predicatori*, (Orvieto, 1853).

SEVEN   INQUISITION, REPRESSION, AND TOLERATION

1. See Luigi Fumi, ed., "Cronaca di Luca di Domenico Manenti," in *Ephemerides Urbevetanae*, vol. 15, pt. 5 of *Rerum Italicarum Scriptores*, ed. L. A. Muratori (Città di Castello, 1910), p. 307, for the year 1262.

2. On the shift of power that facilitated the repression of heresy, see Raoul Manselli, "La fin du catharisme en Italie," *Cahiers de Fanjeaux* 20 (1985), pp. 101–18.

3. Istrumentari 868 (Galluzzo) 55r; CD, no. 363, p. 226.

4. Ibid., 53r; CD, no. 375, p. 232.

5. Ibid., 54v; CD, no. 361, p. 225. The funds were explicitly owed because of a loan, "ex causa mutui."

6. The structure is termed a *calcistructium*. The text raises the possibility that the lineage had the use of a shop that actually belonged to the commune: it is described as located "adjoining the piazza of the commune and adjoining the tower of the commune and adjoining the other shops of the commune" ("iuxta plateam comunis et iuxta turrim comunis et iuxta alias apothecas comunis"). The emphasis in the petition on their renunciation of any rights established by the construction of the structure reinforces this possibility. However, the Filippeschi

shop is explicitly called their shops—"eorum apothece" and "dicta sua apo-teca"—suggesting ownership.

7. Ibid., 56v; CD, no. 381, p. 237; Fumi's citation is an error.

8. See Daniel Waley, *Medieval Orvieto*, (Cambridge, 1952), pp. 43–49.

9. On Italian heresy inquisitions see Jean Guiraud, *Histoire de l'Inquisition au moyen âge*, vol. 2 (Paris, 1938), especially pp. 519–21 on Orvieto. For a critique of the assumptions shaping the literature on inquisitions, see Henry Ansgar Kelly, "Inquisition and the Prosecution of Heresy: Misconception and Abuses," *Church History* 58: 4 (December 1989), pp. 439–51. See Mariano d'Alatri, ed. *L'Inquisizi-one francescana nell'Italia centrale del Duecento* (Rome, 1996).

10. Agostino Turreni, in a 1965–66 laureate thesis, argued that the inquisi-tion was continuous from the time of Innocent IV's 1254 replacement of the Dominicans with Franciscans; it seems to me that there is not enough evidence to sustain this view. See Agostino Turreni, "La condizione giuridica degli eretici patarini in Orvieto," (laureate thesis, Università degli Studi di Perugia, Facoltà di Giurisprudenza, 1965–66).

11. Mary Henderson listed and categorized these actions, "Medieval Orvieto: The Religious Life of the Laity, c. 1150–1350" (Ph.D. diss., University of Edin-burgh, 1990), pp. 215–17.

12. Again, these encounters are listed in ibid., pp. 220–22.

13. Liber donationum, 90r.

14. "[M]anifesta confessa quod ad petitionem et preces Dyambre olim famule sue fecit venire duos patarenos ad domum suam pro consolatione dicte Dyambre tunc infirme qui heretici consolaverunt eam sub solario domus viri sui iuxta pravam hereticorum consuetudinem detestandam. Receptavit in domo sua Riccam patarenam per unam noctem et audivit monitiones ipsius ibidem et misit hereticis panem et vinum." Liber inquisitionis, 24r.

15. "Reservata semper Romane Ecclesie nobis et aliis Inquisitoribus pro-videndi de bonis predictis filiabus dicte domine Adalascie iuxtam nostram provisi-onem et penam." Liber inquisitionis, 12r.

16. Ibid., 19v.

17. Ibid., 4r and 27v.

18. "[A]d presentiam fratris Jordanis . . . personaliter accedens dolose con-fessus quod locutus fuit Stefano Narnensis heretico et sotio suo in Monte Mar-ano recepit ab eo consilium pro sua infirmitate ac etiam alias locutus fuit patar-enis morantibus in Castellonclo et dixit interrogatus quod nullo tempore fuit credens hereticorum erroribus." Ibid., 4r.

19. Elisabeth Carpentier, *Orvieto à la fin du XIIIe siècle: Ville et campagne dans le cadastre de 1292* (Paris, 1986), p. 286, n. 417.

20. Liber inquisitionis 32v. He appeared not of his own choice but because he was cited.

21. "[A]ctendentes quod honestati sanctissimi ordinis penitentium a beato Francisco patre nostro condi[to] derogatur infama eisdem si aliquis heretica labe respersus dictorum fratrum habitum sane portet et eorumdem privilegio gaudeat libertatis." Ibid., 32v.

22. ". . . xxv pauperes induat indigentes ita quod xl soldos valeant quolibet indumentum. Rome unam proximam faciat quarentana secuturus stationes per Romanos pontifices institutas, jejunet vi feria toto tempore vite sue et alia ieiunia servet per romanam ecclesiam instituta ita quod sextis feriis quadragesimarum maiorum nil cottum commedat preter panem, dicat inter diem et noctem cum ave maria quinquagies paternoster confiteatur ter in anno pro anima sua discreto confessori de ordine fratrum minorum quem sibi dixerit eligendum." Ibid., 32v.

23. Locto's sentence is Ibid., 32v. Henderson, "Medieval Orvieto," p. 95, argues that he, like Dominico, was a tertiary. But his penitential sentence may have been due to his voluntary confession: the text reads: "constet legitime ex propria confessione Locthi filii Surdi coram nobis sponte facta ab eodem." He also was sentenced to wear the cross, to fast once a week for his entire life, to keep the other fasts of the Roman Church, to say twenty-five Pater Nosters and Ave Marias a day, to attend divine services on Sundays (when the apostolic interdict is lifted[!]) and to confess every four months. Unlike the case of Domenico Petri Rosse, a Franciscan confessor was not specified, again suggesting Locto was not a tertiary. Petrutio Miscinelli was to wear the cross, travel at his own expense to aid the Holy Land within a year, clothe one-hundred paupers, after his return from the Holy Land perform two quarentenas, apparently 40 day penances, fast every sixth day for the rest of his life, keep the other fasts of the Roman Church, and say twenty-five Pater Nosters and Ave Marias a day. There is no indication of voluntary confession, and the rationale for the sentence is unstated. Liber inquisitionis, 29r.

24. The marginalia reads: "sententia Petri Guidi Becci et condemnatione eius de C libras. satisfactum est comuni." Ibid., 16r.

25. "Satisfactum est comuni." Ibid., 23v.

26. James Given, "The Inquisitors of Languedoc and the Medieval Technology of Power," *American Historical Review* 94: 2 (April 1989), pp. 336–61; these quotations are from pp. 360–61. See also his "A Medieval Inquisitor at Work: Bernard Gui, 3 March 1308 to 19 June 1323," in *Portraits of Medieval and Renaissance Living*, ed. Samuel Cohn and Steven Epstein (Ann Arbor, 1996), pp. 207–32.

27. For a more positive assessment of the applicability of this view in an Italian community, see Robert Brentano, *A New World in a Small Place: Church and Religion in the Diocese of Rieti, 1188–1378* (Berkeley, Los Angeles, and London, 1994), pp. 236–37.

28. The 1325 Carta del Popolo required the Seven to have twenty retainers, including a cook, a porter, and police. See CD, Carta del Popolo, no. 5, p. 742.

On the problems of police power and social control, see Andrea Zorzi, "Controle social, ordre public et répression judiciaire à Florence à l'époque communale: éléments et problèmes," *Annales E.S.C.* 45 (1990), pp. 1169–88, and the path-breaking article by William Bowsky, "The Medieval Commune and Internal Violence: Police Power and Public Safety in Siena, 1287–1355," *American Historical Review* 73 (1967), pp. 1–17

29. The extant copy of the sentence does not always explicity state that the person was absent, and I have not included those that are unclear on this count. In most cases, like that of Ranucetto Toste or Miscinello Ricci Miscinelli, they were almost certainly absent. When a person was present, the notary was careful to record it.

30. Ibid., 27v.

31. See Giudiziario Busta I, fasc. 3, 7r: "Peruccius Guidonis Bechi publicus banditor comunis stans super scallas palatii comunis Urbisveteris," dated 4 November 1272.

32. See also Giudiziario, Busta I, fasc. 13, 1r, fasc. 16, 1r; Registro I, 64v; the last mention I have seen is Busta II, fasc. 4, 8v, dated 1291. See the discussion in Henderson, "Medieval Orvieto," pp. 74–76.

33. Giudiziario, Busta I, fasc. 1 bis, 12v (3 May 1269).

34. Giudiziario, Busta I bis, 24r–v. The tax in question was the *libra*, used to assess the number of horses owed for the *cavalcata*, a levy of horses and riders for the civic militia. The heirs of Amideo had been expected to supply three horses. On the exgravator, see M. Caponeri Rossi, "Nota sulle fonti giudiziarie medioevali conservate presso la sezione di Archivio di Stato di Orvieto," *Bollettino istituto storico-artistico orvietano* 38 (1982), pp. 3–7.

35. Tocco, no. 25, pp. 73–78.

36. See Giudiziario, Busta I, fasc, 14, 1v for his fine for carrying a knife; Busta I, fasc. 15, 3v, for his absolution for theft. Registro I, 83r, records his fine for taking his hand off the "bancha."

37. Giudiziario, Registro I, 148v. The marginalia indicate that because she had demonstrated to the court that she had none of her son's property, the judge ordered that she not be burdened.

38. See Carpentier, 281 n.

39. Giudiziario, Registro I, 107v mentions an unpaid judicial fine by "Raynucceptus Cristofori Tosti de Ficulle."

40. This grandson was Lippo Ranucepti Toste: Riformagioni, 77, 160r.

41. Their 1292 catasto returns show very substantial property: Catasto 399, 3v–4r, 5v, 10r–v, 17v, 45r. Catasto 401, 22r–v, 25r, lists their property confiscated for Ghibellinism. See Elisabeth Carpentier, *Orvieto*, 281 n.

42. See *Les Registres de Boniface VIII: Recueil des bulles de ce pape*, ed. Georges Digard, Maurice Faucon, Antoine Thomas and Robert Fawtier, Bibliothèque des Écoles

Françaises d'Athènes et de Rome, 2nd series vol. 4 (Paris, 1904), vol. 4, no. 2740, cols. 216–17, Archivio del Duomo di Orvieto, Diplomatico, parchment 60a; both are printed by Henderson, "Medieval Orvieto," pp. 256–59.

43. Given's phrase "technologies of power" derives from Michel Foucault, who argued for the inseparability of power and knowledge.

44. See Antonio Oliver, *Tactica de propaganda y motivos literarios en las cartas antiheréticas de Inocencio III* (Rome, 1957), pt. 2. On the demonization of heretics and the idea that heresy is corrupting, see Grado Merlo, "Membra del diavolo': la demonizzazione degli eretici," reprinted in *Contro gli eretici* (Bologna, 1996), ch. 2.

45. "Receptaculum sordium que fuit latibulum perfidorum." See for example the sentence of Cristoforo Toste, Liber inquisitionis, 1v.

46. See, for example, ibid., 2r "tanquam canis ad vomitum reddiens"; 3v "a progenitoribus suis dampnati erroris tanquam virulenta progenies et genimina viperarum nephariam contrahens."

47. Robert I. Moore has shown, in *The Formation of a Persecuting Society* (Oxford, 1987), that a stereotypical account of heretics as dirty, sexually voracious, and so forth closely resembled the vicious contemporary stereotypes of lepers and Jews. I would argue that the emphasis on filth was a particularly apt way to respond to Catharism because it denied the reputation for purity that made the perfects so attractive.

48. "Filius patareni salati;" "latro e patareno." See Giudiziario Registro I, 120r, 323v, 370v, 472v.

49. Ibid., 79v mentions Peter the son of Cristofano, otherwise called Patarene: "Petrum Cristofani alius vocatur Patarenum." See Henderson, "Medieval Orvieto," p. 199. Was he a son of Cristoforo Toste? The only possible evidence I have seen is hardly conclusive: the catasto record of the holdings of Ranuccio Toste, Catasto 399, 21v, mentions property adjoining a "Petrus Cristofani," who may have been a Toste, perhaps his brother, and the person nicknamed as well. Ranuccio was surely the Ranuccio Cristofani Toste mentioned in the 1280–81 Istrumentari 878.

50. For a discussion of the appearance of the term *patarene* see Gabriele Zanella, *Itinerari eretical: Patari e catari tra Rimini e Verona*, Istituto storico italiano per il medio evo, Studi storici (Rome, 1986), p. 11. The term became a proper name in Vicenza: see Franceso Lomastro Tognato, *L'eresia a Vicenza nel Duecento*, Fonti e studi di storia veneta, no. 12 (Vicenza, 1988), pp. 20–21. On judicial insults see Daniel Lesnick, "Insults and Threats in Medieval Todi," *Journal of Medieval History* 17 (1991), pp. 71–89.

51. Moore in *Formation of a Persecuting Society* analyzes this process in a somewhat different way.

52. "[D]ictus frater Ioannes in tribus diebus fecit comburi et cremari in foro et plaza de Verona 51 ex melioribus inter masculos et feminas de Verona, quos ipsos condemnavit de haeretica pravitate." Parisii de Cereta, "Chronicon Ver-

onese," in *Rerum Italicarum Scriptores*, vol. 8 (Milano, 1726), col. 627. See Andrè Vauchez, "Une campagne de pacification en Lombardie en 1233. L'action politique des ordres mendiants d'après la réforme des statuts communaux et les accords de paix," *Mélanges d'archéologie et d'histoire* 78:2 (1966), pp. 503–48.

53. See Lorenzo Paolini, *L'eresia catara alla fine del duecento, in L, eresia a Bologna fra XIII e XIV secolo,* Istituto storico italiano per il medio evo, Studi storici, 93–96 (Rome, 1975), pp. 44–45; 135–36.

54. "Item bene scivit quod dictus inquisitor ivit personaliter ad domum dicte Rosaflore et ad examinandum eam de crimine heresis, et dictus inquisitor habebat eam sicud relapsam in heresim, et ad examinandum eciam Bonafiglam, neptem dictorum Bonigrini et Rosaflore, de dicto crimine. Iterum bene scivit quod dictus inquisitor fuit expulsus cum multo vituperio et multis cominationibus usque ad periculum mortis de dicta domo, ita quod non potuit perficere dictam examinationem." Lorenzo Paolini and Raniero Orioli, *Acta S. Officii Bononie ab anno 1291 usque ad annum 1310,* Fonti per la storia d'Italia, vol. 106 (Rome, 1982), part I, no. 15, pp. 37–39.

55. See Paolini, *L'eresia catara*, pp. 40–44; 9v etc. For the text of her will, see Paolini, "Bonagrino da Verona e sua moglie Rosafiore," in *Medioevo ereticale*, ed. Ovidio Capitani (Bologna, 1977), p. 227 n.

56. This action was in keeping with the papal decree that punished church burial of heretics; see "Liber Sextus," in *Corpus Iuris Canonici*, ed. Aemilius Friedberg (Graz, 1959) vol. 2, p. 40 n.

57. Paolini and Orioli, *Acta Sancti Officii Bononie*, no. 564, p. 299. See Paolini, *L'eresia catara*, pp. 40–44.

58. See Paolini and Orioli, *Acta Sancti Officii Bononie*, nos. 328, 329, 330, 333, 345. I do not think his angry and unreflective comment about not fearing God really implies atheism.

59. "[Q]uia in dicta sententia continebatur quod corpus dicte Roxeflore sive ossa deberent extumulari et conburi, dicta soror Agnex dixit quod erat malum opus illud quod faciebat inquisitor, et dicta Roxaflore fuerat bona mulier et de melioribus, que essent in contrata illa." Ibid., no. 122, p. 149; see no. 123, p. 150–51.

60. Her remark is odd in the notary's Latin translation: "Comedatus comedat illum sacerdotem," literally, "having been eaten up, let him eat up that priest."

61. A young noble testified that he heard "Francescum Pasqualis de Agubio notarium . . . dicentem cum clamore, quod inquisitor qui condempnaverat eos et fratres magis essent digni conburi, quam ipsi Bonpetrus et Iulianus et quod bonum esset ire ad domum fratrum et ponere ignem in domo et conburere inquisitorem et fratres et facere sicud factum fuit Parme." Ibid., no. 150, p. 164. It is not clear whether the notary's statement was on the day of the sentence or the following day, the day of the execution.

62. See Giuliano Bonazzi, ed., *Chronicon Parmense*, in *Rerum Italicarum Scriptores*, ed. Ludovico Antonio Muratori, vol. 9: 9 (Città di Castello, 1902), p. 35.

63. "[L]acrimatus fuit ex conpassione" Paolini and Orioli, *Acta Sancti Officii Bononie*, no. 147, pp. 162–63. Vallariano was accused of arguing, in the presence of Bompietro and Giuliano and the populace, that the inquisitor had committed a sin because Bompietro asked for the sacrament, but was denied it. He paid a fine of one hundred libre in Bolognese currency.

64. The exact curses and blasphemy, unfortunately, are not recorded: for example, Belda, daughter of Roland the well-cleaner, "Dixit suo sacramento dixisse quod magnum pecatum erat id quod fiebat de Bompetro patareno, iudicato ad mortem, et quod maledixit fratribus." Ibid., no. 223, p. 187.

65. "Domina Garsendina, uxor Martini . . . dixit . . . quod posset esse quod societates irent ad domum fratrum." Ibid., no. 300, p. 212.

66. See Paolini, *L'eresia catara*, pp. 29–32. He suggests that the fact that so many people voluntarily confessed suggests the threat of excommunication, p. 67. He discusses popular accusations against the inquisitors, pp. 63–79. He suggests that about 337 people were accused or accused themselves of a part in the riot, p. 66.

67. See Paolini and Orioli, *Acta Sancti Officii Bononie* part I, nos. 132, p. 155; 139–40, pp. 158–59; 273, pp. 204–5; 328, pp. 219–20.

68. "Michael condam Santi . . . calzolarius . . . dixit quod ipse Bompetrus erat bonus homo et fuerat bonus vicinus." Ibid., no. 221, p. 186.

69. "Que truffe sunt iste?" Ibid., no. 272, p. 204.

70. "Diana magistri Gerabelli . . . dixit suo sacramento quando ossa quondam Rosaflore fuerunt conbusta: 'Quid prodest facere derisionem de ossis?'" Ibid., no. 235, p. 192. Both women lived in Sancta Maria de Mascharella.

71. See ibid., no. 325, p. 217.

72. "Soror Luchexia, filia Luchixini . . . dixit 'Quid est comburere ossa, ex quo persone mortue sunt?'" Ibid., no. 323, p. 217.

73. "Soror Agnexia, que moratur cum domina Iacobina de Broilo . . . dixit suo sacramento quod nichil ascendebat conburere ossa, quando fuerunt conbusta ossa Roxaflore." Ibid., no. 315, p. 215.

74. "Domina Diana filia condam Domini Alberti de Schalamis . . . dixit de ossis condam Rosaflore quod malum erat et melius fuisset comburere vivos quam mortuos." Ibid., no. 239, p. 193.

75. Ibid., no 206, p. 162.

76. Paolini prints the text of the bull, *L'eresia catara*, p. 32 n.

77. *Acta Sancti Officii Bononie*, no. 197, p. 180.

78. See Ibid., no. 316, p. 215.

79. Ibid., no. 238, p. 193.

80. "[D]ixit quod fratres erant plus heretici quam ipse Bompetrus, et quod

Christus hostendebat miracula pro eo, quia non fuit illa die iudicatus, et dixit quod doluit de sacerdote Sancti Thome, qui condempnatus fuit." Ibid., no. 238, p. 193.

81. On his status, see Paolini, *L'eresia catara*, p. 56. He was matriculated in the cordwainers' guild, probably not because he actually was involved in the trade but, like Dante in Florence, because it qualified him for civic office. Still, his membership in a leatherworkers' guild suggests he surely knew the executed men.

82. This version is taken from the testimony of an inquisitorial nuncio, Nascimbene Adelardi of Bologna. He testified: "quod cum ipse frater Guido inquisitor faceret legi et publicari sententias suas latas contra Bompetrum et Iulianum bursarios, condemnatos de crimine heresis et relictos iuditio seculari . . . in ecclesia Sancti Martini de Aposa, quando missa maior dicebatur, post evangelium, coram populo, dominus Paulus Trintinellus, cappelle Sancti Martini predicti, detrasit dictis sententiis ipsius inquisitoris . . . dicendo quod illud quod fiebat et factum erat de predictis Iuliano et Bompetro erat malum opus et quod inquisitor poterat facere scribi illa quod volebat, et quod ipse non daret de illis scripturis unam fabam. Et dominus Pax de Saliceto, qui erat presens, dixit dicto domino Paulo Trintinello: 'Vos male dicitis et estis excomunicatus propter verba que dicitis' et dictus dominus Paulus respondit: 'Inquisitor non potest excommunicare, nec credo quod excommunicatio eius valeat aliquid.' Et dicebat quod dictus Bompetrus fuerat bonus homo et quod iniuste erat condempnatus et quod magnum peccatum erat factum de eo, et magnum peccatum erat exheredare filios dicti Bompetri et destruere familiam suam. Iterum dicebat quod illi fratres de Carmelo, qui morantur in dicto loco Sancti Martini, fuerant viles et miseri, quia dictus Bompetrus dabat eis vinum pro sacrificio et ipsi non deffenderunt eum nec excusaverunt eum, nec iuverunt ipsum Bompetrum." *Acta Sancti Officii Bononie*, no. 22, p. 49; see also no. 21, pp. 47–48.

83. Messer Paolo when questioned by Fra Guido initially denied all; see Ibid., no. 179, pp. 174–75. He was condemned for aiding and defending heretics and threatened with excommunication, but the sentence was mitigated to a fine of 200 libre and penance. He was, among other things, required to beg mercy from the inquisitor on his knees. His sentence is no. 569, pp. 312–14; see also no. 45, p. 75–76.

EIGHT   CORPUS DOMINI AND THE CREATION OF ADAM AND EVE

1. Emile Durkheim, *The Elementary Forms of the Religious Life*, (originally published 1913; trans. Joseph Ward Swain, New York, 1965), p. 356.

2. On Urban's visit, see Luigi Fumi, ed., "Cronaca di Luca di Domenico Manenti," in *Ephemerides Urbevetanae*, vol. 15, pt. 5 of *Rerum Italicarum Scriptores*, ed.

L. A. Muratori (Città di Castello, 1910), p. 307. Urban IV was in residence 1262–64; Clement IV in 1266; Gregory X in 1272 and 1273; Martin IV from 1281–84; Nicholas IV in 1290 and 1291. The most evocative account of the papal curia in the period, see Robert Brentano, *Two Churches: England and Italy in the Thirteenth Century* (Berkeley, 1968; rev. ed. 1988). See Agostino Paravicini Bagliani, *La cour des papes au XIII siècle* (Paris, 1995).

3. On the travels of the curia, see Agostino Paravicini Bagliani, "La mobilità della Curia romana nel secolo XIII. Riflessi locali," in *Società e istituzioni dell'Italia comunale. L'esempio di Perugia (secoli XII–XIV)* (Perugia, 1988), pp. 155–278. He calculates that the curia spent a total of seven years and nine and a half months in Orvieto in the thirteenth century.

4. See Daniel Waley, *Medieval Orvieto* (Cambridge, 1952), p. 48.

5. For the rents, see Michele Maccarone, "Orvieto e la predicazione della crociata," in *Studi sul Innocenzo III*, (Padua, 1972) and Paravicini Bagliani, *La cour*, pp. 61–66. For the luxury trades, see Elisabeth Carpentier, *Orvieto à la fin du XIIIe siècle: Ville et campagne dans le cadastre de 1292* (Paris, 1986), ch. 3, pt. 2.

6. Martin IV was elected podestà in 1284, but refused the office; Nicholas IV held both offices in 1290–91. See Waley, *Medieval Orvieto*, pp. 48, 59. Boniface VII was elected Capitano del popolo in 1297 and 1301; see Riformagioni, vol. 72, 18v–20r, 76r. On Italian civic religion and the rise of local cults supported by the town government, see André Vauchez, *Les laics au moyen âge: Pratiques et expériences religieuses* (Paris, 1987), ch. 15.

7. On the Orsini, see Sandro Carocci, *Baroni di Roma: Dominazioni signorii e lignaggi aristocratici nel duecento e nel primo trecento* (Rome, 1993), (Collection de l'École française de Rome, no. 181), pp. 387–403.

8. The March 1298 council vote is Riformagioni, vol. 71, 15v–19v, dated 28–29 March 1298. See Marilena Caponeri Rossi, "Il Duomo e l'attività edilizia dei Signori Sette (1295–1313)," *Il Duomo di Orvieto*, ed. by Lucio Riccetti (Rome, 1988), 29–80. On the papal palace, see Luigi Fumi, *Il palazzo Soliano o de' papi* (Rome, 1896).

9. See Riformagioni, vol. 70; references to these preparations appear between 22r and 51v. Daniel Waley, "Pope Boniface VIII and the Commune of Orvieto," *Transactions of the Royal Historical Society* 4: 32 (1950), pp. 121–39.

10. Giudiziario Busta I, fasc. 6, 7v.

11. Margaret Aston argues that the feast was intended to counter heresy and explores the significance of the timing of the English Peasants' Revolt on the feast day; "Corpus Christi and Corpus Regni: Heresy and the Peasants' Revolt," *Past and Present* 143 (May 1994), pp. 3–47. On the development of imagery of the Last Supper and the Eucharist, see Dominique Rigaux, *À la table du Seigneur: L'Eucharistie chez les Primitifs italiens 1250–1497* (Paris, 1989).

12. Miri Rubin, *Corpus Christi: The Eucharist in Late Medieval Culture* (Cambridge, 1991), pp. 54–59.

13. Jean-Claude Schmitt, *La raison des gestes* (Paris 1990); on the Mass, pp. 330–355.

14. See Rubin, *Corpus Christi*, ch. 3.

15. Waley, *Medieval Orvieto*, p. 45; see *Les Registres d'Urbain IV*, ed. Jean Guiraud (Paris 1897–1958), vol. 2, nos. 853–60. Waley cites a papal letter in Edmund Martène and Ursin Durand, *Thesaurus Novus Anecdotorum*, vol. 2, 82–86.

16. Eugene Mangenot, "Hugues de Saint-Cher," in *Dictionnaire de théologie catholique*, ed. Andre Vacant, vol. 7, pt. I, col. 226.

17. The worst threat had passed with the death in mid-July of Manfred's vicar-general and the flight of his army. See Waley, *The Papal State in the Thirteenth Century* (London, 1961), pp. 172–73, and *Les Registres d'Urbain IV*, ed. Jean Guiraud, vol. 2, no. 858.

18. For examinations of the evidence see Andrea Lazzarini, *Il miracolo di Bolsena. Testimonianze e documenti dei secoli XIII e XIV* (Rome, 1952) and F. Buchicchio, "La 'storia del miracolo di Bolsena' e le sue vicende," *Bolletino istituto storico-artistico orvietano* 29 (1973), pp. 3–45. See *Eucaristia: Il mistero dell'altare nel pensiero e nella vita della Chiesa*, ed. Antoine Piolanti (Rome, 1957).

19. "Detto anno in la chiesa di Santa Christina de Bolsena apparvi il miraculo del Corpus Domini et portato in Orvieto per il vescovo de la ciptà con sollenne cirimonia posato in Santa Maria Prisca, come al presenti si vede." *Ephemerides Urbevetanae*, pp. 308–9.

20. Jaroslav Polc, "Il miracolo di Bolsena e Pietro di Praga: Un'ipotesi," *Rivista di storia della chiesa in Italia* 45: 2 (1991), pp. 437–49.

21. "[E]t scias quod nos huiusmodi festum cum omnibus fratribus, Romane videlicet Ecclesie cardinalibus, nec non cum omnibus archiepiscopis, episcopis, ceterisque ecclesiarum prelatis tunc apud sedem apostolicam commorantibus, ad hoc ut videntibus et audientibus de tanti festi celebritate salubre preberetur exemplum, duximus celebrandum." Quoted by Buchicchio, "La 'storia del miracolo di Bolsena,' " p. 33 n.

22. There is a precise discussion of Aquinas's role in the curia and the Dominican convent in Orvieto, in James A. Weisheipl, *Friar Thomas d'Aquino: His Life, Thought and Works* (Washington, D.C., 1974), pp. 147–63.

23. There is an extensive discussion in the proceedings of a conference held at Orvieto in 1964 on the bull that established the feast: *Studi eucaristici*, Atti della settimana internazionale di alti studi teologici e storici, Orvieto, 21–26 settembre 1964 (Torino, 1966); see especially Angelus Walz, "La presenza di San Tommaso a Orvieto e l'ufficiatura del Corpus Domini," pp. 321–55. For a summary of the debate, see Pierre-Marie Gy, "L'Office du Corpus Christi et S. Thomas d'Aquin:

état d'une recherche," *Revue des sciences philosophiques et théologiques* 64 (1980), pp. 491–507.

24. Pierre-Marie Gy, "L'Office du Corpus Christi et la théologie des accidents eucharistiques, *Revue des sciences philosophiques et théologiques* 66 (1982), pp. 81–86.

25. See Louis-Jacques Bataillon, "Le Sermon inédit de Saint Thomas 'Homo quidam fecit cenam magnam,' introduction et édition," *Revue des sciences philosophiques et théologiques* 67 (1983), pp. 353–69.

26. Buchicchio in "La 'storia de miracolo di Bolsena'" argues that it was copied from a version recorded by ser Cecco di Pietro in 1362.

27. Andrea Lazzarini, "La data originaria della sacra rappresentazione dl miracolo di Bolsena," *Bolletino istituto storico-artistico orvietano* 6 (1950), pp. 1–5. See A. Giannoti, "Forme drammatiche nell'Orvieto medievale" (laureate thesis, Università di Roma, 1983–84).

28. The text is Vincenzo de Bartholomaeis, ed., *Laude drammatiche e rappresentazioni sacre* (Florence, 1943), vol. I, pp. 368–81. On the procession's route see Riccetti, *La città costruita: Lavori pubblici e immagine in Orvieto medievale* (Florence, 1992), pp. 176–78.

29. There is an extensive literature on ritual processions in late medieval Italy, most importantly Edward Muir, *Civic Ritual in Renaissance Venice* (Princeton, 1981) and Richard Trexler, *Public Life in Renaissance Florence* (New York, 1980).

30. On the Orvietan courts and cases of sexual morality, see Carol Lansing, "Gender, Adultery and Authority: Sexual Regulation in a Medieval Italian Town," *Journal of Social History* forthcoming (Sept. 1997).

31. Pucius de Montefalco . . . maledisserat deum et sanctos suos et ecclesia romana." Giudiziario, Busta I, fasc. 15.

32. See Sarah Blanshei, "Criminal Law and Politics in Medieval Bologna," *Criminal Justice History*, p. 19, n. 9.

33. Giusdiziario, Registro I, 165r, 117r.

34. She is termed a "paupercula mulier Rosa olim de Bisenzio." Giudiziario, Exgravator II, 4v. An exgravator was active in Orvieto in March of 1260: see Diplomatico A63 (9 March 1260).

35. Her lack of identification by neighborhood, patronymic, or even matronymic suggests a person of very low status, perhaps a vagrant.

36. See Giudiziario Registro I, 382v.

37. Ibid., 297r.

38. Giudiziario, Busta II, fasc. 9, 15v; 73r records the conviction of Cola, nicknamed Rotanello. For further examples of blasphemy fines, see Guidiziario, Registro I, 15r, 231r, 275r (a Lombard), 330v, 358r, 362v–63r.

39. On the courts' treatment of marginals in Bologna, see Blanshei, "Criminal Law," especially p. 6.

40. Riformagioni, vol. 69 (1295), 139r.

41. The phrase derives from a petition of the capitano del popolo, that "Bernardus Staiulis . . . detinetur in carcere dicti comuni . . . placeat vobis [dominis septem consulibus . . . civitatis Urbisveteris] ipsum intuitu domini nostri Ieshu Christi et beatissime gloriose assumptionis Sancte Marie virginis in ipso festo ipsum Bernardum exhibere et donare et offere ecclesie nove dicte gloriose virginis Sancte Marie, ut ipsa conservet populum et comunem Urbevetanum." The full text is printed by Marilena Caponeri Rossi, "Il Duomo e l'attività edilizia dei Signori Settle (1295–1313)" in Riccetti, Il Duomo, appendix, no. 22, pp. 58–59.

42. Caponeri, appendix, no. 13, pp. 54–55.

43. For a recent survey of the evidence concerning medieval Orvietan confraternities, see the thesis of Mary Henderson, "Medieval Orvieto: The Religious Life of the Laity, 1150–1350" (Ph. D. dissertation, University of Edinburgh, 1990), pt. B.

44. CD, no. 354, p. 222.

45. Henderson found that the fraternity's inventory, Codice Vittorio Emanuele 528, f, 1r, refers to a list of those who had died or left the group. See Henderson, "Medieval Orvieto," p. 312 and 337 n. 1. The codex has been published, but without a matriculation list or a later necrology: "Sacre Rappresentazioni per le Fraternitate d'Orvieto nel Cod. Vittorio Emanuele 528," in Bollettino della (regia) Deputazione di Storia patria per l'Umbria, appendix 5 (Perugia, 1916). On death confraternities, see James Banker, Death in the Community: Memorialization and Confraternities in an Italian Commune in the Late Middle Ages (Athens, Ga., and London, 1988).

46. Michael D. Taylor, "The Prophetic Scenes in the Tree of Jesse at Orvieto," Art Bulletin 54 (1972), pp. 403–17; see also his "A Historiated Tree of Jesse," Dumbarton Oaks Papers 34–35 (1980–81), pp. 125–76.

47. See John White, "The Reliefs of the Facade of the Cathedral of Orvieto," Journal of the Warburg and Courtauld Institutes 2 (1959), pp. 254–302.

48. David Gillerman, "The Evolution of the Design of Orvieto Cathedral, ca. 1290–1310," Journal of the Society of Architectural Historians 53 (September 1994), pp. 300–321.

49. Photographs of the sketches are generally too faint to make this clear, but see the line drawings based on the sketches in Luigi Fumi, Il Duomo di Orvieto e i suoi restauri (Rome, 1891).

50. The Latin is "ad instar;" Luigi Fumi, Statuti e Regesti dell'Opera di Santa Maria di Orvieto (Rome, 1891), p. 86; see Julian Gardner, "Pope Nicholas IV and the decoration of Santa Maria Maggiore," Zeitschrift für Kunstgeschichte 36 (1973), pp. 1–50. As Gardner points out, this statement referred originally to the plan of the church, but was perhaps later extended to the iconography, most significantly the Coronation of the Virgin on the facade.

51. John Pope-Hennessey, *Italian Gothic Sculpture*, 3d. ed. (New York, 1985), p. 20. Pope-Hennessey attributes only the reliefs on the two outer piers to Maitani: they were carved in a style closely associated with that of the bronze statues on the facade that are known to be Maitani's work.

52. On Genesis iconography, Edward B. Garrison argued for an Umbro-Roman group in which (among other characteristics) the scene of the Creation of Adam and Eve includes the Creator seated to the left on the globe. The group dates from the eleventh and twelfth century but the iconography persisted, with few changes, in late thirteenth-century frescoes, including the upper church of San Francesco at Assisi; see Edward B. Garrison, "Note on the Iconography of Creation and of the Fall of Man in Eleventh- and Twelfth-Century Rome," in *Studies in the History of Mediaeval Italian Painting*, by Edward B. Garrison, vol. 4 (Florence, 1960), pp. 201–10.

53. Roberto Salvini, *Il Duomo di Modena* (Modena/Milan, 1972), pp. 118–19 and plates 6 and 7.

54. They are illustrated in *Andrea, Nino e Tommaso scultori pisani*, ed. Mariagiulia Burresi (Milan, 1983), p. 57.

55. See the brief discussion of the handling of trees and drapery in Anita Moskowitz, "Studies in the Sculpture of Andrea Pisano: Origins and Development of His Style," (Ph.D. diss., New York University 1978), pp. 136–37.

56. Marvin Trachtenberg, *The Campanile of Florence Cathedral: "Giotto's Tower"* (New York, 1971), pp. 91–96.

57. The figures of Adam, while more linear, recall the heroic male nude of Strength carved by Nicola Pisano for the baptistry pulpit in Pisa, completed in 1259; see Pope-Hennessey, *Italian Gothic Sculpture*, p. 3.

58. See Olga Raggio, "The Myth of Prometheus," *Journal of the Warburg and Courtauld Institutes* 21 (1958), 44–62. I owe both the insight and the reference to Patricia Simons.

59. See Caroline Bynum, *Jesus as Mother* (Berkeley, 1982), especially pt. 4.

60. Giudiziario Busta II, fasc. 9, 21v–23r. See Riccetti, *La città costruita*, pp. 198–99.

61. Riformagioni, vol. 70, 3r, dated 1297.

62. The most important study is Charles Trinkaus, *In Our Image and Likeness: Humanity and Divinity in Italian Humanist Thought* (Chicago, 1970).

Works Cited

MANUSCRIPT SOURCES

Archivio di Stato di Orvieto

Archivio Notarile
    Registers I/1–I/5: Angelo di Pietro Grazia (1296–1340).
Diplomatico
Statuti civici
Riformagioni
    69 (1295)   74 (1303)
    70 (1297)   75 (1306–7)
    71 (1298–1301) 76 (1307–9)
    72 (1300–4)   81 (1294–1331)
    73 (1303–4)
Istrumentari
    865: Titolario A (1190–1249)   869: Titolario B (1248–95)
    866: Codice Caffarello (1170–1250) 870: Codice Savello (1203–85)
    867: Codice Catalano (1171–1257) 871: Codice de Bustolis
    868: Codice Galluzzo (1171–1265)   (1168–1285)

Catasti
  399: 1292 catasto (city)
  400: 1292 catasto (contado)
  401: 1313 communal property acquired from rebels
Insinuazioni delle Donazione
  Liber donationum I (34 fascicles, 1202–1329)
Giudiziario

Busta I: 17 fascicles (1266–1287)	Busta III: 7 fascicles (1306–1320)
Busta Ibis: Exgravator (1269)	Busta V: in disorder (1271–1565)
Busta II: 10 fascicles (1270–1298)	Registro I: c.807 pages (1286–1289, with documents of 1278)

Liber Inquisitionis

Archivio Vescovile di Orvieto

Codice A: c. 255 pages (1257–1331)
Codice B: c. 208 pages (1024–1388)
Codice C: c. 194 pages (1250–1378)

Archivio dell'Opera del Duomo di Orvieto

Diplomatico (1221–1784)

Archivio di Stato di Firenze

Diplomatico

Archivio di Stato di Siena

Caleffo vecchio
Diplomatico, Riformagioni

Archivio di Stato di Bologna

Comune, Curia del Podestà

Biblioteca Nazionale di Firenze

Manoscritti xxxv, 222 (Giordano of Pisa, Prediche)

PUBLISHED SOURCES

Primary Sources

Angela of Foligno. *Il libro della Beata Angela da Foligno.* Ed. Ludger Thier and Abele Calufetti. Spicilegium Bonaventurianum, 25. Grottaferrata: Editiones Collegii S. Bonaventurae ad Aquas Claras, 1985.

Adams, Norma and Charles Donahue. *Select Cases from the Ecclesiastical Courts of the Province of Canterbury, c. 1200–1301.* London: Selden Society, 1981.

Andreani, Laura. "Un frammento di statuto del comune di Orvieto (1313–1315). Note a margine." *Bollettino istituto storico-artistico orvietano* 42 (1986–87): 123–72.

Augustine of Hippo. *La Genèse au sens littéral en douze livres.* Ed. Paul Agaesse and Aime Solignac. Bibliothèque augustinienne. Vol. 49. Paris: Declèe de Brouwer, 1972.

Bartholomaeis, Vincenzo de. *Laude drammatiche e rappresentazioni sacre.* Florence: F. Le Monnier, 1943.

Bazzochi, Dino. *La eresia catara: saggio storico filosofico con in appendice 'Disputationes nonnullae adversus haereticos.' Codice inedito del secolo XIII della Biblioteca Malatestiana di Cesena.* Bologna: 1919–20.

Boccaccio, Giovanni. *Decameron. Tutte le opere di Giovanni Boccaccio.* Ed. Vittore Branca. Vol. 4. Milan: A. Mondadori, 1976.

Bozòky, Edina, ed. *Le livre secret des cathares: Interrogatio Iohnnis. Apocryphe d'origine bogomile.* Paris: Beauchesne, 1980.

Cecchini, Giovanni, ed. *Il Caleffo vecchio del comune di Siena.* Siena: Archivio di Stato di Siena, 1931.

Digard, Georges, Maurice Faucon, Antoine Thomas, and Robert Fawtier, eds. *Les Registres de Boniface VIII: recueil des bulles de ce pape publiées ou analysées d'après les manuscrits originaux des archives du Vatican.* 5 vols. Bibliothèque des Écoles françaises d'Athènes et de Rome, 2nd ser. 2, vol. 4. Paris: E. De Boccard, 1904.

Dondaine, Antoine, ed. "La Hiérarchie cathare en Italie, I: Le 'De Heresi Catharorum in Lombardia;' II. Le 'Tractatus de hereticis' d'Anselme d'Alexandrie, O.P.; III: Catalogue de la hiérarchie cathare d'Italie." *Archivum fratrum praedicatorum* 19 (1949): 280–312; 20 (1950): 234–324.

———. *Un Traité néo-manichéen du XIIIe siècle: Le 'Liber de Duobus Principiis.'* Rome, Istituto storico domenicano Santa Sabina, 1939.

Douais, Célestin, ed. *Documents pour servir à l'histoire de l'Inquisition dans le Languedoc.* 2 vols. Paris: H. Champion, 1900.

———. *La somme des autorités à l'usage des prédicateurs méridionaux au XIIIe siècle.* Paris: 1896.

———. *Les sources et l'histoire de l'inquisition dans le Midi de la France au XIIIe et XIVe siècles* Paris: 1881.

Duchesne, Louis, ed. *Liber Pontificalis.* Paris: E. de Boccard, 1955.

Durandus of Huesca. *Une Somme anti-cathare: Le Liber contra Manicheos de Durand de Huesca*. Ed. Christine Thouzellier. Louvain: Spicilegium sacrum Lovaniense, Études et documents, 32, 1964.

Duvernoy, Jean, ed. *Le Registre d'Inquisition de Jacques Fournier èveque de Pamiers (1318–1325)*. Toulouse: Edouard Privat, 1965.

Fabre, Paul,. and Louis Duchesne, eds. *Le Liber Censuum de l'église romaine*. Bibliothèque des Écoles françaises d'Athènes et de Rome, ser. 2, vol. 6. Paris, Thorin, 1910–52.

Friedberg, Aemilius, ed. *Corpus iuris canonici*. 2 vols. Leipzig: 1879–81; rpt. 1922.

Fumi, Luigi, ed. *Codice diplomatico della città di Orvieto: Documenti e regesti dal secolo XI al XV, e la Carta del Popolo: codice statuario del comune di Orvieto*. Documenti di storia italiana. Vol. 8. Florence: G. P. Viesseux, 1884.

———. *Ephemerides Urbevetanae. Rerum Italicarum Scriptores*. Ed. Ludovico A. Muratori. Vol. 15, part 5. Città di Castello: 1910.

———. *Statuti e Regesti dell'Opera di Santa Maria di Orvieto*. Rome: Tipografia Vaticana, 1891.

"Gesta Innocenti Papae III." *Patrologia cursus completus, Series Latina*. Ed. Jacques-Paul Migne. Paris, 1844–1891. Vol. 214.

Jacobus de Voragine. *The Golden Legend: Readings on the Saints*. Trans. William Granger Ryan. 2 vols. Princeton: Princeton University Press, 1993.

Lazzarini, Andrea, ed. *Il miracolo di Bolsena. Testimonianze e documenti dei secoli XIII e XIV*. Rome: Edizioni di storia e letteratura, 1952.

Maccarone, Michele. "La notizia della visita di Innocenzo III ad Orvieto nel cod. M465 della Morgan Library di New York." *Studi sul Innocenzo III*. Italia Sacra. Vol. 17. Padua: Editrice Antenore, 1972.

Marredu, P. Vincenzo. *Leggenda della Beata Giovanna detta Vanna d'Orvieto del Terz'Ordine di San Domenico scritta dal Ven. P. Giacomo Scalza Orvietano de Predicatori*. Orvieto: 1853.

Martène, Edmund, and Ursin Durand, eds. *Thesaurus novus anecdotorum*. Paris: 1917. Reprint ed. New York: B. Franklin, 1968.

Natalini, Vincenzo, ed. *San Pietro Parenzo. La Leggenda scritta dal Maestro Giovanni canonico di Orvieto*. Rome: Facultas Theologica Pontifici Atheniae Seminarii Romani, 1936.

Paolini, Lorenzo, and Raniero Orioli, eds. *Acta Sancti Officii Bononie ab anno 1291 usque ad annum 1310*. Fonti per la storia d'Italia. Vol. 106. Rome: Istituto storico italiano per il Medio Evo, 1982.

Perali, Pericle, ed. *La cronaca del vescovado orvietano (1029–1239) scritta dal vescovo Ranerio*. Orvieto: 1907.

"Processus Canonizationis B. Ambrosii Massanii." *Acta Sanctorum*. Paris: V. Palme, 1863–1919. Vol. 66. (10 November.)

Ricchini, Thomas A., ed. *Monetae Cremonensis adversus Catharos et Valdenses libri quinque. Descriptio fidei haereticorum*. Rome: Typographia Palladis, 1743. Reprint Ridgewood, N.J., 1964.

Roman, J. "Summa d'Huguccio sur le Décret de Gratien d'après le Manuscrit

3891 de la Bibliothèque Nationale. Causa 27, Questio 2 (Théories sur la formation du mariage)." *Revue historique de droit française et étranger* 2: 27 (1903): 745–805.

"Sacre Rappresentazioni per la Fraternitate d'Orvieto nel Cod. Vittorio Emanuele 528." *Bolletino della (regia) Deputazione di Storia Patria per l'Umbria.* Appendix 5. (Perugia, 1916).

Santini, Pietro, ed. *Documenti dell'antica costituzione del comune di Firenze.* Documenti di storia italiana. Vol. 10. Florence: G. P. Vieusseux, 1895.

Thomas Aquinas. "Le Sermon inédit de Saint Thomas 'Homo quidam fecit cenam magnam:' Introduction et édition." Ed. Louis-Jacques Bataillon. *Revue des sciences philosophiques et théologiques* 67 (1983): 353–69.

Thouzellier, Christine. *Une Traité inédit du début du XIIIe siècle d'après le 'Liber contra manicheos' de Durand de Huesca.* Bibliothèque de la Revue d'histoire ecclésiastique, 37. Louvain, 1961.

Tocco, Felice. *Quel che non c'è nella Divina Commedia, o Dante e l'eresia.* Bologna: N. Zanichelli, 1899.

Tognato, Francesca Lomastro. *L'eresia a Vicenza nel Duecento.* Fonti e studi di storia veneta, no. 12. Vicenza: Istituto per ricerche di storia sociale e di storia religiosa, 1988.

Velluti, Donato. *La cronica domestica di Donato Velluti.* Ed. Isidoro del Lungo and Guglielmo Volpi. Florence: Sansoni, 1914.

Villani, Giovanni. *Cronica.* Ed. Giovanni Aquilecchia. Turin: Einaudi, 1979.

Secondary Sources

Abels, Richard and Ellen Harrison. "The Participation of Women in Languedocian Catharism." *Medieval Studies* 41 (1979): 215–51.

Aston, Margaret. "Corpus Christi and Corpus Regni: Heresy and the Peasants' Revolt." *Past and Present* 143 (May 1994): 3–47.

Banker, James. *Death in the Community: Memorialization and Confraternities in an Italian Commune in the Late Middle Ages.* Athens, Georgia: University of Georgia Press, 1988.

Becker, Marvin B. "Heresy in Medieval and Renaissance Florence: A Comment." *Past and Present* 62 (1974): 153–61.

———. *Medieval Italy: Constraints and Creativity.* Bloomington, Indiana: Indiana University Press, 1981.

Bell, Catherine. *Ritual Theory, Ritual Practice.* New York: Oxford University Press, 1992.

Bellomo, Manlio. *Ricerche sui rapporti patrimoniali tra coniugi: Contributo alla storia della famiglia medievale.* Milan: Giuffre, 1961.

Bertelli, Sergio. *Il corpo del re: Sacralita del potere nell'Europa medievale e moderna.* Florence: Ponte alle Grazie, 1990.

Blanshei, Sarah. "Criminal Law and Politics in Medieval Bologna." *Criminal Justice History* 2 (1981): 1–30.

Boissevain, Jeremy. "When the saints go marching out: Reflections on the decline of patronage in Malta." *Patrons and Clients in Mediterranean Societies.* Ed. Ernest Gellner and John Waterbury. London: Center for Mediterranean Studies of the American Universities Field Staff, 1977.

Bolton, Brenda. "Tradition and temerity: Papal attitudes to deviants, 1159–1216." *Schism, Heresy and Religious Protest.* ed. Derek Baker. Studies in Church History. Vol. 9. Cambridge: Cambridge University Press, 1972.

Bornstein, Daniel, and Roberto Rusconi, eds. *Mistiche e devote nell'Italia tardomedievale.* Naples: Liguori, 1992. Trans. Margery Schneider as *Women and Religion in Medieval and Renaissance Italy.* Chicago: University of Chicago Press, 1996.

Borst, Arno. *Die Katharer.* Stuttgart: Hiersemann,1953. Trans. Ch. Roy as *Les Cathares.* Paris: Payot, 1974.

Bourdieu, Pierre. *Outline of a Theory of Practice.* Trans. Richard Nice. Cambridge: Cambridge University Press, 1977.

Bowsky, William. "The Medieval Commune and Internal Violence: Police Power and Public Safety in Siena, 1287–1355." *American Historical Review* 73 (1967): 1–17.

Boyle, Leonard. "Montaillou Revisited: Mentalité and Methodology." *Pathways to Medieval Peasants.* Ed. J. Ambrose Raftis. Toronto: Pontifical Institute of Mediaeval Studies, 1981.

Brentano, Robert. *A New World in a Small Place: Church and Religion in the Diocese of Rieti, 1188–1378.* Berkeley: University of California Press, 1994.

———. *Two Churches: England and Italy in the Thirteenth Century.* Princeton, N.J.: Princeton University Press, 1968.

Brooke, Christopher. *The Medieval Idea of Marriage.* Oxford: Clarendon Press, 1989.

Brown, Peter. *The Cult of the Saints: Its Rise and Function in Latin Christianity.* Chicago: University of Chicago Press, 1981.

Brundage, James. *Law, Sex and Christian Society in Medieval Europe.* Chicago: University of Chicago Press, 1987.

Buchicchio, F. "La storia del miracolo di Bolsena' e le sue vicende." *Bolletino istituto storico-artistico orvietano* 29 (1973): 3–45.

Burresi, Mariagiulia, ed. *Andrea, Nino e Tommaso scultori pisani.* Milan: Electa, 1983.

Butler, Judith. *Bodies That Matter: On the Discursive Limits of "Sex".* New York: Routledge, 1993.

Bynum, Caroline. *Fragmentation and Redemption: Essays on Gender and the Human Body in Medieval Religion.* New York: Zone Books, 1991.

———. *Holy Feast and Holy Fast: The Religious Significance of Food to Medieval Women.* Berkeley: University of California Press, 1987.

———. *Jesus as Mother: Studies in the Spirituality of the High Middle Ages.* Berkeley: University of California Press,1982.

———. *The Resurrection of the Body in Western Christianity 200–1376.* New York: Columbia University Press, 1995.

Cadden, Joan. *Meanings of Sex Difference in the Middle Ages.* Cambridge: Cambridge University Press, 1993.

Cammarosano, Paolo. "Aspetti delle strutture familiari nelle città dell'Italia comunale (secoli XII–XIV)." *Studi medievali* 16 (1975): 417–36.

Capitani, Ovidio. *L'eresia medievale.* Bologna: Il Mulino, 1971.

———. "Legislazione antiereticale e strumento di costruzione politica nelle decisioni normative di Innocenzo III." *Bollettino della società di studi valdesi* 140 (1976): 31–53.

———. *Medioevo ereticale.* Bologna: Il Mulino, 1977.

———. "Patari in Umbria: Lo 'status quaestionis' nella recente storiografia." *Bolletino istituto storico-artistico orvietano* (1983): 37–54.

Carocci, Sandro. *Baroni di Roma: Dominazioni signorili e lignaggi aristocratici nel duecento e nel primo trecento.* Rome: École française de Rome, 1993.

———. "Le Comunalie di Orvieto fra la fine del XII e la metà del XV secolo." *Mélanges de l'École Française de Rome* 99:2 (1987): 701–28.

Carpentier, Elisabeth. *Une Ville devant la peste: Orvieto et la peste noire de 1348.* Paris: S.E.V.P.E.N., 1962. Revised ed. Brussels: De Boeck Université, 1993.

———. *Orvieto à la fin du XIIIe siècle: Ville et campagne dans le cadastre de 1292.* Paris: Éditions du Centre National de la Recherche Scientifique, 1986.

Cherubini, Wanda. "Movimenti patarinici in Orvieto." *Bollettino istituto storico-artistico orvietano* 15 (1989): 3–42.

Corsi, Dinora. "Firenze 1300–1350: 'Non conformismo' religioso e organizzazione inquisitoriale." *Annali dell'istituto di storia.* Università di Firenze, Facoltà di Magistero I (1979): 29–66.

———. " 'Les secréts des dames:' " Tradition, traduction." *La culture sur le marché. Médiévales: langues, textes, histoire* 14 (Spring 1988): 47–58.

———. "Per la storia dell'inquisizione a Firenze nella seconda metà del secolo XIII." *Bolletino della società di studi valdesi* 3 (December 1972).

Le Credo, la Morale et L'Inquisition. Cahiers de Fanjeaux. Vol. 6. Toulouse: Privat, 1971.

D'Alatri, Mariano. *Eretici e inquisitori in Italia: studi e documenti.* Rome: Collegio San Lorenzo da Brindisi, Istituto storico dei Cappuccini, 1986–87.

D'Alatri, Mariano, ed. *L'inquisizione francescana nell'Italia centrale del Duecento: con il testo del 'Liber inquisitionis' di Orvieto, trascritto da Egidio Bonanno.* Biblioteca seraphico-cappuccina. Vol. 49. Rome: Istituto storico dei Cappuccini, 1996.

Dameron, George. "Conflitto rituale e ceto dirigente fiorentino alla fine del Duecento: l'ingresso solenne del vescovo Jacopo Rainucci nel 1286." *Ricerche storiche* 20: 2–3 (May–Dec. 1990): 263–86.

———. *Episcopal Power and Florentine Society, 1000–1320.* Cambridge, Massachusetts: Harvard University Press, 1991.

D'Angelo, Franco. "Concia e conciatori nella Palermo del Duecento." *Schede medievali* 6–7 (1984): 111–26.

Davidsohn, Robert. *Storia di Firenze.* 8 vols. Berlin: 1896–1927. Trans. G. B. Klein. Florence: Sansoni, 1956–68.

Delort, Robert. *Le commerce des fourrures en occident à la fin du moyen âge (vers 1300–vers 1450).* Rome: École française de Rome, Palais Farnese, 1978.

De Rosa, Daniela. *Alle origini della repubblica fiorentina: Dai consoli al 'Primo popolo.'* Florence: Arnaud, 1995.

Diehl, Peter. "The Papacy and the Supression of Heresy in Italy, 1150–1254." Ph.D. dissertation, U.C.L.A., 1991.

Diehl, Peter, and Scot Waugh. *Christendom and Its Discontents: Exclusion, Persecution and Rebellion, 1000–1500.* Cambridge, England: Cambridge University Press, 1996.

Döllinger, Ignatius von. *Beiträge zur Sektengeschichte des Mittelalters.* Munich: Beck, 1890. Reprint, New York, 1960.

Donahue, Charles. "The Policy of Alexander III's Consent Theory of Marriage." *Proceedings of the Fourth International Congress of Canon Law.* Ed. Stephan Kuttner. Monumenta Iuris Canonici, series C: Subsidia 5 (Vatican City, 1976): 251–81.

Douglas, Mary. *Natural Symbols.* New York: Pantheon Books, 1982.

Duby, Georges. *The Knight, the Lady and the Priest: the Making of Modern Marriage in Medieval France.* Trans. Barbara Bray. New York: Pantheon Books, 1983.

Dupré-Theseider, Eugenio. "L'eresia a Bologna nei tempi di Dante." *Mondo cittadino e movimenti ereticali nel medio evo.* Bologna: Patron, 1978

Durkheim, Emile. *The Elementary Forms of the Religious Life.* Trans. Joseph Ward Swain. New York: Free Press, 1965.

Effacement du Catharisme? (XIIIe–XIVe siècles). Cahiers de Fanjeaux. Vol. 20. Toulouse: Privat, 1985.

Elliott, Dyan. *Spiritual Marriage.* Princeton, N.J.: Princeton University Press, 1993.

English, Edward. "Emancipation, Succession and Honor: Family Strategies in Medieval Siena." *Medieval Manuscript Studies in Honor of Leonard E. Boyle.* ed. Jacqueline Brown and William Stoneman. Notre Dame: Forthcoming.

English, Edward. "Five Magnate Families of Siena, 1240–1350," Ph.D dissertation, University of Toronto, 1981.

Esmein, Adhemar. *Le mariage en droit canonique.* Paris: L. Larose of Forcel, 1891.

Evans, Austin P. "Social Aspects of Medieval Heresy." *Persecution and Liberty: Essays in Honor of George Lincoln Burr.* New York: Century, 1931. 93–116

Farmer, Sharon. "Matter Out of Place: Elite Perceptions of Single Women in Thirteenth-Century Paris." *Single Women in the European Past.* Ed. Judith Bennett. Forthcoming.

Fineschi, Vincenzio. *Storia di Santa Maria Novella.* Rome: Multigrafica editrice, 1977.

Fiumi, Enrico. *Demografia, movimento urbanistico e classi sociali in Prato dall'età comunale ai tempi moderni.* Florence: L. S. Olschki, 1968.

Fumi, Luigi. *Il Duomo di Orvieto e i suoi restauri.* Rome: Società laziale tipografico-editrice, 1891.

———. *Il palazzo Soliano o de' papi.* Rome: 1896

Galletti, A. I. "I francescani e il culto dei santi nell'Italia centrale." Atti del VII convegno, Società internazionali di studi Francescani. Assisi: Commissione storica internazionale T.O.R., 1981.

Galli, Quirino. "Presente e passato nel Carnevale della Tuscia meridionale. Le Fonti medievali." *Il Carnevale: dalla tradizione Arcaica alla traduzione colta del Rinascimento.* Atti del XIII convegno, Rome, 31 maggio–4 giugno 1989. Ed. M. Chiabo and F. Doglio. Viterbo: Centro studi sul teatro medievale e rinascimentale, 1990.

Gardner, Julian. "Pope Nicholas IV and the Decoration of Santa Maria Maggiore." *Zeitschrift für Kunstgeschichte.* 36 (1973): 1–50.

Garrison, Edward B. "Note on the Iconography of Creation and of the Fall of Man in Eleventh and Twelfth-Century Rome." *Studies in the History of Mediaeval Italian Painting* by Edward B. Garrison. Vol. 4. Florence: Pindar Press, 1960.

Geremek, Bronislaw. "Activité économique et exclusion sociale: les métiers maudits." *Gerarchie economiche e gerarchie sociale, secc. XII–XVIII.* Istituto internazionale di storia economica Francesco Datini, dodicesima settimana di studio, Prato, 22 April 1980.

Giannotti, A. "Forme drammatiche nell'Orvieto medievale." Laureate thesis, University of Rome, 1983–84.

Gillerman, David. "The Evolution of the Design of Orvieto Cathedral, ca. 1290–1310." *Journal of the Society of Architectural Historians* 53 (September 1994): 300–21.

Given, James. "The Inquisitors of Languedoc and the Medieval Technology of Power." *American Historical Review* 94: 2 (April 1989): 336–61.

———. "A Medieval Inquisitor at Work: Bernard Gui, 3 March 1308 to 19 June 1323." *Portraits of Medieval and Renaissance Living.* Ed. Samuel Cohn and Steven Epstein. Ann Arbor: University of Michigan Press, 1996.

Gold, Penny S. "The Marriage of Mary and Joseph in the Twelfth-Century Ideology of Marriage." *Sexual Practices and the Medieval Church.* Ed. Vern Bullough and James Brundage. Buffalo: Prometheus Books, 1982.

Golinelli, Paolo. *Città e culto dei santi nel medioevo italiano.* Bologna: Clueb, 1991.

Goodich, Michael. *Violence and Miracle in the Fourteenth Century.* Chicago: University of Chicago Press, 1995.

Grundmann, John. *The Popolo at Perugia, 1139–1309.* Ph.D dissertation, Washington University. 1974. Published in *Fonti per la storia dell'Umbria.* Vol. 20. Perugia: Deputazione de storia patria per l'Umbria, 1992.

Grundmann, Herbert. *Religiöse Bewegungen im Mittelalter.* 1935. Trans. by Steven Rowan as *Religious Movements in the Middle Ages.* Notre Dame: University of Notre Dame Press, 1995.

Guidoni, Enrico. *La città dal Medioevo al Rinascimento.* Rome-Bari: Laterza, 1981.

Guiraud, Jean. *L'Inquisition au XIII siècle en France, en Espagne et en Italie. Histoire de l'Inquisition au Moyen Age.* Vol. 2. Paris: A. Picard, 1938.

Gy, Pierre-Marie. "L'Office du Corpus Christi et la théologie des accidents eucharistique." *Revue des sciences philosophiques et théologiques* 66 (1982): 81–86.

———. "L'Office du Corpus Christi et S. Thomas d'Aquin: état d'une recherche." *Revue des sciences philosophiques et théologiques* 64 (1980): 491–507.

Heaney, Seamus P. *The Development of the Sacramentality of Marriage from Anselm of Laon to Thomas Aquinas.* Washington, D.C.: Catholic University of America Press, 1963.

Henderson, Mary. "Medieval Orvieto: The Religious Life of the Laity 1150–1350." Ph.D. Dissertation. University of Edinburgh, 1990.

Herlihy, David. *Pisa in the Early Renaissance.* New Haven: Yale University Press, 1958.

Historiographie du catharisme. Cahiers de Fanjeaux. Vol. 14. Toulouse: Privat, 1979.

Jones, Philip. *The Malatesta of Rimini and the Papal State.* Cambridge: Cambridge University Press, 1974.

Kantorowicz, Ernst. *The King's Two Bodies: A Study in Medieval Political Theology.* Princeton: Princeton University Press, 1957.

Kelly, Henry Ansgar. "Inquisition and the Prosecution of Heresy: Misconception and Abuses." *Church History* 58:4 (December 1989): 439–51.

Kent, Dale. *The Rise of the Medici: Faction in Florence, 1426–1434.* Oxford: Oxford University Press, 1978.

Kent, Francis W., and Patricia Simons, eds. *Patronage, Art and Society in Renaissance Italy.* Oxford: Oxford University Press, 1987.

Kieckhefer, Richard. *Magic in the Middle Ages.* Cambridge: Cambridge University Press, 1989.

Kirshner, Julius. "Wives' Claims against Insolvent Husbands in Late Medieval Italy." *Women of the Medieval World.* Ed. Julius Kirshner and Suzanne Wemple. Oxford: Blackwell, 1985.

Klapisch-Zuber, Christiane. *Women, Family and Ritual in Renaissance Italy.* Trans. Lydia Cochrane. Chicago: University of Chicago Press, 1985.

Kuehn, Thomas. *Emancipation in Late Medieval Florence.* New Brunswick, N.J.: Rutgers University Press, 1982.

———. "Some Ambiguities of Female Inheritance Ideology in the Renaissance." *Continuity and Change* 2 (1987): 11–36.

Ladurie, Le Roy. *Montaillou: The Promised Land of Error.* Trans. Barbara Bray. New York: G. Braziller, 1978.

Lambert, Malcolm. *Medieval Heresy: Popular Movements from the Gregorian Reform to the Reformation.* 2nd. ed. Oxford: Blackwell, 1992.

———. "The Motives of the Cathars: Some Reflections." *Religious Motivation: Biographical and Sociological Problems for the Church Historian.* Ed. Derek Baker. Studies in Church History. Vol. 15. Oxford: Blackwell, 1978.

Lansing, Carol. *The Florentine Magnates: Lineage and Faction in a Medieval Commune.* Princeton: Princeton University Press, 1992.

———. "Gender, Adultery and Authority: Sexual Regulation in a Medieval Italian Town." *Journal of Social History.* Forthcoming.

Lattanzi, Bernardino. "La famiglia Lupicini di Orvieto." *Bolletino istituto storico-artistico orvietano* 21 (1965): 74–83.

Lazzarini, Andrea. "La data originaria della sacra rappresentazione di miracolo di Bolsena." *Bolletino istituto storico-artistico orvietano.* 6:1 (1950): 1–5.

Le Bras, Gabriel. "La doctrine du mariage chez les théologiens et les canonistes depuis l'an mille." *Dictionnaire de théologie catholique.* Ed. A. Vacant et al. Vol. 9 (1930–1950): 2196–2217.

Leff, Gordon. *Heresy in the Later Middle Ages.* Manchester: Barnes and Noble, 1967.

Le Goff, Jacques, ed. *Hérésies et sociétés dans l'Europe pré-industrielle, 11e–18e siècles.* Paris: Mouton, 1961.

Lesnick, Daniel. "Insults and Threats in Medieval Todi." *Journal of Medieval History* 17 (1991): 71–89.

Lottin, Odon. *Les théories sur le péché originel de Saint Anselme à Saint Thomas D'Aquin.* Vol. 4. *Psychologie et morale aux XIIe et XIIIe siècles.* Louvain: Abbaye du Mont Cesar, 1954.

Luchaire, Achille. *Innocent III, Rome et l'Italie.* Paris: Librairie Hachette, 1905.

Maccarone, Michele. "Orvieto e la predicazione della Crociata." *Studi sul Innocenzo III.* Italia sacra. Vol. 17. Padua: 1972.

Maire Vigueur, Jean-Claude. *Comune e signorie in Umbria, Marche e Lazio.* Turin: Utet, 1987.

Manselli, Raoul. *L'eresia del male.* Naples: Morano, 1961.

———. "Aspetti e significato dell'intolleranza popolare nei secoli XI–XIII." *Il secolo XII: religione popolare ed eresia.* Rome: Jouvence, 1983.

———. "Evangelisme et mythe dans la foi cathare." *Heresis* 5 (1985): 5–17.

———. "La fin du catharisme en Italie." *Effacement du catharisme? (XIIIe–XIVe siècles)* Cahiers de Fanjeaux. Vol. 20. Toulouse: Privat, 1985. Pp. 101–18.

———. "Per la storia dell'eresia catara nella Firenze del tempo di Dante." *Bollettino dell'istituto storico italiano per il medio evo e Archivio Muratoriano* 62 (1950): 123–38.

Martin, John. *Venice's Hidden Enemies: Italian Heretics in a Renaissance City.* Berkeley: University of California Press, 1993.

McSheffrey, Shannon. *Gender and Heresy: Women and Men in Lollard Communities.* Philadelphia: University of Pennsylvania Press, 1995.

Merlo, Grado. *Contro gli eretici.* Bologna: Il Mulino, 1996.

———. *Eretici ed eresie medievali.* Bologna: Il Mulino, 1989.

———. *Eretici e inquisitori nella società piemontese del trecento.* Turin: Claudiana, 1977.

———. "'Membra del davolo': la demonizzazione degli eretici." Reprinted in *Contro gli eretici.* Bologna: Il Mulino, 1996.

———. "Tensioni religiose all'inizio del duecento." *Tra eremo e citta.* Assisi: Edizioni Porziuncola, 1991.

Milano, Ilarino da. "Il dualismo cataro in Umbria al tempo di San Francesco." *Filosofia e cultura in Umbria tra medioevo e rinascimento.* Atti del IV convegno di studi umbri, Gubbio 22–26 May 1966. Perugia: Centro di studi Umbri presso la Casa di Sant'Ubaldo in Gubbio, 1967.

———. "Summa Contra Haereticos." *Collectanea franciscana* 10 (1940): 66–82.

Miller, Maureen. *The Formation of a Medieval Church: Ecclesiastical Change in Verona, 950–1150.* Ithaca, N.Y.: Cornell University Press, 1993.

Molinier, Charles. "Un Texte de Muratori concernant les sectes cathares: Sa provenance réelle et sa valeur." *Annales du Midi* 22 (1910): 212–16.

Moore, Robert I. *The Formation of a Persecuting Society.* Oxford: Blackwell, 1987.

———. "St. Bernard's Mission to the Languedoc in 1145." *Bulletin of the Institute of Historical Research* 47:115 (May 1974): 1–10.

Moskowitz, Anita. "Studies in the Sculpture of Andrea Pisano: Origins and Development of His Style." Ph.D Dissertation, New York University, 1978.

Muir, Edward. *Civic Ritual in Renaissance Venice.* Princeton: Princeton University Press, 1981.

Mundy, John Hine. *Liberty and Political Power in Toulouse 1050–1230.* New York: Columbia University Press, 1954.

———. *Men and Women at Toulouse in the Age of the Cathars.* Toronto: Pontifical Institute of Mediaeval Studies, 1990.

———. *The Repression of Catharism at Toulouse.* Toronto: Pontifical Institute of Mediaeval Studies, 1985.

Murray, Alexander. "Piety and Impiety in Thirteenth-Century Italy." *Popular Belief and Practice.* Ed. S. J. Cuming and Derek Baker. Studies in Church History. Vol. 8. Cambridge: Cambridge University Press, 1972.

Noonan, John T. *Contraception.* Cambridge, Mass: Belknap Press, 1965.

———. "Power to Choose." *Viator* 4 (1973): 419–34.

Oliver, Antonio. *Tactica de propaganda y motivos literarios en las cartas antiheréticas de Inocencio III.* Rome: Regnum Dei, 1957.

Paolini, Lorenzo. *L'eresia catara alla fine del duecento.* Vol. I. *L'eresia a Bologna fra XIII e XIV secolo,* Istituto storico italiano per il medio evo, Studi storici, fasc. 93–96. Rome: 1975.

Paolini, Lorenzo. "Bonigrino da Verona e sua moglie Rosafiore." *Medioevo ereticale.* Ed. Ovidio Capitani. Bologna: Il Mulino, 1977.

———. "Domus e zona degli eretici: l'esempio di Bologna nel XIII secolo." *Rivista di storia della chiesa in Italia* 35 (1981): 371–87.

———. *Eretici del Medioevo: L'albero selvatico.* Bologna: Patron, 1989.

———. "Italian Catharism and written culture." *Heresy and Literacy, 1000–1530.* Ed. Peter Biller and Anne Hudson. Cambridge: Cambridge University Press, 1994.

Papi, Anna Benvenuti. "Un vescovo, una città: Ardingo nella Firenze del primo Duecento." *Pastori di popolo: Storie e leggende di vescovi e di città nell'Italia medievale.* Florence: Arnaud, 1988.

———. "Umiliana dei Cerchi. Nascita di un culto nella Firenze del Duecento." *Studi Francescani* 77 (1980): 87–117.

Paravicini, Agostino Bagliani. *La cour des papes au XIII siècle.* Paris: Hachette, 1995.

———. "La mobilità della Curia romana nel secolo XIII. Riflessi locali." *Società e istituzioni dell'Italia comunale. L'esempio di Perugia (secoli XII–XIV).* Perugia: 1988.

Pardi, Giuseppe. "Gli Statuti della Colletta del comune di Orvieto (sec. XIV)." *Bolletino Deputazione di storia patria per l'Umbria* 9 (1905): 324–25.

————. "Serie di supremi Magistrati." *Bolletino della società umbra di storia patria* I (1895): 25–86; 4 (1898): 1–46; 10 (1904): 169–97; 11 (1905): 263–380.

Partner, Peter. *The Lands of St. Peter: The Papal State in the Middle Ages and the Early Renaissance.* Berkeley: University of California Press, 1972.

Payer, Pierre. *The Bridling of Desire: Views of Sex in the Later Middle Ages.* Toronto: University of Toronto Press, 1993.

Pellegrini, Letizia. "*Negotium Imperfectum:* Il processo per la canonizazione di Ambrogio da Massa (O.M., Orvieto 1240)." *Società e storia* 64 (1994): 253–78.

Pierotti, Romano. "Aspetti del mercato e della produzione a Perugia fra la fine al secolo XIVe la prima metà del XV: la bottega di cuoiame di Niccolo di Martino di Pietro." *Bolletino della Deputazione di storia patria per l'Umbria* 72:1 (1975): 79–185; 73:1 (1976): 2–131.

Piolanti, Antonio, ed. *Eucaristia: Il mistero dell'altare nel pensiero e nella vita della Chiesa.* Rome: Desclèe, 1957.

Polc, Jaroslav. "Il miracolo di Bolsena e Pietro de Praga: Un'ipotesi." *Rivista di storia della chiesa in Italia* 45:2 (1991): 437–49.

Pope-Hennessey, John. *Italian Gothic Sculpture.* New York: Phaidon, 1985.

Pouchelle, Marie-Christine. *The Body and Surgery in the Middle Ages.* Paris: 1983. Trans. Rosemary Morris. New Brunswick, N.J.: Rutgers University Press, 1990.

————. "Représentations du corps dans la *Legende dorée.*" *Ethnologie française* 6:3–4 (1976): 293–308.

Raggio, Olga. "The Myth of Prometheus." *Journal of the Warburg and Courtauld Institutes* 21 (1958): 44–62.

Raveggi, Sergio, Massimo Tarassi, Daniela Medici, and Patrizia Parenti. *Ghibellini, Guelfi e Popolo Grasso: I detentori del potere politico a Firenze nella seconda metà del Dugento.* Florence: La Nuova Italia, 1978.

Reames, Sherry. *The Legenda Aurea:* A Re-examination of its Paradoxical History. Madison, Wis.: University of Wisconsin Press, 1985.

Reltgen, Anne. "Dissidences et contradictions en Italie." Actes de la 2e Session d'Histoire Médiévale de Carcassonne. *Heresis* 13–14 (1989): 89–113.

Reynolds, Susan. "Social Mentalities and the Case of Medieval Skepticism." *Transactions of the Royal Historical Society* 6th series: I (1991): 21–41.

Riccetti, Lucio. "La cronaca di Ranerio vescovo di Orvieto 1228–1248, una prima ricognizione." *Rivista di storia della chiesa in Italia* 43:2 (1989): 480–509.

————. *La città costruita: Lavori pubblici e immagine in Orvieto medievale.* Florence: Le Lettere, 1992.

————., ed. *Il Duomo d'Orvieto.* Rome: Laterza, 1988.

————. "Note in margine ad un testamento orvietano del trecento: Il testamento di Ugolino di Lupicino." *Bolletino istituto storico–artistico orvietano* 38 (1982): 13–15.

————. "Orvieto: I testamenti del 'Liber donationum' (1221–1281)." *Nolens intestatus decedere: Il testamento come fonte della storia religiosa e sociale.* Archivi dell'Umbria: Inventari e ricerche, 7. Umbria: Editrice Umbra Cooperativa, 1985.

Rigaux, Dominique. *À la table du Seigneur: L'Eucharistie chez les Primitifs italiens 1250–1497* Paris: Cerf, 1989.

Rist, John. *Augustine: Ancient Thought Baptised.* Cambridge: Cambridge University Press, 1995.

Ristori, G. R. "I Patarini in Firenze nella prima metà del secolo XIII." *Rivista storico-critica delle scienze teologiche* I (1905): 15–17.

Rossi, Marilena Caponeri, and Lucio Riccetti, eds. *Chiese e conventi degli ordini mendicanti in Umbria nei secoli XIII–XIV. Inventario delle fonti archivistiche e catalogo delle informazione documentarie. Archivi di Orvieto.* Perugia, Regione dell'Umbria: Editrice Umbra Cooperativa, 1987.

Rossi, Marilena Caponeri. "Il duomo e l'attività edilizia dei Signori Sette (1295–1313)." *Il Duomo di Orvieto.* Ed. Lucio Riccetti. Rome: Laterza, 1988.

Rottenwoher, Gerhard. "Foi et théologie des cathares Bagnolistes." Trans. Jean Duvernoy. *Heresis* 7 (December 1986): 26–31.

Rubin, Miri. *Corpus Christi: The Eucharist in Late Medieval Culture.* Cambridge: Cambridge University Press, 1991.

Salvini, Roberto. *Il Duomo di Modena.* Modena-Milan: Artioli, 1983.

Sayers, Jane. *Innocent III: Leader of Europe, 1198–1216.* London: Longman, 1994.

Schmitt, Jean-Claude. *Medioevo superstitioso.* Trans. Maria Garin. Rome: Laterza, 1992.

————. *La raison des gestes dans l'Occident Medieval.* Paris: Gallimard, 1990.

————. *Religione, folklore e società nell'Occidente medievale.* Trans. Lucia Carle. Rome: Laterza, 1988.

Semkov, Georgi. "Die Katharer von Florenz und Umgebung in der ersten halfte des 13. Jahrhunderts." *Heresis* 7 (1986): 61–75.

Sergiacomi, Giuseppe. *Il miracolo eucaristico di Offida.* Ascoli Piceno: 1957.

Söderberg, Hans. *La Religion des Cathares: Étude sur le gnosticisme de la basse antiquité et du moyen age.* Uppsala: Almquist & Wiksells Boktr., 1949.

Spufford, Peter. *Handbook of Medieval Exchange.* London: Offices of the Royal Historical Society, 1986.

Stanbury, Sarah. "The Body and the City in 'Pearl.'" *Representations* 48 (Fall, 1994): 30–47.

Stephens, John N. "Heresy in Medieval and Renaissance Florence." *Past and Present* 54 (1972): 25–60.

Stella, Alessandro. *La révolte des Ciompi.* Paris: Éditions de l'École des hautes études en sciences sociales, 1993.

Stopani, Renato. *La via Francigena: Una strada europea nell'Italia del Medioevo.* Florence: Le Lettere,1988.

Swanson, Heather. *Medieval Artisans.* Oxford: Blackwell, 1989.

Taylor, Michael D. "The Prophetic Scenes in the Tree of Jesse at Orvieto." *Art Bulletin* 54 (1972): 403–17.

————. "A Historiated Tree of Jesse." *Dumbarton Oaks Papers* 34–35 (1980–81): 125–76.

Tentler, Thomas. *Sin and Confession on the Eve of the Reformation.* Princeton: Princeton University Press, 1977.

Toubert, Pierre. *Les structures du Latium medieval.* Rome: École française de Rome, 1973.

Trachtenberg, Marvin. *The Campanile of Florence Cathedral: "Giotto's Tower".* New York: New York University Press, 1971.

Trexler, Richard. *Public Life in Renaissance Florence.* New York; Academic Press, 1980.

Trinkaus, Charles. *In Our Image and Likeness: Humanity and Divinity in Italian Humanist Thought.* Chicago: University of Chicago Press, 1970.

Turreni, Agostino. "La condizione giuridica degli eretici patarini in Orvieto." Laureate thesis, Università degli Studi di Perugia, Facoltà di Giurisprudenza, 1965–66.

Ullmann, Walter. "The significance of Innocent III's decretal Vergentis." *Études d'histoire du droit canonique dédiées à Gabriel Le Bras.* Paris: Sirey, 1965.

Van Engen, John. "The Christian Middle Ages as an Historiographical Problem." *American Historical Review* 91:3 (1986): 519–52.

Van Oort, Johannes. "Augustine on Sexual Concupiscence and Original Sin." *Studia Patristica.* Vol. 22 (Leuven, 1989): 382–86.

————. "Augustine and Mani on Concupiscentia Sexualis." *Augustiana Traiectiana.* Ed. J. den Boeft and J. van Oort. Paris: Études Augustiniennes, 1987.

Vauchez, André. "Une campagne de pacification en Lombardie en 1233: L'action politique des ordres mendiants d'après la réforme des statuts communaux et les accords du paix." *Mélanges d'archéologie et d'histoire* 78:2 (1966), 503–49.

————. *Les laics au moyen âge: Pratiques et expériences religieuses.* Paris: Cerf, 1987.

————. *La sainteté en occident aux derniers siècles du Moyen Age.* Rome: École française de Rome, 1981.

Vernant, Jean-Pierre. "La belle mort et le cadavre outragé." *La mort, les morts dans les sociétés anciennes.* Ed. Gherardo Gnoli and Jean-Pierre Vernant. Cambridge: Cambridge University Press, 1982.

Violante, Cinzio. "Hérésies urbaines et hérésies rurales en Italie du XIIIe siècle." *Hérésies et sociétés dans l'Europe pré-industrielle, 11e–18e siècles.* Ed. J. Le Goff. Paris: Mouton, 1968.

————. "Premessa." *La storia locale: Temi, fonti e metodi di ricerca.* Bologna: 1982.

Volpe, Giovacchino. *Movimenti religiosi e sette ereticali nella società medievale italiana (sec. XI–XIV).* Florence: Sansoni, 1972.

Wakefield, Walter L. "Burial of Heretics in the Middle Ages." *Heresis* 5 (December 1985): 29–32.

Wakefield, Walter L., and Austin P. Evans, eds. *Heresies of the High Middle Ages.* New York: Columbia University Press, 1969; 2nd ed., 1991.

————. *Heresy, Crusade and Inquisition in Southern France, 1100–1250.* Berkeley: University of California Press, 1974.

————. "Some Unorthodox Popular Ideas of the Thirteenth Century." *Mediaevalia et Humanistica* new series 4 (1973): 25–35.

Waley, Daniel. *Medieval Orvieto.* Cambridge: Cambridge University Press, 1952.

————. *The Papal State in the Thirteenth Century.* London: Macmillan, 1961.

————. "Pope Boniface VIII and the Commune of Orvieto." *Transactions of the Royal Historical Society* 4:32 (1950): 121–39.

Wallace-Hadrill, Andrew, ed. *Patronage in Ancient Society.* London: Routledge, 1989.

Waterer, John W. "Leather." *A History of Technology.* Ed. Charles Singer et al. Oxford: Clarendon Press, 1957.

Weisheipl, James A. *Friar Thomas d'Aquino: His Life, Thought and Works.* Washington, D.C.: Catholic University of America Press, 1983.

White, John. "The Reliefs of the Facade of the Cathedral of Orvieto." *Journal of the Warburg and Courtauld Institutes* 2 (1959): 254–302.

Wickham, Chris J. *Comunità e clientele nella Toscana del XII secolo: Le origini del comune rurale nella Piana di Lucca.* Rome: Viella, 1995.

Wood, Diana, ed. *The Church and Sovereignty c. 590–1918.* Oxford: B. Blackwell, 1991.

Zanella, Gabriele. "Malessere ereticale in valle padana (1260–1308)." *Rivista di storia e letteratura religiosa* 14:3 (1978): 341–90.

————. "L'eresia catara fra XIII e XIV secolo: in margine al disagio di una storiografia." *Bolletino dell'istituto storico italiano per il medio evo e Archivio Muratoriano* 88 (1979): 239–58.

————. "Boni homines, bona opera, bona verba." *Hereticalia: Temi e discussioni.* Centro italiano di studi sull'altomedievo di Spoleto. Collectanea 7. Spoleto: 1995.

————. *Itinerari ereticali: patari e catari tra Rimini e Verona.* Istituto storico italiano per il medio evo, Studi storici. fasc. 153. Rome: 1986.

Zorzi, Andrea. "Contrôle social, ordre public et répression judiciaire à Florence à l'époque communale: éléments et problèmes." *Annales, E. S. C.* 45 (1990): 1169–88.

Index